STEPHEN HALES, D.D., F.R.S.

An Eighteenth Century Biography

Plate I. The Rev. Stephen Hales, D.D., F.R.S., at the age of eighty-one

(From the portrait by Thomas Hudson in the National Portrait Gallery, London)

STEPHEN HALES, D.D., F.R.S.

An Eighteenth Century Biography

BY

A. E. CLARK-KENNEDY, M.D., M.R.C.P.

*Fellow of Corpus Christi College, Cambridge. Assistant Director
of the Medical Unit and Assistant Physician to the
London Hospital*

CAMBRIDGE

At the University Press

1929

CAMBRIDGE
UNIVERSITY PRESS

University Printing House, Cambridge CB2 8BS, United Kingdom

Cambridge University Press is part of the University of Cambridge.

It furthers the University's mission by disseminating knowledge in the pursuit of education, learning and research at the highest international levels of excellence.

www.cambridge.org
Information on this title: www.cambridge.org/9781107475229

© Cambridge University Press 1929

First published 1929
First paperback edition 2014

A catalogue record for this publication is available from the British Library

ISBN 978-1-107-47522-9 Paperback

To

E. C. P.,

C. A. E. P., W. S., and G. G. B.

PREFACE

IN 1927, the Master and Fellows of Corpus Christi College, Cambridge, decided to celebrate the two hundred and fiftieth anniversary of the birth of Stephen Hales, and it fell to my lot, on Corpus Christi day, to give a short account of his life and work. When I came to prepare my address, I collected many more facts than I could possibly make use of, and soon realised that, to do justice to this remarkable character, it would be necessary to write some sort of book. In these pages I have attempted to tell the story of his life in the hope that it may prove of interest to others as well as to botanists and physiologists. I have also endeavoured to give a simple account of his researches such as will be to some extent intelligible to the reader who has no particular knowledge of science.

Short articles have been written about him by Francis Darwin (*Dictionary of National Biography*, and *Makers of British Botany*, Cambridge, 1913), Peter Dawson (*Bulletins of the Johns Hopkins Hospital*, 1904, xv, 185 and 232), and J. Paul de Castro (*Edinburgh Review*, 1920, CCXXXI, 78). From these I have drawn freely. In my account of Georgia, I have made use of Osgood's *American Colonies in the Eighteenth Century* (New York, 1924). My other sources of information are indicated in the text, and in giving quotations either from MSS or print the original punctuation and spelling have been strictly followed. To make his position intelligible to the reader who is not familiar with the history of botany and physiology, it has been necessary to give some account of contemporary scientific knowledge; for this purpose I have employed Von Sachs's *History of Botany* (Garnsey's English translation revised by Balfour, Oxford, 1890), and Michael Foster's *History of Physiology* (Cambridge, 1901).

In the preparation of this book I received much kind assistance. Mr P. E. Towell, of Teddington, put me on to many interesting facts in connection with Hales's life, and Dr H. Godwin, of Clare College, Cambridge, kindly criticised my account of his botanical work. My wife helped me considerably in various ways. The Rev. Herbert Williams showed me the parish registers at Teddington, and Mr C. E. Baker, of Sherwood, Nottingham, the extensive genealogy of the Hales family prepared by the late Mr Hovenden. Vice-Admiral Sir Robert Dixon, K.C.B., R.N., and Sir William Berry, K.C.B., helped me at the Admiralty in looking up the use of Hales's ventilators on board H.M. ships. Mr E. H. Dring, of Sutton, courteously allowed me to see and make use of the Stukeley manuscripts in his possession. The Earl of Shaftesbury gave me permission to reproduce the picture of the Trustees of the colony of Georgia. I am particularly indebted to Mr G. B. Harrison of King's College, and to Dr Charles Singer of University College, for reading my MS and giving me valuable criticisms; also to Dr P. M. Tookey Kerridge for kindly reading the proofs.

A. E. CLARK-KENNEDY

London, October 1st, 1928

CONTENTS

ILLUSTRATIONS

CHAPTER I

THE family of Hales was one of the most ancient and distinguished in Kent. Their earliest ancestor, of whom there is any record, was Tonne, Lord of Hale and Luceby in Norfolk in the time of Edward the Confessor. Among his descendants was Sir Robert de Hales, Prior of the Hospital of St John of Jerusalem in the reign of Edward III, and Admiral of the Fleet and Treasurer of the Exchequer in the reign of Richard II; he was killed when Wat Tyler and his followers broke into the Tower of London. Sir Robert left no children, but the family was continued by his brother, Sir Nicholas Hales. Sir Nicholas had two grandsons; one became the head of the branch of the family that migrated to Coventry; the other continued to reside in Kent, and built Hales Place at Tenterden. Among the descendants of John Hales of Tenterden were Sir Christopher Hales, Attorney-General (1529), Vice-Chancellor, and Master of the Rolls, and Sir John Hales, Baron of the Exchequer (1522–1539). Sir John Hales had three sons. The eldest, another Sir John, received his knighthood at the coronation of Edward VI; his two younger brothers, Thomas Hales of Thanington, and Edward Hales of Tenterden, were the ancestors of the Bekesbourne and Woodchurch branches of the family.

Stephen Hales was descended from the Hales of Bekesbourne. Thomas Hales, the head of this branch of the family, had a son Charles, who was knighted in the reign of James I, and a great-grandson, Robert, who was created a baronet by Charles II at the Restoration. Sir Robert Hales's eldest son, Thomas, married Mary, daughter and heiress of Richard Wood, Esq., of Abbotts Langley in Hertfordshire; by this marriage he had six sons and five daughters. He predeceased his father, and, as his first two sons died young, his third son, Thomas, inherited the family title at his grandfather's death. Sir Thomas Hales, the second baronet, lived at "Howletts", Canterbury, and was Member of Parliament for Kent. At his death, in 1746, the title passed to his son, and then to two of his grandsons; but the baronetcy, like the one in the Woodchurch branch of the family,[1] became extinct early in the nineteenth century.[2]

Stephen Hales was the sixth and last son of Thomas

[1] Among the descendants of the Hales of Woodchurch, the senior branch of the family in Kent, was Sir Edward Hales, Bart., Lieutenant of the Tower, a Lord of the Admiralty, and a Privy Councillor. He was held in special favour by James II, and his connection with the King's attempted flight and abdication is well known. His eldest son supported the cause of the Stuarts, and was killed at the Battle of the Boyne. His second son transferred his allegiance to the House of Hanover, and declined a peerage offered to him by George I, when he was not allowed to assume the title of Earl of Tenterden; this son died fourth baronet. Three generations later the baronetcy became extinct (1829).

[2] This account is based on a manuscript genealogy of the Hales family drawn up by the late Mr Hovenden (now in the possession of Mr C. E. Baker of Sherwood, Nottingham), and on "Brief Notes on the Hales Family" by the Rev. R. Cox Hales, *Archaeologia Cantiana*, London, 1881.

and Mary Hales, and grandson of Sir Robert Hales, the first baronet. The last but one of a family of eleven, he was born at the family home at Bekesbourne in Kent on September 17th, 1677. Of his boyhood there is nothing recorded, except his own statement that he was educated at Kensington under Mr St Clair, and then at Orpington under the Rev. Mr Johnson. Thomas Hales died in his father's lifetime, and at his death the guardianship of Stephen devolved upon the boy's grandfather, Sir Robert Hales of Bekesbourne. Sir Robert and his family were said to be "constant hearers" of sermons preached by the Rev. Thomas Ventris, a graduate of Cambridge University, who had been a scholar on Archbishop Parker's Foundation at Corpus Christi College.

Mr. Ventris at length became possessed of St. *Margaret's* in his native City (Canterbury); where he behaved with so much prudence throughout those Times of difficulty, that at the Restoration, he was treated more kindly both by the Gentry and Clergy than most of his Brethren; but as he could not comply with the Terms of the Act of Uniformity, he was ejected with the rest. He continued his Preaching privately however, as he had opportunity, and at length became Pastor of a Congregation, amongst whom he laboured many years with no small Success: and when not thus employed, he was either at his Studies, or instructing Gentlemen's Sons, many of whom were committed to his Care. Thus profitably did he spend his time till the latter end of the Reign of *Charles* II, when he, like many others of the same Persuasion, met with great Disturbance from some Informers, who were the occasion of their being imprisoned etc. Soon after which Mr. *Ventris* with great serenity quitted his Life for a better, about the 73rd Year of his Age. He was a Person of no small

Learning, especially in History, and withal a very pious man, and very careful of redeeming his Time.[1]

It is likely that it was through his influence with Sir Robert Hales, that Stephen, having been properly instructed in "Grammar Learning", was sent up to Cambridge University in 1696, and, at the age of nineteen, admitted a pensioner of Bene't College (as Corpus Christi was then called) under the Tutorship of Mr Moss, later Dean of Ely.[2]

Stephen Hales entered Bene't College at a prosperous period of its history. Under the Mastership of Dr John Spencer, elected by the Fellows themselves in 1667 after a succession of Masters appointed by Royal Mandate, the College had recovered from the political upheavals of the Civil War, the Commonwealth, and the Restoration, and from the havoc wrought in Cambridge by the Great Plague. Spencer had introduced important educational reforms and disciplinary measures; under his rule the Society is said "to have flourished in reputation and numbers", so that in 1672 those in residence numbered one hundred and forty-five, of whom thirty-seven were scholars. Three years before Hales came to Corpus Christi, Spencer died; he was succeeded at the Lodge by Dr William Stanley. Five years later Stanley was followed in this office by Dr Thomas Greene, who introduced "the use of publick prayers in the Chapel immediately after the locking up of the gates, that he

---

[1] Robert Masters, *The History of Corpus Christi College, Cambridge*, Cambridge, 1753.

[2] When the College was founded, it was called Corpus Christi, but for many centuries (up till about 1820) it was generally known as Bene't College, from its architectural continuity with St Benedict's Church.

might know what Scholars were abroad, and, if need were, visit their chambers ".[1] Theology predominated, but even before Spencer's time science had become well established as a branch of learning. In 1618, Edward Lapworth, M.D., a member of the College, had been appointed "first Reader of Sir William Sedley's Lecture in Natural Philosophy", and "Lynacre's Physick Reader" in the following year.[2] At a later date, Edward Tyson, M.D., F.R.C.P., F.R.S. (1651–1708), had become well known as a comparative anatomist. William Briggs, M.D., F.R.S., elected a Fellow in 1668, had published his *Ophthalmographia*; he was the first in this country to write about vision and the anatomy of the eye.[3] During the same century John Hawys and his grandson of the same name, both Doctors of Medicine, were each for a time Fellows of the College.[4] Nor was scientific study limited to the medical graduates. In 1688, Clement Scott, a Fellow of the College and "Minister of St. Benedict", turned papist:

At the Revolution the mob broke into his rooms and would

[1] Rev. H. P. Stokes, *Cambridge University College Histories: Corpus Christi*, London, 1898.
[2] Robert Masters, *The History of Corpus Christi College*, Cambridge, 1753.
[3] J. Lamb, *Masters' History of Corpus Christi College, Cambridge, with a Continuation to the Present Time*, London, 1831.
[4] Thirty-seven members of the College graduated in medicine between the years 1600 and 1850. Five of them left their mark on the profession. Of these five, two have already been mentioned. Of William Stukeley there will be more to say below. The other two belong to a later date: Dr David Pitcairn, Physician to St Bartholomew's Hospital, the first to point out the relationship between rheumatic fever and heart disease (1749–1780); and Dr Bond, Regius Professor of Physic, who filled that chair with "dignity and distinction" from 1857 to 1882. Arnold Chaplin, *British Medical Journal*, 1928, i, 1109.

probably have seriously injured him had he not escaped from their rage by secreting himself in the cupola. They vented it, however, upon his books and papers, and there is every reason to imagine that several belonging to the College (he being then bursar) were destroyed. It is traditionally reported that upon finding Boyle's *Experiments on Blood* some of them cried out, *See what a bloody-minded dog he is, his books are full of nothing but blood.*[1]

Of Bene't College, as it was in the days when Hales was an undergraduate, the Old Court, connected with St Bene't's Church, alone remains; the main entrance was through the archway in the north-west corner, opening into Bene't Street. The building on the south side (the present Kitchen) was the Hall. The Master's Lodge was in the south-east corner, and a gallery, built by Matthew Parker, connected it with the Chapel and Library. To the west of the Chapel, the "old tennis-court" had been converted into the Pensionary (Plate II). To the south of these buildings there was an open space: from north to south, the Master's flower garden, the kitchen garden, the Fellows' garden and bowling-green, and the "new tennis-court". On the far side the gardens were bounded by Free School Lane, and on the south by St Botolph's Lane.[2] The Fellows occupied the first-floor sets of rooms in the Old Court, and had the use of the attics over them as sleeping places for the

[1] Robert Masters, *The History of Corpus Christi College, Cambridge*, Cambridge, 1753.

[2] With the construction of the new court in the early years of the nineteenth century, Parker's gallery, the Chapel, and the Pensionary, were pulled down. The old Hall was converted into the Kitchen, and the Chapel and the Master's Lodge now stand on ground once occupied by the Fellows' garden and the tennis-court.

Plate II. Corpus Christi College, Cambridge, in the XVIIIth century. The old Chapel and the Pensionary

(From Masters's *History* of the College)

particular pupils allotted to their care. Other undergraduates "kept" in the Pensionary. The scholars lived in the ground-floor rooms of the old quadrangle. This is a brief account of the College to which Hales came as an undergraduate in 1696. His Master was Stanley, and his Tutor Moss. He probably occupied an Old Court attic above his Tutor's rooms. Of his student days no record has been left, but some idea of the education of the period may be gained from the diary[1] of his friend, William Stukeley, who entered the College a few years later, and made "physick" his principal study.

I was matriculated Spring 1704. I staid all that year in College, applying myself to the accustomd studys, & constantly attending Lectures, sometimes twice or thrice a day, & Chappel thrice a day, & scarce missed three times all the while I staid in College. My Tutor, & Mr., now Dr. Danny, afterwards Chaplain to the Chancellor of the University, the Duke of Somerset, now Rector of Spofforth in Yorkshire, joined in reading to their respective Pupils. The former read to us in Classics, Ethics, Logic, Metaphysics, Divinity, & the other in Arithmetic, Algebra, Geometry, Philosophy, Astronomy, Trigonometry. Mr. Fawcett read to us in Tullys offices, the Greek Testament, Maximus Tyrius by Davis, Clerks Logics, Metaphysics, Grotius de jure Belli & Pacis, Pufendorf de Officio Nominis & Civis, Wilkins Natural Religion, Lock of human Understanding, Tullys Orations. Mr. Danny read to us in Wells Arithmetica numerosa & speciosa, Pardies Geometry, Tacquets Geometry by Whiston, Harris's use of the Globes, Rohaults Physics by Clark. He read to us Clarks 2 Volumes of Sermons at Boyles Lectures,

[1] *Family Memoirs of the Rev. William Stukeley, M.D.*, edited by Rev. W. C. Lukis, and published by the Surtees Society, 3 vols. London, 1882.

Varenius Geography put out by Sr Isaac Newton, & many other occasional pieces of Philosophy, & the Sciences subservient thereto. These courses we went thro with so much constancy that with moderate application we could scarce fail of acquiring a good knowledg therein.

Stukeley also tells something of their recreations:

I used to frequent, among the other Lads, the River in sheeps Green, & learnt to swim in Freshmens & Sophs pools as they are called, & sometimes in Paradice, reckoning it a Beneficial Exercise. About 1705 Mr. Hales & Mr. Waller gathered subscriptions to make the cold bath about a mile & a half out of town.

Although most of Hales's fellow-undergraduates, like himself, were ordinands, they all gave some time to classics, mathematics, science, and philosophy. Hales, being intended for the Church, received special instruction in divinity from his Tutor, Mr Moss, and it was on his merits as a student of theology that, after taking his first degree in Arts in 1699, he was pre-elected into a Fellowship on April 16th, 1702: he was to be elected a Fellow of the College as soon as there should be a vacancy.

In this year the Society consisted of twelve Fellows under the Mastership of Dr Thomas Greene. The two senior were Richard Sheldrake, B.D., and Thomas Beck, B.D.; both had been elected soon after the Restoration. The next senior was Charles Kidman, B.D., a celebrated Tutor of the College, and "one of the earliest, if not the first", to introduce the reading of Locke's *Essay on the Human Understanding* in place of the old logic. Kidman is described as "a man of great judgment, candour, and virtue, a steady friend to liberty at all times"; it is said that it was principally owing to him that the College was "so firmly attached to the Revolution, and the succession in the House of Hanover, when principles of a quite different tendency were inculcated".

When Dr. Tenison became Bishop of Lincoln in 1691, he took Mr. Kidman for his Chaplain, but did not carry him to Lambeth upon his promotion to the Archbishoprick of Canterbury; for which among others one reason assigned was, that the clamour raised against him as a person of Latitudinarian principles, from a Sermon preached before the University, on "Private Judgment in Matters of Religion", prevented it.

The fourth Fellow was Robert Moss, D.D., Hales's Tutor, a Chaplain to King William, and Dean of Ely. The next, Henry Williams, B.D., had been elected to the Society at a stormy College meeting. "Nov. 11, 1689. Mr. Williams was then chosen and pronounced Fellow, by the Master, Mr. Beck, Mr. Kemp, Mr. Kidman, the rest (being five) suspended and gave no vote." Mr Williams subsequently caused trouble:

April 4, 1708. Agreed then by all the Fellows present, that every Fellow that is summoned to a meeting by the Master ought to be there. Agreed that Mr. Williams' reasons for not appearing at the Meeting called on Saturday last are not sufficient to excuse his absence. Then the Master of the College admonished Mr. Williams to take care for the future not to be absent from a meeting when summoned thereto.[1]

Mr Williams became senior Fellow some time after,

[1] J. Lamb, *Masters' History of Corpus Christi College, Cambridge, with a Continuation to the Present Time*, London, 1831.

and when, in the Master's absence, the College Order Book was entrusted to his keeping, he seized the opportunity to obliterate this censure that the College had passed on his conduct. The sixth Fellow was Edward Oliver, D.D., Chaplain to the Earl of Northampton; he succeeded in acquiring some notoriety as a bitter opponent of non-conformity:

> Mr. Oliver being exalted to the dignity of the scarf, as a domestic Chaplain to a nobleman, had the honour to preach before Sir H. Edwin, the Lord Mayor, at St. Paul's; when he seized the opportunity to display his ill-timed zeal against the worship of the Nonconformists. For his want of judgment in offering this public affront to a Presbyterian chief magistrate, he met with a proper reproof, in a clever pamphlet, which came speedily to a second edition, and was entitled, "A *Rowland* for an *Oliver*; or A Sharp Rebuke to a Saucy Levite".

The next senior was John Waller, B.D., "the Humanity Lecturer of Bene't, who ordered his sophs to make themes on unheard-of things, and set up for a pretty fellow".[1] He was subsequently appointed Professor of Chemistry in the University in succession to Vigani, and occupied this chair until 1717, when he was succeeded by Mr John Mickleberg, B.D., another member of the College. The eighth was Elias Sydall, D.D., "one of the best candidates ever examined for Holy Orders", and later Bishop of Gloucester. The remaining four were, John Scott, D.D., Michael Bull, B.D., Thomas Fawcett (Stukeley's tutor), and Nicholas Bacon, B.D. It seems

---

[1] Rev. H. P. Stokes, *Cambridge University College Histories: Corpus Christi*, London, 1884.

strange that, when a few years afterwards two new
Fellows were elected to this Society, both of whom
subsequently held high office in the Church, Bishop
Greene should have thought it necessary to write
from Norwich and warn them "not to tipple wine
every night at the houses of the Townsmen, to avoid
their names being entered in the gate-bill, and not
to be absent from morning chapels". Politically, led
by the Master and Kidman, the Society was well
united; they were mostly Whigs and supporters of
the Hanoverian Succession. Theology and classics
predominated in the scholarship of Greene, Moss, and
Fawcett, but learning of this kind was varied by
Kidman's philosophy and Waller's chemistry; Danny,
who shortly succeeded Sydall, was a student of
mathematics, physics, and astronomy.

Hales did not have to wait long for a vacancy;
Mr Bull was presented to the living of Brasted in
Kent by Archbishop Tenison, and on February 25th,
1703, Hales was admitted a Fellow of the College. In
the same year he took the degree of Master of Arts,
and on September 19th was ordained Deacon at
Bugden by Dr Gardner, Bishop of Lincoln.[1] As an
undergraduate he had already received a liberal
education; he now came into a more intimate relationship with his teachers. There were arguments on
classics and theology, and discussions on the University topics of the day, the rise of the Newtonian
philosophy and the fall of the Cartesian, Bentley's
recent attack on the atheists, and his impending prosecution by his own Fellows. Controversies were

[1] *Gentleman's Magazine*, 1799, LXIX, 267.

frequent between Kidman, with his Latitudinarian principles, and Oliver, the bitter opponent of individualism in matters of belief. Waller was studying chemistry and Danny physics, and it was during the early years of his Fellowship that Hales began to take a serious interest in science. He continued his theological studies, however, and some years later took the degree of Bachelor of Divinity. On June 19th, 1709, he was ordained Priest at Fulham by Dr Compton, Bishop of London.

The study of science at Bene't College was but a single instance of a movement that was rapidly developing in the University as a whole. Newton, born in the year that Galileo died, had entered Trinity College as an undergraduate in 1661, and within eight years had succeeded to the Lucasian Chair of Mathematics vacated by Dr Barrow. When Hales came to Bene't College, Newton was still at Trinity, but four years later Newton left Cambridge to take up his new appointment as Governor of the Mint; shortly afterwards he resigned his Lucasian Professorship in favour of his deputy, Whiston, of Clare College. In 1700, the year in which Newton left Cambridge, Richard Bentley, the classical scholar and Regius Professor of Divinity in the University, was appointed Master of Trinity, and played an active part in developing the Cambridge school of natural science which Newton had founded. When the Plumian Professorship of Astronomy was endowed in 1706, Bentley, wishing Trinity to be "a house of all kinds of good letters", and being anxious to continue in the College the scientific tradition that Newton had established, succeeded in procuring the unanimous election of Roger Cotes, one of the junior Fellows.

No sooner had he accomplished this point than he undertook to build a noble observatory, that the study of Astronomy promoted by such a Professor, and aided by such advantages, might become naturalised and permanent in Trinity College. For this purpose he instituted a subscription among members of the College and lovers of science throughout the University, by means of which he succeeded in erecting over the beautiful entrance of the College, called the King's Gate, an Observatory stored with the best astronomical instruments which science could at that period produce. It was at this time his favourite object to make Trinity College the focus of all the science in the University. With this view he procured for Professor Whiston chambers in the College adjoining the King's Gate, from which he and his pupils enjoyed the full advantage and convenience of the observatory.[1]

In 1703, a Grace had been passed by the Senate "investing with the title of Professor of Chemistry, John Francis Vigani, a native of Verona, who has taught chemistry with reputation for 20 years previously". Bentley, "to serve the purposes of science and promote the dignity of the College", now succeeded in transplanting Vigani from Queens' to Trinity, where he fitted up "an elegant Chymical Laboratory made out of a ruinous Lumber-Hole, the thieving House of the Bursars of the Old Set, who in spite of frequent orders to prevent it, would still embezzle the College-Timber". This laboratory, said to be the first of its kind in Cambridge, was constructed by Bentley on the bowling-green in the face of vigorous opposition on the part of the Fellows of

---

[1] J. H. Monk, *Life of Richard Bentley*, D.D., London, 1833.

the College, who considered it an unwarrantable encroachment upon their comfort. Here, Vigani gave his lectures and demonstrations for several years.

The important part played by the Cambridge school of natural science in determining the course and nature of Hales's researches will become apparent later. At this time there was another influence to which he was subjected, for in 1703, just a few months after he had been elected to his Fellowship, William Stukeley came as an undergraduate to Bene't College.

I (*Stukeley*) was admitted Pensioner in Corpus Christi, or Bennit College, Cambridg, Nov. 20. 1703. I was examined by my countryman old Mr. Beck, the senior Fellow, & Mr. Waller; my Tutor was Mr. Thomas Fawcett recommended by Mr. Dodson, Bro^r to my Uncle Dodson, at that time Butler of Kings College. I went to reside there about Lady day following, & kept in the ground chamber in Katherin Hall Court, next the Walk that leads to the Gate, my study was the first corner of the College on the right hand going from the street to the gate. Mr. John Brand, now living near Norwich, was my chum & at that time Janitor & Chappel Clerk. I was, soon after, Scholar of the House & removed into my Scholarship Chamber, the ground room on the left hand, the first stair case on the right hand of the Court beyond the corner; my study that in the room, & bed that next the fire place. I had not been a month in the University before I made a map of the whole Town....

I turned my mind particularly to the study of Physick, & in order thereto began to make a diligent & near inquisition into Anatomy & Botany, in consort with Hobart, a senior Lad of our College who was entered into that study, & since dead. With him I went frequently a simpling, & began to steal dogs & dissect them & all sorts of animals that came in our way. We saw too, many Philosophical Experiments in Pneumatic Hydrostatic Engines & instruments performed at that time by Mr. Waller, after parson of Grantchester, where he dy'd last year beeing professor of chymistry, & the doctrine of Optics & Telescopes & Microscopes, & some Chymical Experiments, with Mr. Stephen Hales then Fellow of the College, now of the Royal Society. I contracted acquaintance with all the Lads (& them only) in the University that studyd Physic, & Swallow of Pembroke who took his Batchelor of Physics degree while I was there, & since practised near or at Bp Stortford, now dead; Child of Magdalen who now practises at Lavenham Suffolk, & Parry Humphry, who both took the same degree, the latter now lives in North Wales; Joseph Sparkes, of St. Johns, who now lives at Peterburgh; Henry Stebbing, of Katherin Hall, who since took Orders, & has signalised himself ag^t the Bp. of Bangor; Kitchener of Queens' College, since dead; Dr. Ashenhurst, now living in Trinity College; Dr. Addenbrook, now dead. I was acquainted with Dr. Crask, since dead, at Bury St. Edmonds. With these I used to range about once or twice a week the circumjacent country, & search the Gravel & Chalk pits for fossils. Gogmagog hills, the Moors about Cherry Hinton, Grantchester, Trumpington, Madingley Woods, Hill of Health, Chesterton, Barnwell, were the frequent scenes of our simpling toyl, armed with Candleboxes & Rays catalogus. We hunted after Butterflys, dissected frogs, usd to have sett meetings at our chambers, to confer about our studys, try Chymical experiments, cut up Dogs, Cats, & the like. I went to Chymical Lectures with Seignor Vigani at his Laboratory in Queens' College. I took down all his Readings in Writing, & have them in a Book with Drawings of his manner of building Furnaces of Dry Bricks without Iron or Mortar, & his manner of regulating the Fire to any degree of heat.

Stukeley's father died early in 1706, and in consequence he was absent from Cambridge for a while.

At that time I sett myself to work in dissecting Dogs, & Herons, & all sorts of Animals that came in my Way. We

had an old Cat in the house, which had been a great Favorite
of my Fathers & the whole Familys, & by my Mothers leave
I rid her of the infirmitys of age, & made a handsom sceleton
of her bones, which I carryd to Cambridg with me the next
Journey thither, & after I had taken my Degree & was leaving
the University I buryed her in a high walk by the side of the
Lane leading from the Spittle house Conduit & the bridge
in the road to Gogmagog hills, where I used frequently to
walk. I likewise sceletonised several different sorts of birds,
& made air pumps & 20 inventions to try mechanical &
philosophical experiments I had learnt in my Academical
Lectures....We took up old Hoyes that hangd himself &
was buryed in the highway, & dissected him, & afterwards
made a sceleton of his bones, & put them into a fine Glass
case with an inscription in Latin....At this time my Tutor
gave me a Room in the College to dissect in, & practise
Chymical Experiments, which had a very strange appearance
with my Furniture in it, the wall was generally hung round
with Guts, stomachs, bladders, preparations of parts &
drawings. I had sand furnaces, Calots, Glasses, & all sorts
of Chymical Implements. I then tryd a good experiment of
blowing up the lungs thro a heated gun barrel for a day
together, a pair of bellows being tyd to the wind pipe, & a
pan of charcoal under the barrel, so that the lungs being
thro'ly dry I pourd into them melted lead which filld up all
their ramifications like the branches of a tree, then rotting
the substance of them with water I had the finest animal
plant that ever was seen which was mightily admired, but
I pulld it all to bits to give away little portions of it among
my acquaintance. Here I & my Associats often dind upon
the same table as our dogs lay upon. I often prepard the
pulvis fulminans & sometime surprizd the whole College
with a sudden explosion. I cur'd a lad once of an ague with
it by fright. In my own Elaboratory I made large quantitys
of sal volatile oleosum, Tinctura Metallorum, Elixir Proprietatis, & such matters as would serve to put into our Drink.
I usd to distribute it with a plentiful hand to my Tutors

Fawcet & Danny, to Mr. Kidman who was their Tutor, then Senior Fellow & President, to Mr. Williams, & Bacon acquaintance of my Tutors since dead (the two last), & to any of the Lads I kept Company withal....I visited the Apothecarys shop to make my self perfect in the knowledge of Drugs, & Officinal Compositions & exercised a little Gratis Practise among the poor people that depended upon the College, & such lads as would trust themselves to my Care. I prescribed often to one Smith, who was our Joyner, & the Fellow in gratitude promised me his body to dissect when he dyd, which happening next Spring when I was out of College he expressed much concern that I could not have the benefit of his Promise.[1]

Hales was ten years older than Stukeley, seven years senior to him in the University, and already a Fellow of the College; in spite of this they soon became acquainted. When Fawcett gave Stukeley a room in College for his dissections and experiments, Hales became an interested spectator of his strange pursuits. He began to offer advice, and make suggestions; Stukeley's method of obtaining a cast of the bronchial tree in lead was his idea. Then, anxious to direct Stukeley's widely scattered interests into more profitable channels, Hales and others suggested that he should bring out a revised edition of Ray's catalogue of Cambridge plants:

When I came back to Cambridg I found Mr. Rolf dissecting there, & he was declard Professor of Anatomy in the University. He was very curious too in the knowledge of Botanics. Mr. Step. Hales, & he & I, & Mr. Sherwin, Fellow

[1] *Family Memoirs of the Rev. William Stukeley, M.D.*, edited by Rev. W. C. Lukis and published by the Surtees Society, 3 vols. London, 1882. The original diary is now in the possession of E. H. Dring, Esq., The Ridgeway, Sutton.

of Christs, & several more of us, usd to goe a simpling
together. I had drawn a Map of the County of Cambridg
to put into Rays Catalogus which I carryd about with me
(*Plate III*). They put me upon dressing up a new Edition
of that famous Restorer of Botany among us, whereto should
have been prefixd a Map, & they would procure the large
Additions to the work of plants observd there since his
time, but my short stay there prevented any such thoughts
being put in execution.[1]

Before long a close friendship grew up between
Hales and Stukeley, and of this, Peter Collinson,
their contemporary, gives some account:

They rambled over *Gogmagog Hills* and the bogs of *Cherry-
Hunt-Moor* to gather simples with Ray's *Catalogus Plantarum
circa Canterbrigiam nascentium* in their pockets, to which
Stukeley, who was always a ready draughtsman, had added a
map of the country, the better to direct them in their peregri-
nations; in some of these expeditions they collected fossils from
the gravel and chalk-pits; and in others they hunted butterflies
having contrived an instrument for taking them. *Hales* also
in conjunction with his friend *Stukeley* applied himself to
the study of anatomy, frequently dissecting frogs, and other
animals, in their herbarising walks. They proceeded also to
the dissection of dogs, and *Hales* contrived a method of
obtaining a preparation of the lungs in lead, of which Dr.
Stukeley now has several specimens. They applied themselves also to chymistry and repeated many of Mr. *Boyle's*
experiments, making flowers of *benzoin, pulvis fulminans,
elixir proprietatis*, and various preparations, some of use,
others of curiosity: but besides what they did between
them, they attended the chymical lectures that were then
read by the public Professor Signior Vigani in *Queens
College* Cloysters, and went also to see the chymical operations which he performed in a room at Trinity College,
which had been the laboratory of Sir *Isaac Newton*, and

[1] Stukeley's Diary.

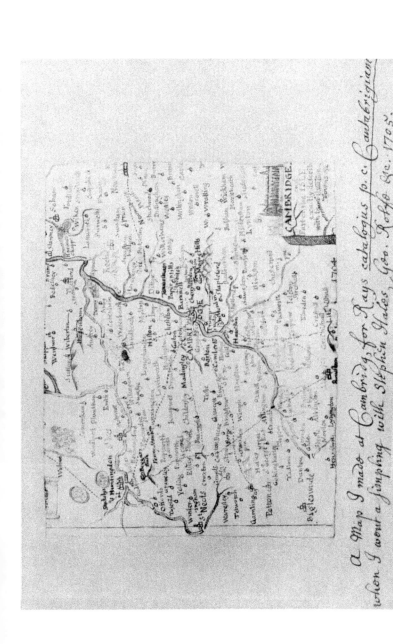

A Map I made at Cambridg, for Rays catalogus &c. Cantabrigiam
when I went a simpling with Stephen Hales, &c. Roffo &c. 1705.

Plate III. Stukeley's map of the country round Cambridge
(From the original in the Bodleian Library)

in which, unfortunately for the world, Sir *Isaac Newton's* manuscript concerning chymical principles was accidentally burned.[1]

When it was completed, they worked in the laboratory on the bowling-green at Trinity, and it was at Whiston's classes on "Hydrostatics and Pneumatics" that they repeated Robert Boyle's experiments. They also attended Roger Cotes's lectures on astronomy, and used the telescopes installed in the observatory over the Great Gate at Trinity.

Hales was equally assiduous and successful in the study of astronomy, for having acquired a perfect knowledge of the *Newtonian* system, he contrived a machine to demonstrate it, which was constructed of brass and moved by wheels, so as to represent the motions of all the planets, upon the same principles, and nearly in the same manner as the machine afterwards constructed by Mr. *Rowley*, Master of Mathematics to King George I, which was absurdly called an *Orrery*, because an Earl of *Orrery* was *Rowley's* patron. This machine was supposed to be the first of its kind, but it appeared that Dr. *Cumberland*, Rector of *All-Saints* at *Stamford*, and afterwards Bishop of *Peterborough*, had constructed one of them before, when he was fellow of *Magdalene College, Cambridge*. *Stukeley*, at the request of his friend *Hales*, made a drawing of the sphere he invented. (*Plate IV.*)[1]

The University and the College taught Hales physical science; but it was William Stukeley, the undergraduate and medical student, who started his interest in biology. Credit is due to Fawcett, the classical Tutor of Bene't, for allowing Stukeley a free hand, and giving him active assistance in follow-

[1] Peter Collinson, *Gentleman's Magazine*, 1764, xxxiv, 273; *Annual Register*, 1764, vol. vii, Characters, 42.

ing out his own inclinations. Stukeley did not altogether fulfil his early promise; but the influence that Stukeley, thus encouraged, exerted on Hales, who subsequently exceeded in scientific achievement anything that could have been expected of him in those early days, justified Fawcett's action.

In 1709, after taking his degree of Bachelor of Medicine, Stukeley left Cambridge, and their companionship ceased.

In December 1708 I went again to College, where I prepard myself for taking my Degree. I enterd then into Fellows Commons. My Questions were in Catamenia pendent a plethora, upon which I made a Thesis when I kept my Act, Monday 24. Jan. 1708–9. Mr. Danny was my Far as we call it, and opend the Dispute with a jocular speech, according to custom, wherein he expatiated on my Dissecting the Old Man of Holbech. Mr. Waller, another Fellow of our College, was my Prompter, as the Method is, he being Devoted to Physic. The exercise being over I kept my Feast where the Professor Dr. Green, & his namesake the Mr of our College, favord me with their Company among the Rest of the Faculty in the University, & the Professor observd to me the next day that he never was so merry, nor staid so long at any Entertainment before. The Young Gentlemen of the University, who were Students in our Faculty or of my Acquaintance, I treated at the same time very plentifully in my own Chamber, & I think I went to bed the soberest of all the company.[1]

Stukeley went down from Cambridge in January, and Hales left Bene't College a few months later. On

[1] Stukeley's Diary. Stukeley afterwards became a Fellow of the Royal Society and a Fellow of the Royal College of Physicians; he delivered the Goulstonian Lectures [on the spleen]. In later life, being, as he said, "of a religious turn of mind from his youth", he gave up medicine and took Holy Orders. He also relinquished

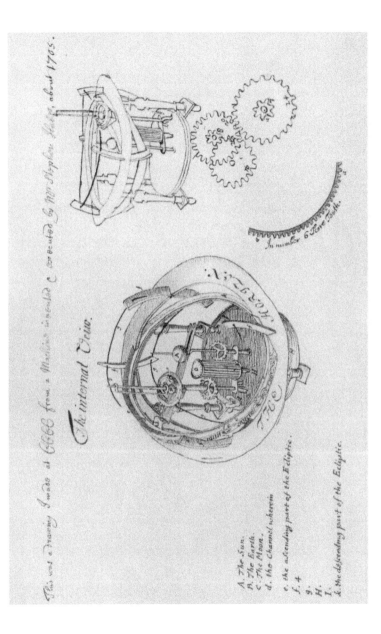

This was a Drawing I made at 6666 from a Machine invented & executed by Mr Stephen Hales, about 1705.

The internal View.

MORGEN

A. The Sun.
B. The Earth.
c. The Moon.
d. the Channel wherein
e. the ascending part of the Ecliptic.
f. +
g.
H.
k. the descending part of the Ecliptic.

In number 6 Score Teeth.

Plate IV. Stukeley's drawing of the machine which Hales constructed to demonstrate the movements of the planets

(From the original in the Bodleian Library)

August 10th, 1709, he was appointed "Perpetual Curate", or Minister, of the parish of Teddington in the County of Middlesex. The reason why he left the University without waiting for a College living is not altogether apparent. Perhaps he found life at Cambridge intolerable now that Stukeley had left; in his close association with him he may have lost touch with the other Fellows of the College; or it is possible that the Society did not altogether approve of the unconventional way in which he spent his time. The considerations responsible for his decision can only be surmised, but it is significant that his leaving should have followed so closely on Stukeley's departure. He retained his Fellowship for some years longer, and it appears from the College Order Book that he continued to visit Cambridge occasionally.

science and natural history for antiquarian studies, a field in which his powers of draughtsmanship found adequate scope. He became Secretary of the Society of Antiquaries, devoted much time to the collection of Greek and Roman coins, and published works on Stonehenge, Avebury, heathen mythology, and an account of the eclipse predicted by Thales. He survived Hales, and died in 1765.

CHAPTER II[1]

Animal Physiology. Blood Pressure. Cardiac Output. Blood Flow through the Tissues. Muscular Movement. The Spinal Reflex.

AT about this time, Hales began researches on the physiology of the circulation of the blood in animals. Throughout this chapter the reader must remember that his experiments were performed alone and unaided in the Parsonage at Teddington. These researches extended over many years; his life as a country parson will form the subject of the next chapter, but, since this work was the direct result of the education he had received at the University, it is natural to give some account of it at this point.

At Cambridge he had been well grounded in the Newtonian physics and astronomy of his day, and, by the time he left the University, had acquired a thorough knowledge of physical and chemical science, and the laws of mechanics as then understood. Of physiology he had been taught little; but contact with Stukeley had stimulated his interest in biology, and his education as a whole had shown him the value of the experimental method:

In so complicated a subject as the animal body, all things are wisely adjusted in number, weight and measure, yet with such complex circumstances as require many *data* from ex-

---

[1] This chapter is of necessity technical, and it is not possible to make it altogether intelligible to anyone who is unfamiliar with anatomy and physiology. It may also be repellent to the reader who is not accustomed to experiments on animals, but it can be omitted without interfering seriously with the story of his life.

periments, whereon to found just calculations: but though
many of the following calculations are founded only on such
inaccurate mensurations as the nature of the subject would
allow of; yet may we thence fairly draw many rational de-
ductions in relation to the animal oeconomy.[1]

Since the work of Harvey, knowledge of the mechanics of the circulation had advanced considerably.
Malpighi had described the capillary vessels, which
connect the ends of the arteries with the beginnings
of the veins. Borelli had pointed out that the beat of
the heart was a muscular contraction, comparable to
that of a skeletal muscle, and that the elastic recoil of
the arteries during diastole played an important part
in promoting the onward flow of blood. He had also
calculated the blood pressure from measurements of
the capacity of the heart and the dimensions of the
vessels, but they led him to the entirely erroneous conclusion that the force of each heart beat was 135,000
pounds! In his *Tractatus dè Corde*, Lower had given
an accurate description of the structure of the heart
and the distribution of its nerve supply, and had
shown that the heart would beat for a while after
being cut away from all its bodily connections. He
had also extended Harvey's exposition of the circulation of the blood with the help of the new and
exact physics, which had come to hand since Harvey
wrote his book, and had computed, from anatomical
measurements, the output of the ventricles and the
velocity of the blood in the arteries. As yet, however,
although attempts had been made to calculate it, the
blood pressure had not been directly measured. The

[1] Hales, *Haemastatics*, 3rd ed. Preface.

vaguest ideas were still prevalent as to its magnitude, and, the source of muscular energy being then unknown, the lateral swelling of a muscle during contraction was attributed to the force of the blood in the nutrient vessels dilating the muscle fibres.[1]

Hales knew that this explanation was completely unsupported by experimental proof:

> Having read the unsatisfactory conjectures of several, about the cause of muscular motion, it occurred to me, that by fixing tubes in the arteries of live animals, I might find pretty nearly, whether the blood, by its mere hydraulic energy, could have a sufficient force, by dilating the fibres of the acting muscles, and thereby shortening their lengths, to produce the great effects of muscular motion. And hence it was, that I was insensibly led on from time to time, into this large field of statical and other experiments.

This method, "his statical way of investigation", ran through all his subsequent experimental work, and was in a large measure responsible for the successes he achieved in many branches of physiology: "since the animal fluids move by *hydraulic* and *hydrostatic* laws, the likeliest way therefore to succeed in our inquiries into the nature of their motions, is by adapting our experiments to those laws". Hence his classical experiments on blood pressure:

> In December I caused a *mare* to be tied down alive on her back; she was 14 hands high, and about 14 years of age, had a fistula on her withers, was neither very lean nor very lusty: having laid open the left crural artery about 3 inches from her belly, I inserted into it a brass pipe whose bore was 1/6 of an inch in diameter; and to that, by means of another brass

[1] Sir Michael Foster, *Lectures on the History of Physiology*, Cambridge, 1901.

pipe which was fitly adapted to it, I fixed a glass tube, of nearly the same diameter, which was 9 feet in length: then untying the ligature on the artery, the blood rose in the tube 8 feet 3 inches perpendicular above the level of the left ventricle of the heart: but it did not attain to its full height at once; it rushed up about half way in an instant, and afterwards gradually at each pulse 12, 8, 6, 4, 2, and sometimes 1 inch: when it was at its full height, it would rise and fall at and after each pulse 2, 3, or 4 inches; and sometimes it would fall 12 or 14 inches, and have there for a time the same vibrations up and down, at and after each pulse, as it had, when it was at its full height; to which it would rise again, after forty or fifty pulses.[1]

I laid a common field gate on the ground, with some straw upon it, on which a white *mare* was cast on her right side, and in that posture bound fast to the gate; she was 14 hands and 3 inches high, lean, tho' not to a great degree, and about 10 or 12 years old. This and the above-mentioned horse and mare were to have been killed as being unfit for service. Then laying open the left jugular vein, I fixed to that part of it which comes from the head, a glass tube, which was four feet and 2 inches long. The blood rose in it, in 3 or 4 seconds of time about a foot, and then was stationary for 2 or 3 seconds; then in 3 or 4 seconds more, it rose sometimes gradually, and sometimes with an unequally accelerated motion, 9 inches or more, on small strainings of the mare: then upon greater strainings, it rose about a yard, and would subside 5 or 6 inches: then upon a larger strain or struggle of the mare, it rose so high, as to flow a little out of the top of the tube; so that had the tube been a few inches higher, it would have risen probably to that height. Then laying bare the left carotid artery, I fixed to it towards the heart the brass pipe, and to that the windpipe of a goose; to the other end of which a glass tube was fixed, which was 12 feet 9 inches long. The design of using

---

[1] Hales, *Haemastatics*, 3rd ed. p. 1.

the wind-pipe was by its pliancy to prevent the incon-
veniences that might happen when the mare struggled; if
the tube had been immediately fixed to the artery, without
the intervention of this pliant pipe. The blood rose in the
tube in the same manner, as in the case of the two former
horses, till it reached to 9 feet 6 inches height.[1]

He realised that one criticism could be levelled
against this method of determining the blood
pressure:

It may be objected to this method of estimating the
force of the blood, that by thus fixing tubes to these large
veins and arteries, the course of a considerable stream of
blood was for that time stopped; and that consequently
the force of the blood must be proportionately increased
in all the veins and arteries: and doubtless to some
degree it is so. To obviate therefore this inconvenience,
I fixed tubes laterally to the jugular veins and arteries of the
dog, Numb. 13, in the following manner: viz. I took two
cylindrical sticks which were $\frac{1}{2}$ inch diameter, and $1 + \frac{1}{2}$ inch
in length; and having bored holes through them from end
to end, something larger than those of veins and arteries;
I then slit them in halves length-ways, and bored another hole
through the middle of one of them into its cavity, into which
lateral hole the brass pipe entered; which was, at its other end,
adapted to fit another pipe which was cemented to a glass
tube. Then having laid the vein or artery bare, I drew a linen
cloth under it, to wipe it very dry; and then placed under it
one of the above-mentioned slit pieces of wood, laying the
vein or artery in its cavity, which was covered with pitch,
that was at that instant afresh melted with a small warm iron
rod; then pouring melted pitch not very hot, over the vein
or artery, I immediately put on the other half of the split
wood, which had the hole bored thro' it, and tied them fast
together: then entering the slender point of a pen-knife into
the above-mentioned hole, I cut an orifice in the vein or

[1] Hales, *Haemastatics*, 3rd ed. p. 13.

artery, and then immediately fixed the brass pipe and tube to receive the following blood, which rose from the jugular vein of the thirteenth dog, first, six inches, and on straining $9 + \frac{1}{2}$ inches, and from the artery four feet eleven inches.[1]

He had now measured the blood pressure in the large arteries and veins. In the arteries, this is the result of two forces: the output of the heart, and the peripheral resistance. His next step was a detailed investigation of these two factors, and his subsequent researches fall into two divisions: attempts to determine the output of the heart, and an investigation into the mechanics of the peripheral circulation.

The output of blood from the heart per minute is the output at each beat multiplied by its rate of beating. Not only does the pulse rate alter from time to time, but the output per beat varies under different conditions of exercise and rest. He seems to have been well aware of this. The following passage shows that he had a clear idea of the importance of the muscular and respiratory movements in promoting the return of venous blood to the heart, and of the

---

[1] Hales, *Haemastatics*, 3rd ed. p. 33. His experiments are all undated, but the following passage in his book shows that his work on the circulation was the first research in which he engaged, although it was not published until several years after he had completed his later researches on vegetable physiology. " I endeavoured about twenty-five years since, by proper experiments, to find what was the real force of the blood in the crural arteries of dogs, and about six years afterwards I repeated the like experiments on two horses, and a fallow doe" (*Haemastatics*, Introduction). A comparison of dates shows that his first observation on the blood pressure of the dog must have been performed before he left the University, possibly in Vigani's laboratory at Trinity, but more probably in the seclusion of Stukeley's room at Bene't College. His experiments on the arterial and venous blood pressure of horses were carried out at the Parsonage in Teddington.

principle underlying Starling's law: the direct response of the heart to increased diastolic filling by
augmented systolic output. Continuing his description of his experiment on the white mare, he writes:

The violent straining to get loose, did, by the acting of
most of her muscles, especially the abdominal, impel the
blood from all parts to the *vena cava*, and consequently there
was a greater supply for the heart, which must therefore
throw out more at each pulsation, and thereby increase the
force of the blood in the arteries. For the same reason too,
it would be somewhat increased in height upon deep sighing,
because the lungs being then put into greater motion, and
more dilated, the blood passed more freely, and in greater
quantity, to the left auricle, and thence to the ventricle.

The determination of the output of the heart per
minute has always been, and still is, a matter of considerable difficulty. Hales came to the conclusion
that an approximate idea of it under resting conditions could be obtained by injecting the interior of
the left ventricle with melted wax at a pressure comparable to that which was maintained during life in
the great veins near the heart. For these experiments
he used a mare, an ox, a "fat gelt sheep or wether",
and twenty dogs of different weights. The pulse rate of
the animal under resting conditions was counted; as
this would be considerably disturbed by the pain and
terror of the experiment, care was taken to do this
before the experiment was begun. He could not
record satisfactorily the pulse of the ox, and so he
took instead the rate of the heart beat in "a very
gentle cow which was not terrified or disturbed while
its pulse was counted". In the case of the fallow doe
he came to the conclusion that it was impossible to

obtain "in that timorous creature the just number of pulses in a minute"; the fallow doe was therefore omitted from his subsequent calculations. After the pressures in the carotid artery and jugular vein had been determined during life, the animal was bled to death. A third vertical tube, four feet high, was then tied into the pulmonary vein, and melted wax poured down it. The wax flowed into the left auricle, passed through the mitral valve, entered the left ventricle, forced the aortic valve, and appeared in the tube tied into the carotid artery; the aorta was now ligatured, and the wax allowed to harden *in situ*. By this method the ventricle was kept distended, while the wax was hardening, by a hydrostatic pressure approximately equal to the venous pressure which normally opens the mitral valve and fills the ventricle during diastole: "So that this piece of wax thus formed, may reasonably be taken to be nearly commensurate to the quantity of blood received into this ventricle at each *diastole*, and is thence propelled into the *aorta* at the subsequent systoles". The wax cast was now cut out of the left ventricle, and its volume and surface area measured; the former he took to be equal to the output of the heart per beat under resting conditions, the latter to the internal surface area of the ventricle at the commencement of ventricular systole. From these measurements he made the following calculations:

(1) The pressure sustained by the whole internal surface of the left ventricle at the commencement of systole = internal surface area of left ventricle × arterial blood pressure.

(2) The ventricular output per minute = ventricular output per beat × number of pulses in a minute.

(3) The velocity of the blood at the orifice of the aorta during ventricular systole (assuming the systole of the ventricle to occupy one-third of the cardiac cycle)

$$= \frac{\text{ventricular output per minute}}{\text{area of cross-section of aorta}} \times 3.$$

(4) The time that the heart takes to throw out a weight of blood equal to the weight of the animal

$$= \frac{\text{weight of animal}}{\text{ventricular output per minute} \times \text{density of blood}}.$$

In his book there is an extensive table[1] summarising his results; a few representative experiments have been abstracted from it, and set out in a semi-modernised form below:

	Ox	Horse No. 3	Sheep	Dog No. 1	Dog No. 4
Weight of animal in pounds	1600	825	91	52	12·5
Pulse rate: beats per minute	38	36	65	97	148
Pressure of blood in jugular vein in inches of blood	—	12–52	5–9	6	4
Pressure of blood in carotid artery in inches of blood	—	114	77	80	39
Internal surface area of left ventricle at commencement of systole in square inches	—	26	12·35	11	1·2
Weight of blood sustained by whole surface of contracting left ventricle in pounds	—	113	36·6	33·6	11·1
Ventricular output per beat in cubic inches	12·5	10	1·85	1·17	0·5
Ventricular output per minute in cubic inches	475	360	120	114	74
Systolic velocity of the blood at the aortic orifice in feet per minute	77	87	175	145	210
Time taken by the heart to expel a weight of blood equal to that of the animal's body in minutes	88	60	20	12	7

[1] Hales, *Haemastatics*, 3rd ed. p. 42.

These experiments brought out certain facts that are now regarded as fundamental in the comparative physiology of the circulation in different animals. The pulse rate is more rapid in small animals than large, while the blood pressure is more or less proportional to the size of the animal. "As in bigger animals", he writes, "the blood has a longer course to go, and must therefore meet with a greater resistance; so we may observe in this table, by comparing the perpendicular heights of the blood in the tubes fixed to the arteries, that the force of it in the arteries is in the main greatest in the largest animals ". The output of the ventricle cannot be determined with any great degree of exactness by injecting the heart of the dead animal with wax, but the method seems to have been sufficiently accurate to establish another important law. His table shows that, while the ventricular output per beat is more or less proportional to the size of the animal, the heart of a small animal, in consequence of its greater rapidity of action, throws out a weight of blood equal to the weight of its body in less time than a big one. The output of the heart per minute is therefore relatively greater in small animals than in large. This is now regarded as an important and well-established fact, but, in the absence of any clear conception of respiration and metabolism, he did not realise the significance of his observations: "I do not see, by comparing the weights of these animals, and the several quantities of blood which pass thro' their hearts in a given time, that we can thence form any rule that is fixed, for the proportioning the quantities of flowing blood to their different sizes ". To this, however, he adds: " These quantities in large animals are very disproportionate to the bulk of their bodies, in comparison of what they are in lesser animals, as estimated in this table ".

He had now gained some idea of the cardiac output in different animals in relation to their weight and blood pressure, and he proceeded to an investigation of the second factor on which arterial blood pressure depends: the resistance offered to the onward passage of the blood by the small arteries, capillaries, and veins. The mechanics of the peripheral circulation are very complicated. The peripheral vessels are of many different sizes, and their calibre varies from time to time. At each systole of the heart a certain volume of the blood is propelled into the aorta; part of the energy of each beat is used up in effecting forward movement of the blood; the rest is expended in stretching the aorta. The following passage shows that he accepted as correct Borelli's explanation of the mechanism by which the intermittent flow of blood in the vessels near the heart is converted into an even flow throughout the cardiac cycle in the smaller arteries:

This velocity (*systolic*) is only the velocity of the blood at its first entering into the aorta, in the time of *systole*; in consequence of which the blood in the arteries, being forcibly propelled forward, with an accelerated *impetus*, thereby dilates the canal of the arteries, which begin again to contract at the instant the *systole* ceases: by which curious artifice of nature the blood is carried on in the finer capillaries, with an almost even tenor of velocity, in the same manner as the spouting water of some fire-engines is contrived to flow with a more even velocity, notwithstanding the alternate *systoles* and *diastoles* of the rising and falling *embolus* or force.

When he came to investigate the anatomy of the cardio-vascular system in detail, measurements showed that in the bifurcation of an artery the sum of the areas of the cross-sections of the two branches was invariably greater than the area of the cross-section of the parent trunk. The "bed" of the vascular system therefore increased with each new bifurcation, and for this reason the actual velocity of the blood became progressively less as the arteries got smaller: the smaller the diameter of the vessel, the slower was the movement of the blood inside it. But with decreasing calibre of the individual vessels, in spite of the fact that the total bed of the vascular system was getting larger, the total resistance to the flow of blood was becoming greater. To gain some idea of this resistance offered to the onward passage of the blood by the small arteries, he performed an interesting experiment. He first measured the arterial blood pressure in a dog by tying a tube into the carotid artery as in his previous experiments. The animal was then killed, and the output of the ventricle was determined by injecting the left side of the heart with melted wax. He then ligatured the two crural arteries, divided the descending thoracic aorta, exposed the guts, and slit them open along their whole length opposite the line of mesenteric attachment. A glass tube was now tied into the peripheral end of the cut aorta, and the "slit guts" were perfused with warm water at a pressure equal to the normal arterial pressure. Under these conditions, 342 cub. in. of water passed through the preparation in 6·6 minutes.

This water passed off thro' the orifices of innumerable small capillary vessels, which were cut asunder thro' the whole length of the slit gut. But notwithstanding it was impelled with a force equal to that of the arterial blood in a live dog, yet it did not spurt out in little distinct streams, but only seemed to ouze out at the very fine orifices of the arteries, in the same manner as the blood does from the capillary arteries of a muscle cut transversely.

The mesenteric arteries were then cut close to the intestines; the same volume of water now passed through in 2·3 minutes. When the crural arteries were severed, and the mesenteric and "emulgent" arteries divided close to their origins from the aorta, this quantity of water passed through in 0·4 minute. He now weighed the intestines, and then the rest of the soft parts of the body, and, as the cardiac output per minute was known, he was able to calculate the amount of blood that had flowed through unit weight of the body of the animal during life. Under the conditions of his experiment (before the arteries were cut), the blood flow through the intestines was thirteen times as great. He attributed this increase to the removal of the resistance of the "succeeding series's of exceedingly small ramifications, thro' which the blood passes in its further progress towards the veins, as also to the want of resistance of the venal blood, which rising six inches in the tube fixed to the jugular vein is 1/13·33 or 0·075th part of the force of the arterial blood, and must therefore proportionately retard its motion".

From this experiment we see how greatly the velocity of
the water is retarded in passing thro' the several branchings
of the arteries, notwithstanding the sum of the areas of their
transverse section is considerably greater than that of the
aorta. For although the velocity of the blood at its first entrance into the *aorta*, depends on the proportion the area of
its orifice bears to the quantity thrown into it at each *systole*,
and also on the number of those *systoles* in a given time: yet
the real force of the blood in the arteries, depends on the
proportion, which the quantity of blood thrown out of the
left ventricle in a given time, bears to the quantity which
can pass thro' the capillary arteries into the veins, in that
time. But the resistance which the blood meets with in those
capillary passages, may be greatly varied, either by the different
degrees of viscidity or fluidity of the blood, or by the several
degrees of constriction or relaxation of those fine vessels.
And as the state of the blood or blood-vessels is in these
respects continually varying from divers causes, as motion,
rest, food, evacuations, heat, cold etc. so as probably never
to be exactly the same any two minutes, during the whole life
of an animal; so the blood in passing thro' the muscular, the
membranous, and other parts of the animal, must be carried
on with innumerable different degrees of velocity, and consequently in different quantities, thro' dissimilar parts.

He now proceeded to make a closer study of some
of the chemical and physical factors which influenced
the degree of constriction of the small vessels. He
added different substances to the perfusion fluid, and
noted the time it took to flow through the intestines
of a recently killed dog: a rate of flow below the
normal indicated that the substance added to the
perfusion fluid constricted the vessels; an increase
that the vessels had been dilated. Hot water increased the rate of flow, and therefore caused vaso-
dilatation; but cold water, decoctions of Peruvian

bark, "chamomel flowers", and cinnamon, all de-creased the rate of flow, and therefore caused vaso-constriction. Alcohol also had a constrictor effect:

I first poured in seven pots full of warm water, the first of which passed off in 52 seconds, and the remaining six gradu-ally in less time, to the last, which passed in 46 seconds. Then I poured in five pots of common brandy, or unrectified spirit of malt, the first of which was 68″ in passing, the last 72″. Then I poured in a pot of warm water, which was 54″ in passing. Hence we see, that brandy contracts the fine capil-lary arteries of the guts, and that water soon relaxes them again, by diluting and carrying off the spirituous part of the brandy.

So far he had concerned himself entirely with the systemic or greater circulation; but the blood flow through the lungs, the lesser circulation, still re-mained to be considered. The actual blood pressure in the large systemic arteries could be measured directly, but the pulmonary artery and its branches were not open to direct experiment, and the pressure in the latter could only be inferred. The volume of the blood that passes through the lungs must, he realised, always be equal to the quantity which flows through the systemic circulation in the same time:

The area of the transverse section of the pulmonary artery being in one part, before it divaricates into branches, of the same dimension with the orifice of the *aorta*, the velocity of the blood in that part may be accounted the same as in the orifice of the *aorta*. But though the quan-tities and velocities of the blood, in passing out of both ventricles, be the same, yet it does not thence follow, that their expulsive forces must be both the same: for if the blood in passing into the pulmonary artery, finds less resistance from the preceding blood, than the blood does in entering into the *aorta*, then a less force will expel it out of the right ventricle with equal velocity; and accordingly, as there is not so much force required to drive the blood thro' the lungs, as thro' the rest of the whole body, so we may observe, that the substance of the muscle of the right ventricle has not near the thickness of that of the left.

His inference was correct: relative to the pressure in the aorta, the pressure in the pulmonary artery is low; relative to the rest of the body, the resistance to the flow of blood through the lungs is small.

The lungs are a small fraction of the body weight, and since the same amount of blood passes through the lungs as through the rest of the body in unit time, he argued that the actual velocity of the blood in the lungs must be greater than in the capillaries of the other tissues. To gain some idea of this velocity, he cut out the lungs of a dead calf just above the bifurcation of the trachea, and, by blowing them up under water in a graduated vessel, found their internal volume, when inflated, to differ from their internal volume, when collapsed, by 166·5 cub. in. This volume, however, included the anatomical dead space (trachea, bronchi, and bronchioles), and during life was encroached upon to some degree by distension of the vessels with blood. The volume of the former (measured by pouring water into the trachea) was 41 cub. in.; the latter was estimated arbitrarily at 25·5 cub. in.; the total volume of all the alveoli during life was therefore 166·5 − (41 + 25·5) = 100 cub. in. He then examined the lungs with a microscope, and estimated the average lung alveolus to be 0·01 in.

across, in which case, assuming the alveolus to be cubical, he calculated that there would be 600 sq. in. of surface in each cubic inch of lung substance. There were therefore 60,000 sq. in. of surface in the lungs as a whole, but one-third of this must be deducted, he said, "to make allowance for the absence of two sides in each little vesicular cube, that there might be a free communication among them for the air to pass to and fro". The reason for his choosing a calf for this experiment is not apparent; but, assuming the same relationship to exist between body weight and lung surface in all animals, he calculated that in a dog of known weight, in which he had determined the cardiac output per minute to be 114 cub. in., the inward surface of the lungs would be 12,000 sq. in. The diameter of a lung capillary was approximately twice that of a red blood corpuscle; the diameter of a red blood corpuscle according to Leewenhoeck was 1/3240 in.; the diameter of an average lung capillary was therefore 0·0006 in. The volume of blood expelled from the heart of the dog in one minute (114 cub. in.), when all in lung capillaries, would therefore occupy a surface area of about 114/0·0006, i.e. approximately 200,000 sq. in. The total surface area of the lungs of the animal was 12,000 sq. in.; half this surface, he thought, would be occupied by capillaries, and the other half by the spaces between them. The actual capillary surface area of the lungs was therefore only 6000 sq. in. It followed that a volume of blood equal to thirty times (200,000/6000) the volume of the capillaries in the lungs must pass through the lungs in a minute. "We see by this calculation", he writes, "as well as by the small proportion that the lungs bear to the rest of the body, that the velocity of the blood must needs be very much accelerated in them."

This calculation is interesting; but it involved a number of assumptions, and was based on experimental procedures of doubtful accuracy. He was able, however, to verify his conclusion, that the velocity of the blood was relatively great in the capillaries of the lungs, by direct experiment. He actually succeeded in viewing with a microscope the capillaries in the muscles of the abdomen and in the lungs of a living frog, and measured by direct observation the speed at which the corpuscles moved: in the straight muscles of the abdomen they traversed a distance of 1/10th in. in a minute and a half; in the lungs they moved five times as fast.

As a frog's heart has but one ventricle, the blood is thrown by the same ventricle, at the same instant, both into the lungs and all over the body; then since its velocity is, in arteries of equal diameters, five times greater in the lungs than in the muscles, notwithstanding it is impelled by one common impetus; this evidently shows, that it must have freer passage through the lungs. Accordingly the left ventricle of the heart is made much stronger, thereby to impel the blood with a greater force than the right ventricle does.

His researches had now carried him very far from his original starting-point, and his initial problem still remained unsolved. Was the pressure of the blood in the capillaries of the muscles sufficiently great to account for muscular action? He had measured the pressure in the arteries and veins of living animals by direct experiment; but, as he could see no way in which he could actually determine the capillary blood pressure, he proceeded to calculate it along the following lines. Making the same assumptions as to the diameter of an average capillary as before, he calculated its cross-section to be 0·000003 sq. in. If the arterial blood pressure in a dog was 80 in. of blood, the effect of this arterial blood pressure in the capillary would be 80 times this, i.e. 0·00024 cub. in. of blood, equal to 0·51 grain. If the venous pressure was 6 in. of blood in the great veins near the heart, the opposite effect of the venous pressure would be 6/80ths of this, i.e. 0·03 grain.

The remainder 0·48 grain is the force with which the blood would be impelled into such a capillary by a column of blood of eighty inches height, supposing it were in a stagnant state; to which also must be added the velocity which the blood has acquired at its first entrance in the capillary vessel, which can be but small, as appears by the great resistance it meets with in the capillary vessels in these experiments. Whence we see, both from experiment and calculation, that the force of the blood in these fine capillaries can be but very little; and the longer such capillaries are, the slower will be the motion of the blood in them. From this very small force of the arterial blood, among the muscular fibres, we may with good reason conclude, how short this force is of producing so great an effect, as that of muscular motion. This wonderful and inexplicable mystery of nature must therefore be owing to some more vigorous active energy, whose force is regulated by the nerves: but whether it be confined in canals within the nerves, or acts along their surfaces like electrical powers, is not easy to determine.[1]

He performed many other experiments which cannot be followed out in detail. He studied the

---

[1] Hales, *Haemastatics*, 3rd ed. p. 55.

effects of progressive dilution of the blood with water, and produced ascites and anasarca by intravenous injection. He prevented the blood from clotting by adding nitre. He performed experiments on the effects of the respiratory movements on the intra-pleural pressure. He measured the force required to burst the arteries, veins, and guts, and the tensile strength of bones, ligaments, and tendons. He observed the contraction of individual muscle fibres:

If the skin be stripped off the belly of a live frog, and the abdomen opened on each side, so as that its strait muscles may, by drawing a little on one side, have a strong focal light cast on the inside of them; if in this posture these muscles be viewed thro' a good microscope, the parallel fibres of the muscle are plain to be seen, with the blood running alternately up and down, between each fibre, in capillary arteries so fine that only a single globule can pass them. If the muscle happened to act while thus viewed, then the scene is instantly changed from parallel fibres, to series's of *rhomboidal pinnulae*, which immediately disappear as soon as the muscle ceases to act. It is not easy to get a sight of this most agreeable scene, because that on the action of the muscle, the object is apt to get out of the focus of the microscope; but those who are expert in the use of those glasses may readily move them accordingly.[1]

A few lines further down he writes: "stimulating the foot of the frog will sometimes make it contract these muscles". To this significant remark he adds nothing. Spinal reflexes, the responses of the skeletal muscles to sensory stimulation of the skin brought about by nervous impulses passing through the intact spinal cord of animals in which the brain has

[1] Hales, *Haemastatics*, 3rd ed. p. 59.

been removed, had not yet been described. Short of this remark, there is nothing in any of his writings to suggest that Hales had observed them, but more than twenty-five years later Robert Whytt wrote in his *Physiological Essays*[1]:

The very ingenious Dr. *Hales* writes me, that, having many years since, tied a ligature about a frog's neck, to prevent any effusion of blood, he cut off its head, and, thirty hours after, observed the blood circulating freely in the web of the foot: the frog also at this time moved its body when stimulated: but, on thrusting a needle down through the spinal marrow, the animal was strongly convulsed, and, immediately after, became motionless.

Hales, therefore, observed reflexes in spinal frogs, and their abolition by destruction of the cord, before Whytt gave his celebrated description of reflex action in 1757.

[1] Edinburgh, 1755, p. 176.

CHAPTER III

Perpetual Curate of Teddington. Parish Work. Rector of
Farringdon. Elected a Fellow of the Royal Society.

IN the seventeenth century, the patronage of the
curacy of Teddington was vested solely in the
hands of the Lord of the Manor. The annual
stipend was only six pounds four shillings, but the
value of the living had been recently augmented;
a few years previously the alternate presentation had
been acquired by Sir Orlando Bridgeman for his
heirs, when he had offered to increase its value with
fee-farm rents to eighty pounds. When Hales was
appointed to Teddington, it was Sir John Bridgeman's turn to present:

Nominated Feb. 21. 1709 to the donative of Teddington,
in the County of Middlesex, by the late Edward Hill Esq.
for and as the turn of Sir John Bridgeman Bart. of Castle
Bromige, Warwickshire, it being from that time an alternate
nomination; had a license from the Bp. of London to serve
that cure Aug. 10. 1709.[1]

His income from the living was eighty pounds a
year, but as he came of a family which was at any rate
once wealthy, it is likely that he possessed some
private means.

Teddington was a country village with a population of less than five hundred persons.[2] It was
situated on the north bank of the Thames between
Twickenham and Hampton, and fifteen miles from

---

[1] *Gentleman's Magazine*, 1799, LXIX, 267. A copy of the agreement relating to the patronage of the curacy of Teddington is to be
found in the parish register.

[2] Rev. Daniel Lysons, *Environs of London*, III, 503, London, 1795.

London. In those days the riverside was fashionable; many of the aristocracy had their country houses in the neighbourhood, and in summer time members of the Royal Family lived at Richmond, Kew, and Hampton Court. The parish itself was widely scattered, but the register shows that there were a number of houses in the vicinity of the church, and that their occupiers were held responsible for the upkeep of successive sections of the churchyard wall. Among these were Mr William Redford who lived near "the Old Maypole", Mr Ashby who owned the malt-houses, and Mr John Goodchild the wax chandler. There were four public-houses in the village: the Greyhound, the King's Head, the Royal Oak, and the Three Bells; the chief inn, the Greyhound, was in close proximity to the church, as the landlord, Mr Grimes, was among those responsible for the upkeep of the churchyard wall. The Parsonage was situated some little way up the village street away from the river; nothing of it now remains but the cellars and part of the garden wall. Edward Hill was Lord of the Manor; at a later date the Manor rights were acquired by Matthias Perkins, but he never lived in the village, and the Manor House was let to Mr William Belitha. Sir Orlando Bridgeman's son, Sir Francis, lived in the parish, and Sir Charles Duncombe, Lord Mayor of London in 1709, owned a house in the village which, some years later, was leased to Lord Thanet. Among Hales's parishioners was Miss Margaret Woffington, who made her reputation as an actress by playing the part of Polly Peacham in Gay's *Beggar's Opera*.

It is likely that Hales, influenced by Kidman at Bene't College, and by the scientific education he had received at Cambridge, was to some extent in agreement with the new school of Latitudinarian divines. They paid little attention to the differences of doctrine and ceremony which divided the high church party from the dissenters, but, avoiding dogmatic teaching, attempted to rationalise religion along the lines of ordinary common sense. Hales was no theologian, and in his discourses from the pulpit made little appeal to authority. His sermons consisted of moral dissertations, based on the teaching of the gospels, and authoritative pronouncements on the wisdom and goodness of God, supported by arguments drawn from natural science. These made their appeal, the attendance at the services at Teddington was soon greater than it had ever been before, and within five years it became necessary to enlarge the church:

Mem: That in the year 1716 the main Beams which support the Roof of the Church being decayed, the Expense of repairing of which and of inlarging the Church with a new Building and Gallery on the south west corner of the Church, viz. from the Church door to the Tower cost £172. 06. 10.

The money for these repairs was largely raised by the sale of pews which were appointed to their prospective purchasers, "their heirs, executors, administrators, and assignees", *for ever*, upon the execution of a legal agreement, signed by the church-wardens, and witnessed by the minister. The seating accommodation of the church was being rearranged, and the existing rights of the parishioners, who already owned pews, had to be safeguarded. The sale of the new pews, and the redistribution of the old, now became a matter of great complexity, as the following extract from the parish register shows:

A Copy of an instrument whereby a Pew was Appointed to Thomas Horseley.

We Edward Hill and Ralph Mountague, Church Wardens of the Parish and Parish Church of Teddington in the county of Middlesex do by these Presents assign and appoint unto Mr. Thomas Horseley of the said Parish one Pew situated in the South Side of the body of the said church and being in length within side from north to south six feet five inches and in breadth 2 feet five inches and containing in all fourteen square feet and three quarters of a foot. Its south end being eight feet nine inches from the south wall of the church and its east end twenty four feet nine inches from the east wall of the church. We the said Church Wardens do assign and appoint Give and Grant to the said Thomas Horseley the sole use and property in the said Pew unto him his heirs Executors Administrators and assignees for ever. Being in exchange for a lesser Pew which belonged to the said Thomas Horseley and which was in length four feet six inches and in breadth two feet two inches and containing in all nine square feet and three quarters of a foot. The said Thomas Horseley having moreover paid to the said Church Wardens the summe of one pound one shilling and sixpence in consideration that this new assigned Pew contains five square feet of ground more than the old lesser Pew which upon inlarging the church and altering the Pews was of necessity taken into other Pews.

In witness thereof we have set our hands and seals this 11th day of January 1716.

Signed.   Edward Hill
          Ralph Mountague.

Signed, sealed and delivered
   in the presence of
   Stephen Hales, Minister.
   Ri: Tudor.

During his life at Teddington he kept the parish register with great care. Each page of births, marriages, and deaths, is signed at the foot, "Stephen Hales, Minister", and among them some quaint entries are to be found:

John Rolt who was murdered in fighting for the May Pole: buried May 23, 1710. Twickenham. Stephen Hales, Minister.

Hester was Baptised April 15, 1737, being a Foundling dropped at Mr. Everett's Door; her surname is Cradle. (*The underlining of "Cradle" is his.*) Stephen Hales, Minister.

James Parsons who had oft eat a shoulder of Mutton and a peck of Hasty Pudding at a Time, which caused his Death, buried March 27. 1744. Aged 35. Stephen Hales. Minister.

Besides the routine entries of births, marriages, and deaths, with occasional quaint comments, there are detailed records of any particular events in the parish that intimately concerned the church. They show the conscientious way in which he carried out his parish duties, while devoting so much time to his experiments. The register has already told how the church was enlarged and repaired in 1716, and the money for the purpose partly raised by the careful sale of the new pews. It also shows that he provided a new water supply for the village:

1754. Mem.—That in order to have a constant stream of fresh water thro' the town, a channel or drain was dug about ten feet deep and 64 yards long from the north side of the road just where it enters the gravel pits, which intercepting all the main springs in that length, a constant stream of water was obtained which runs at the rate of about 30 tuns in 24 hrs; and probably double that quantity of water might be procured if the channel was dug 64 yards further. The whole expense of this was £45. 8. 3½, 15 guineas of which was paid by the Lord of the Manor, the rest by the contribution of the Gentlemen of three guineas each.

But in the year 1755 the above mentioned thirty four tuns of water, not being found sufficient to prevent the sinking of the water in the lower pond in summer time, a new ditch was cut from the upper pond 220 yards long almost up to the brick cart bridge in expectation that the water would not soak away so fast as in the side ditch under the hedge. But this method not being sufficient to keep the lower pond full and flowing down the town ditch, in the year 1755 the drain was cut 64 yards more in length across the springs which produced double the quantity viz: sixty tuns of water in 24 hrs. And if more water shall hereafter be desired, it may be had by lengthening the drain further across the springs.

The labour of cutting the 64 yds cost	£5.	2. 0.
The bricks	2.	11. 0.
The 220 yds long ditch cost	3.	3. 0.
The former expense in the year 1754	45.	8. 3½
	56.	4. 3½

The quantity of water which ran from the springs was estimated by fixing in clay at the mouth of the covered drain a small trough, and placing inside it a vessel containing two quarts which was filled in three swings of a pendulum beating seconds, which pendulum was 39 + 2/10 inches long from the suspending nail to the middle of the plumbet or bob. By which means it was found that more than sixty tuns of water ran there in 24 hours, allowing 53 gallons Winchester measure to the hogshead.

His hold over his parishioners must have been strong; he often succeeded in making offenders of either sex do public penance for immorality:

Persons who have done Public Penance in the Parish.

Anne Clarke Spinster for Adultery	10. Feb. 1722.
William Whiting for Fornication	
Hannah Hill Widow for Fornication	18. April 1732.
Frances Honeywell for Fornication	
Sarah Fuller for Fornication	13. June 1733.
Frances Honeywell for Fornication	16. Oct. 1737.

Eliz. Mansell of Hampton, Feb. 8. 1740, got with child by Joshua Mitchins of London.

Stephen Hales, Minister.

The vestry minutes, of which unfortunately only a few fragments remain, record some of the purposes to which he devoted collections at services in church:

1711.	For Patrick Hele lost by Fire at Edinburgh	4s. 1d.
1715.	For the Cowkeepers' brief	£1. 15s. 0d.
1716.	For a Fire in Thames St., London	8s. 9d.
1716.	For the reformed Episcopal Churches in Great Poland and Polish Russia	£2. 4s. 6d.
1722.	An Inundation in Lancashire	18s. 2d.
1731.	For Llandaff Cathedral	9s. 1d.
1738.	Loss by Fire at St. John's, Wapping	5s. 8d.
1739.	Loss by Hail in Hertfordshire	£1. 5s. 5d.
1740.	A Flood in Essex	15s. 0d.
1742.	Faversham Oyster Dredgers	16s. 6d.
1750.	Loss by Hail in Southwark	7s. 4d.

As a general rule, however, the offertory on Sunday was devoted to the relief of paupers in the village. Abject poverty was common; unemployment was prevalent, and the aged, orphans, and deserted children, such as "the foundling dropped at Mr. Everett's door", added to the numbers who came to the parish for relief. At that time the relationship of

C-K H 4

the church to the poor was not merely one of charity, as the vestry were responsible for providing the poor with food and clothes, and the sick with medicines. Money for this purpose came from the church collections, and was supplemented by a village poor rate which was levied on all householders on a rentage system; it was fixed by the vestry, and approved by the Justices of the Peace. Hales attended the meetings of the vestry which were held at frequent intervals in one of the public-houses in the village, the Greyhound, the King's Head, or the Royal Oak. Their first care was to keep the poor rate as low as possible. The parish workhouse served as a deterrent to keep the lazy off the rates, a few of the genuinely unemployed could be put on to do gate duty at the houses of the resident nobility and gentry, and strenuous efforts were made to prevent vagrants from entering the parish. The detailed work of collecting money and administering relief was left to the overseers of the poor, who, according to the law, had to be nominated from among the local house-holders by two or more Justices of the Peace; in practice the vestry nominated the overseers, and their appointments were then approved by the Justices. In many parishes the overseers were corrupt, and little attempt was made to control them, but, at Teddington, the vestry kept a strict and accurate check on their work:

1750. Agreed and ordered that Mr. Barnaby Church-warden and Mr. William Redford Overseer, doe go to Edward Hill and make an Inquiry how he expended the five shillings given him by the overseers on Tuesday night last, and had none left on Thursday morning, and to inquire of ye Baker, Butcher or Chandler shop what was paid them by Edward Hill.[1]

In 1694, the Middlesex Court of Quarter Sessions, having been informed that a great number of paupers went begging in other parishes, ordered the church-wardens and overseers to provide badges, or tokens, of some durable metal for all the parish poor. These badges were to indicate the parish from which the pauper came, and were to be worn "at the end of the left sleeve".[2] Teddington continued to adopt this method:

Oct. 30. 1750. Ordered that all who do receive alms of this parish and are on ye collection, do wear the Badge of the Parish on their upper Garment.

Nov. 3. 1750. Edward Hill attended this vestry and refused to wear the Badge. Therefore ordered to quit his apartment in the Alms House immediately.

For offenders of this kind further punishment was always ready:

1751. Ordered that the Stocks be put into repair.[1]

During his early years at Teddington, Hales continued to pay occasional visits to Bene't College where he was still a Fellow; his name sometimes appears in the Order Book among the list of members of the Society who attended a College meeting. On these occasions he would see his old masters again. Vigani was dead, but Waller of his own College was teaching chemistry at the laboratory in

[1] Teddington Vestry Minutes.
[2] Dorothy Marshall, *The English Poor in the Eighteenth Century*, London, 1926.

Trinity. Whiston was still Lucasian Professor, and Rolfe, Stukeley's friend, was now Professor of Anatomy. But in 1718 Hales finally severed his connection with the College with which he had been associated, as a Fellow or an undergraduate, for over twenty years. At that time the system of pluralities was in vogue in the Church of England. The better educated and more influential divines held two or more livings at a time, residing themselves in the best, and leaving the other to the care of a hired curate; but by statute a Fellow who became a pluralist had to vacate his Fellowship. Cowper, the Lord Chancellor, now offered him the living of Porlock in Somersetshire. He accepted it, and became a pluralist: Perpetual Curate of Teddington and Rector of Porlock. He was therefore compelled to resign his Fellowship, and there is no record that he ever revisited Bene't College.

Porlock, on the borders of Exmoor, was a hundred and fifty miles from London, a long and arduous journey before the days of railways. He probably never even went to see his new parish. He continued to reside at Teddington, and, as was the custom, put in a hired curate to do the work at Porlock; the balance left over, after the curate had been paid, added to his income. His Rectorship of this remote parish was however of brief duration. Four years later William Cage, Esq., of Milgate, offered him the living of the more accessible village of Farringdon near Winchester. He now resigned at Porlock, and was instituted at his new parish on February 9th, 1722.[1]

[1] *Gentleman's Magazine*, 1799, LXIX, 267.

His first action was to appoint the Rev. Mr Newlyn, Rector of the neighbouring parish of East Tysted on the main London-Southampton road, to be curate-in-charge at Farringdon. When Newlyn died in 1725, he was succeeded at East Tysted by the Rev. Richard Lipsett who, like his predecessor, was appointed to look after Farringdon. The visiting curate came over to take a service on Sundays, but the register shows that during the week Farringdon was often left to look after itself. Mr Lipsett was frequently not available, and the occasional offices of the church, such as funerals and baptisms, had to be performed by one or other of the neighbouring clergy who could be induced to come over for the purpose. The most frequent visitor on these occasions was Mr White, Vicar of the adjoining parish of Selborne, and father of Gilbert White the naturalist. A few years later, at increased expense to himself, Hales persuaded Mr Lipsett to resign the Rectorship of East Tysted, to devote himself entirely to the village of Farringdon, and for this purpose to live in the parish. Even then he would not leave his parishioners entirely to the care of his curate. "The late Dr. Stephen Hales", wrote Gilbert White thirty years later, "was my most valuable friend, and in former days near neighbour during the summer months. For though his usual abode was at Teddington, yet he did for many years reside for about two months at the Rectory of Farringdon, and was well known to my grandfather and father, as well as myself".[1]

[1] J. E. Harting, *Gilbert White's Natural History of Selborne*, 2nd ed. with letters not included in any previous edition of the work, London, 1876.

These annual journeys to and from Farringdon were arduous undertakings. Sixty miles along the London-Winchester road in the stage-coach took two days under the best conditions. There were frequent stops to change the teams, and delays at the turnpikes to pay the tolls. The highways were deplorable, and in wet seasons the coach sometimes stuck in the mire at the roadside until extra horses had been fetched to pull it out. Farringdon was ten miles off the main road at Alton, and the last part of the journey could only be accomplished on horseback. The Parish Register at Farringdon, however, confirms Gilbert White's statement. The routine entries themselves were mostly made by Newlyn or Richard Lipsett, but, between the years 1723 and 1741, every page of births, marriages, and deaths, is signed "Stephen Hales, Rector", and scattered among them, between the months of May and August each year, are some of his characteristic notes:

The field adjoining the Garden is two Acres.

John Trent, the Son of John Trent and Mary his Wife, Vagabonds, was baptised May 25th. 1722.

Mary Holdaway performed Penance for fornication. Aug. 1731.

George Frost   performed Penance
and Eliz. Westbrook   1736 for fornication.

Mary Neal, Widdow, performed Penance for fornication. Sept. 4. 1743.

A strange custom prevailed in the parish. The oak beams of the roof of the church were hung with garlands in honour of the young women of the parish who had died virgins. "The clerk's wife used to cut out of white paper the resemblances of gloves and ribbons to be twisted into knots and roses which were used to decorate these memorials of chastity."[1] At Farringdon, as well as at Teddington, he devoted much time to farming, and he contributed a number of articles to the *Gentleman's Magazine* on agricultural matters. Among his inventions was a winnowing machine, or "back-heaver", which, he said, would "winnow and clean corn both much sooner and better than by the common method of doing it". At a later date, this machine was improved, so that it would "clean and clear it of very small corn, seeds, blacks, and smut balls, to such perfection as to make it fit for seed corn".[2]

In 1719, Alexander Pope the poet moved from Chiswick, and bought a house and five acres of land at Twickenham. He was one of the few at that time who wrote against cruelty to animals and the prevalent passion for brutal amusements. He was now a near neighbour to Hales at Teddington, and, though Pope was a Roman Catholic and had a horror of Hales's experiments, they became friends. Visits to each other's houses were frequent; Pope appealing for expert advice on some horticultural problem, and Hales assisting in laying out Pope's grotto garden. "I shall be very glad to see Dr. Hales", he is reputed to have said, "and always love to see him, he is so worthy and good a man. Yes, he is a very good man, only I'm sorry he has his hands so much imbued in blood". "What, he cuts up rats?" inquired Spence.

---

[1] Gilbert White, Harting's edition.
[2] *Gentleman's Magazine*, 1745, XV, 353; 1747, XVII, 316.

"Ay! and dogs, too. Indeed, he commits most of these barbarities with the thought of being of use to man. But how do we know that we have a right to kill creatures that we are so little above as dogs, for our curiosity?"[1]

Pope was not the only critic of his experiments. Garbled accounts of them proved a frequent subject of the gossip of the neighbourhood, and they feature in a poem entitled *The Boat*, an account of a voyage up the Thames, by the Rev. Thomas Twining:

> Green Teddington's serene retreat
> For Philosophic studies meet,
> Where the good Pastor Stephen Hales
> Weighed moisture in a pair of scales,
> To lingering death put Mares and Dogs,
> And stripped the Skins from living Frogs.
> Nature, he loved, her Works intent
> To search or sometimes to torment.

The reader, who, at first sight, feels inclined to criticise Hales's work on the grounds of cruelty, must remember that Bacon had recommended vivisection as a scientific method, and the discovery, partly through this means, of the circulation of the blood had brought it into prominence. The success of the method had been demonstrated, but anaesthetics had not been discovered, and Hales was compelled to work on unanaesthetised animals. At that time even operations on man had to be performed without anaesthesia; the standards of unavoidable pain and

---

[1] Joseph Spence, *Anecdotes, observations and characters of books and men, collected from the conversation of Mr. Pope*, London, 1820, p. 293. On December 12th, 1743, Hales was a witness to Pope's will. The other two witnesses were the Earl of Radnor and Joseph Spence.

suffering were naturally rather different then from those existing now. His experiments were performed to advance science, but it is important to remember that in those days cruelty to animals for quite useless purposes was general; bull-baiting was patronised by the aristocracy, bear-baiting and the brutal sport of cock-throwing were popular amusements among the lower classes, and only isolated voices, such as those of Pope, Gay, and Steele, had been raised in protest.[1] From the point of view of cruelty, his work must be judged according to the standards of the period, and not by the ideas that prevail to-day. The question whether vivisection is justifiable to advance science still remains to a large extent a matter of personal conviction, and it would serve no useful purpose to enter into this controversy. Whatever views the reader may hold, the fact remains that Hales, by experiments on living animals, made great contributions to physiology: accurate records of the blood pressure, a clear account of the mechanics of the circulation, important observations on the comparative physiology of the heart in different animals, and the discovery of spinal reflex action. Of their value in promoting the advancement of medical science, in the narrow sense of the treatment of disease, it is more difficult to speak, more particularly as, in spite of the remark that Spence attributes to Pope, this was not their primary intention. Their starting-point had been the academic problem of muscular movement. At this time he was essentially

[1] W. E. H. Lecky, *History of England in the XVIIIth Century*, London, 1893, II, 194.

a pure scientist; his concern was with physiology as a branch of science, and not with medicine, of which he knew nothing. Accurate physiological knowledge is, however, the foundation on which medical science is built, and the physiology of one generation finds practical application in the medicine of the next. The direct measurement of the blood pressure of animals filled in a gap in biological knowledge, and his work as a whole contributed to the progress of medical science.

These remarkable researches soon came to the attention of the Royal Society, where he attended his first meeting at the age of forty, as is shown by the following entry in the Society's minutes:

March 14. 1717. Sir Hans Sloane in the Chair. Mr. Hale of Teddington had leave to be present at the Meeting.

In the following year he was elected a Fellow of the Society, not only on the nomination of, but strangely as it appears, on the same day as, the friend and companion of his Cambridge days, William Stukeley (Plate V):

March 6. 1718. The President in the Chair. (*Sir Isaac Newton.*) Mr. Stephen Hale proposed candidate by Dr. Stukeley.

March 13. 1718. The Duke of Mountague, Dr. Websted, Dr. Wagstaff, Dr. Stukeley and Mr. Stephen Hale were chosen Members, the four latter by ballot.

For some reason he was not admitted a Fellow until some months later:

Nov. 20th. 1718. Sir Hans Sloane, Vice President in the Chair. Mr. Hale having been formerly elected, and lapsed the time of his admission, the same was dispensed with by the Society, and he subscribed the obligation and was admitted accordingly.

Plate V. William Stukeley, M.D., F.R.C.P., F.R.S., at the age of thirty-four
(From the print by J. Smith, after the portrait by Sir Godfrey Kneller, Bart. 1721)

CHAPTER IV

The Physiology of Plants. The Flow of Sap. Transpiration and
Capillarity. Root Pressure. Papers to the Royal Society.

HALES'S work on the circulation of the blood in
animals remained unpublished for twenty
years. A few days after his election he read
his first paper to the Royal Society on an entirely
different subject:

> March 15. 1718. The Rev. Mr. Hale inform'd ye President
> that he had lately made a new Experiment upon the Effect
> of ye Sun's warmth in raising ye Sap in trees. Mr. Hale was
> desired to prosecute these experiments, and had thanks for
> communicating this first Essay.[1]

This was the beginning of his researches on the
physiology of plants and trees.

His immediate predecessors in botany were Ray,
Grew, and Malpighi. Ray (1627–1705) had concerned himself particularly with systematic botany
and the classification of plants; it was with Ray's
Catalogus in their pockets that Hales and Stukeley
went "a simpling". Malpighi (1628–1694) and Grew
(1628–1671) were plant anatomists, but they both
speculated as to the function of the different parts.
Malpighi, guided more by anatomical considerations
than by experiments, had perceived that the green
leaves were concerned with nutrition, and that the
fibrous constituents of wood conducted the nutrient
sap up to the developing leaves and flowers. In 1583,
Cesalpino had attempted to explain the absorption of

---

[1] *Royal Society Journal Book*, 1714–1720, XII, 289.

water by the roots and the flow of sap along physical lines; he compared these phenomena with the imbibition of water by substances such as linen, sponge, and powder. To physical speculation of this kind Malpighi and Ray added the clearer conception of capillarity, and employed capillary glass tubes to illustrate the movement of fluid in the stems of plants. Nevertheless, the *continuous* flow of sap up the trunk of a tree, a phenomenon which seemed to defy the laws of physics, still remained unexplained.

Transpiration, the loss of water by evaporation from the surfaces of plants, had been little studied; the magnitude of it had not been realised, and its physiological significance was not yet understood. Hales's early experiments were designed to gain an idea of the actual amount of water that flowed through a plant at any time, and *Vegetable Statics* opens with an account of his researches on transpiration: "Experiments showing the quantities of moisture imbibed and perspired by plants and trees". He planted a sunflower in an ordinary garden pot. When it was fully grown, to prevent any evaporation of water except through the plant itself, he covered over the top of the pot with a sheet of lead which was firmly cemented down to the sides of the pot and to the stem of the sunflower where this passed through. There was a hole in the lead plate, with a cork to fit it, to permit of the plant being watered as required (Plate VI, fig. 1). No steps were taken to prevent the evaporation of water through the sides of the pot, but, at the end of the experiment, he cut off the plant, cemented the stump over, and then found that the unglazed porous pot "perspired" 2 oz. in 12 hours; for this he made due allowance. The sunflower and pot were weighed every night and morning for fifteen days. During sunny days and fine warm nights the sunflower would lose weight from "perspiration" of water. On wet days and dewy nights the sunflower would gain weight by "imbibition" of water. Taken all round, the loss of weight from "perspiration" exceeded the gain of weight by "imbibition", and the plant had lost water by transpiration from the leaves at an average rate of 34 cub. in. in twelve hours. He then cut off all the leaves, and measured their total surface area; he also estimated the surface area of the roots, and measured the cross-section of the main stem. It was now possible to calculate the actual velocity of the flow of sap in different parts of the plant, just as he had determined the speed of the blood in the arteries, capillaries, and veins of animals. The transpiration rate divided by these areas gave the actual velocity of the flow of sap across unit area in the leaves, roots, and stem respectively:

	Area	Relative Velocities	Actual Velocities
Leaves	5616 sq. in.	1/5616	1/165 cub. in. per sq. in. in 12 hours
Roots	2276 ,, ,,	1/2276	1/67 ,, ,, ,,
Stem	1 ,, ,,	1	34 ,, ,, ,,

The flow of the sap was most rapid in the stem, intermediate in the roots, and slowest of all in the leaves; this corresponded to the rate of movement of the blood in the arteries, veins, and capillaries of animals. His method was sound, but these calculations are unreliable, because he did not know that only a small part of the root actually absorbs, and that its surface area is enormously increased by the presence of root hairs. He pointed out, however, the explanation of the common practice of cutting off some of the branches of a transplanted tree when many of the roots have been destroyed in digging it up: the leaf area must be cut down to correspond to the diminished area of root surface, or the tree will lose water too rapidly, wither away, and die.

Transpiration might vary in different species. In his next experiments he employed the same method to determine the average "perspiration rate" in a number of other plants and trees. He began by investigating a vine, a cabbage, an apple tree, and a lemon tree, and compared his results with the average "perspiration rate" of man as determined by Dr Keill:

Perspiration of water per square inch of leaf or body surface in twelve hours.[1]

Lemon Tree	1/248 cubic inches	
Vine	1/191 „	„
Sunflower	1/165 „	„
Apple Tree	1/102 „	„
Cabbage	1/80 „	„
Man	1/50 „	„

These and other observations showed that evergreens "perspired" much less than plants and deciduous trees:

By comparing the very different degrees of perspiration, in these 5 plants and trees, we may observe, that the lemon-tree, which is an ever-green, perspires much less than the sun-flower, or than the vine or the apple-tree, whose leaves

[1] Hales, *Vegetable Statics*, 4th ed. p. 21.

fall off in the winter; and as they perspire less, so are they better able to survive the winter's cold, because they want proportionately but a very small supply of fresh nourishment to support them; like the exanguous tribe of animals, frogs, toads, tortoises, serpents, insects, etc. which, as they perspire little, so do they live the whole winter without food. And this I find hold true in 12 other different sorts of evergreens, on which I have made experiments.

When he came to contrast the rate at which a man lost water from the surface of his skin, with the speed at which moisture evaporated away from the leaves of the sunflower, he found that the "perspiration rate" of the former was three times as great as that of the latter. He attributed this to the higher temperature of the human body. If, however, the comparison was made weight for weight, the "perspiration rate" of the sunflower was seventeen times that of man: "The fluid which is filtrated thro' the roots immediately from the earth, is not near so full freighted with nutritive particles as the chyle which enters the lacteals of animals; which defect it was necessary to supply by the entrance of a much greater quantity of fluid".

He had now gained some idea of the quantity of sap that flowed through different plants and trees. What were the forces responsible for it? Capillarity, suggested by Malpighi and Grew, explained the sap rising to a certain height, but it would not account for its continuous movement. Capillarity might control the quantity of moisture which evaporated away from the surface of the leaves, but it seemed more probable that transpiration, which depended largely on the temperature and humidity of the atmosphere, was responsible for the continuous movement of fluid through the plant. Capillarity started it, and transpiration kept it going. Leaf surface would then be an important factor in the elevation of the sap, in which case the leaves had a function that Malpighi and Grew had not realised. The following are a few examples of the numerous experiments which he carried out to test this theory:

(1) He cut off two branches of approximately similar size and shape from several varieties of fruit trees. From one of each pair, cut from the same tree, he stripped off all the leaves, and then set each branch in a separate vessel containing a measured quantity of water. The branches with leaves imbibed 15 to 30 oz. of water during the night; those without leaves took up only an ounce or so. Capillarity might cause fluid to rise to a certain height, but evidently the leaves determined the amount of sap which flowed in a given time.

(2) He selected a stem 2 in. long bearing twelve leaves and an apple; this, standing in water, imbibed 4/5 oz. in three days. Another stem of the same length with twelve similar leaves, but no apple, imbibed 3/4 oz. in the same time. A similar stem without leaves, but with two apples, each of approximately the same size as before, drew up 1/4 oz.

In this experiment, the apple and the leaves imbibe 4/5 of an ounce; the leaves alonè near 1/4, but the two large apples imbibed and perspired but 1/3 so much as the 12 leaves; the one apple imbibed the 1/6 part of the 12 leaves; therefore two leaves imbibe and perspire as much as one apple; whence the perspirations seem to be proportional to their surfaces; the surface of the apple being nearly equal to the sum of the upper and under surfaces of two leaves. Whence it is probable that the use of these leaves (which are placed, just where the fruit joins the tree) is to bring nourishment to the fruit. And accordingly I observe, that the leaves, next adjoining to blossoms, are, in the spring, very much expanded, when the other leaves, or barren shoots, are but beginning to shoot: so provident is nature in making timely provision for the nourishing the yet embryo fruit.

(3) A branch of an apple tree was tied into a wide glass tube 9 ft. long, turned upside down, completely immersed under water in a large glass vessel, and the glass tube filled up with water to the top (Plate VI, fig. 3). Twelve hours later the level of the water had dropped only 6 in. When the branch was taken out of the water, so that its leaves were exposed to air again, the level of the water in the vertical glass tube fell 26 in. in the next twelve hours. "This experiment", he writes, "shows the great power of perspiration; since when the branch was immersed in the vessel of water, the 7 feet column of water in the tube above the surface of the water, could drive very little thro' the leaves till the branch was exposed to the open air".

(4) He tied a similar branch into a long glass tube as before, again turned it upside down, and filled the vertical tube with water. This time he left the surface of the leaves exposed to air, and the level of water in the tube fell rapidly. He then cut through the main stem above the leaves, and set the part of the branch bearing the leaves upright in a vessel of water; the short leafless part of the stem was left in position with the hydrostatic pressure of the water in the tube

above it (Plate VI, figs. 4 and 5). The branch now imbibed 18 oz. of water upwards against gravity in twelve hours, but in the same time a hydrostatic pressure of 7 ft. of water caused only 6 oz. to percolate through the stem.

The importance of transpiration and leaf surface in promoting the continuous flow of sap was now established; but it was still possible that the capillary vessels of the stem and roots played some part in this phenomenon, although it was certainly not the only part, as other botanists had supposed. He therefore took the trunk of a young apple tree, stripped off all the leaves and lateral branches, placed its lower or great end in water, and cemented the other into a vertical glass tube. After standing for a considerable time, the upper end still remained moist. This showed that water was being continuously imbibed by the stem to make good the loss by evaporation above. No water rose in the tube, however, and water poured into it percolated freely downwards through the stem. Evidently the capillary sap vessels were able to imbibe water, but they had no power to protrude it without the assistance of the leaves. He then repeated the experiment on a growing cherry tree which he cut off close above the ground for this purpose. The stump of the cherry tree remained moist, but again no water rose in the tube.

I then dug up the tree by the roots, and set the root in water, with the glasses affixed to the top of the stem; after several hours nothing rose but a little dew; yet it is certain by many of the foregoing experiments, that if the top and leaves of the tree had been on, many ounces of water would

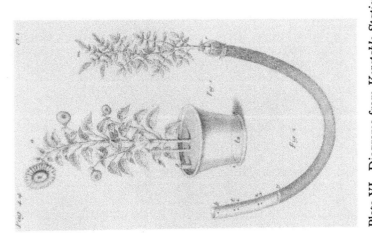

Plate VI. Diagrams from *Vegetable Statics*, illustrating Hales's experiments on transpiration

in this time have passed through the trunk, and been evaporated through the leaves. These last experiments all show, that though the capillary sap-vessels imbibe moisture plentifully; yet they have little power to protrude it farther, without the assistance of the perspiring leaves, which do greatly promote its progress.

His next set of experiments were designed "to find out the force with which trees imbibe moisture". The method was the outcome of an accidental observation:

About twenty years since I made several haemastatical experiments on dogs; and six years afterwards repeated the same on horses and other animals, in order to find out the real force of the blood in the arteries: at which time I wished I could have made the like experiments to discover the force of the sap in vegetables; but dispaired of ever effecting it, till about seven years since, by mere accident I hit upon it, while I was endeavouring by several ways to stop the bleeding of an old stem of a vine, which was cut too near the bleeding season, which I feared might kill it. Having, after other means proved ineffectual, tied a piece of bladder over the transverse cut of the stem, I found the force of the sap did greatly extend the bladder; whence I concluded, that if a long glass tube were fixed there in the same manner, as I had before done to the arteries of several living animals, I should thereby obtain the real ascending force of the sap in that stem, which succeeded according to my expectation: and hence it is, that I have been insensibly led on to make farther and farther researches by variety of experiments.

He now proceeded to investigate the "imbibing force" of the plants and trees in which the phenomenon of transpiration had been studied. He divided the root, branch, or main stem, of the particular plant or tree under investigation, and tied the upper end into a wide glass tube full of water; this was connected below to a mercury manometer (Plate VII). When the sun was out and the air warm, the mercury would be drawn rapidly up the limb of the mano- meter as the plant imbibed the water out of the wide glass tube. If there was no sunshine, the air cool, and transpiration from the leaves slow, it rose less quickly. If the sun went in during an experiment, the mercury would cease to rise, or fall again. The following table gives some idea of his experiments, and of the pressures which he recorded:

Experiment No.	Subject	Height Mercury Reached
XXVI.	Branch of a golden pippin, 3 ft. long with several large lateral branches.	11 ins.
XXI.	Root of a pear tree.	8 ins.
XXII.	Branch of a young apple tree, 3 ft. long.	6 ins.
XXIII.	One year old shoot of a vine, 2 yds. long.	4 ins.
XXIV.	Branch of an apple tree with twenty apples, 2 ft. long.	4 ins.
XXV.	Old apple tree branch, 12 ft. long.	4 ins.
XXX.	Apple with stalk 1½ in. long, & 12 leaves.	4 ins.
	Apple with stalk 1½ in. long, but no leaves.	3 ins.
	Stalk 1½ in. long, but no apples or leaves. (See Plate VII, fig. 15.)	¼ in.

This method could be adapted to throw light on the debated question of the circulation of the sap. Harvey's work was now nearly a century old, and many botanists inclined to the view, first elaborated by Major of Breslau in 1665, that there existed in plants some sort of circulation of the sap comparable to that of the blood in animals. According to the circulation theory, the sap ascended in the substance of the older wood, and descended again in the layer of recent wood and between the wood and bark. The essence of the mechanism of the circulation of the blood in animals was that the direction of its movement could not be reversed, but was it possible to reverse the normal flow of sap in trees as Malpighi had supposed? To answer this question Hales selected a dwarf golden pippin tree with a suitable pliant branch which was cut through below the origin of its laterals. The part still attached to the tree was bent down, and cemented into a wide glass tube of water connected below with a mercury manometer. The detached part of the branch was turned upside down, the original top twig cut off, and its stump connected through water with another manometer. The cut end of the stump, still part of the tree, now imbibed water in the reverse direction, and drew the mercury up 5 in.; the branch itself imbibed water, also in the opposite direction to the normal flow of sap, and drew the mercury up 11 in. "This experiment proves that branches will strongly imbibe from the small end immersed in water to the great end; as well as from the great end immersed in water to the small end". He then cut deep holes one above the other into the wood of a number of different branches; these were arranged alternately on opposite sides, so as to intercept somewhere all the ascending sap vessels. The rate of transpiration remained largely unaffected, and he concluded that the sap must pass laterally between the gaps in its upward path, and that there must be free lateral communication between the sap vessels. These facts, the reversibility of the flow of sap, and lateral communication between the vessels, made the existence of a definite circulation of the sap unlikely.

In addition to these experiments he measured the pressure of the sap and the average transpiration rate in a number of other plants and trees. His results were fairly consistent. Those trees which habitually "perspired" the most, such as the pear, plum, quince, cherry, and peach, would develop the greatest pressures, 3 to 6 in. of mercury, in their roots and stems; others in which transpiration was as a rule less rapid, the elm, oak, horse-chestnut, for instance, would only raise the mercury an inch or so; the evergreens which "perspired" less than any of the deciduous trees often failed to lift the mercury at all. "Imbibing force" and "perspiration rate" therefore ran more or less parallel. This supported his idea that transpiration from the leaves was the most important factor in the elevation of the sap, and he now had a theory to account for this phenomenon supported by a considerable amount of experimental evidence. Capillarity, the automatic rise of fluid in a capillary tube due to surface tension, explained the passive rise of the sap in the vessels of the stem to a height inversely proportional to the diameter of the individual sap vessels. This did not account for the actual flow. The continuous movement of the sap was due to transpiration of water from the leaves. As water evaporated away from their surfaces, sap rose continuously by capillarity in the capillary sap vessels, and made good the loss.

By this principle (*capillarity*) it is that plants, imbibe moisture so vigorously up their fine capillary vessels; which moisture, as it is carried off in perspiration, (by the action of warmth) thereby gives the sap-vessels liberty to be almost continually attracting of fresh supplies; which they could not do, if they were full saturate with moisture: for without perspiration the sap must necessarily stagnate, notwithstanding the sap-vessels are so curiously adapted by their exceeding fineness, to raise a sap to great heights, in a reciprocal proportion to their very minute diameters. Though vegetables (which are inanimate) have not an engine, which, by its alternate dilatations and contractions, does in animals forcibly drive the blood through the arteries and veins; yet has nature wonderfully contrived other means, most powerfully to raise and keep in motion the sap.

There was another factor, however, besides transpiration and capillarity which was responsible for the elevation of the sap in the early spring before the leaves develop. He returned to his accidental observation on the bleeding vine, and proceeded to investigate this phenomenon more closely. That some trees bleed, when cut at certain seasons of the year, must have been common knowledge, but Hales was the first to measure root pressure:

March 30th at 3 p.m. I cut off a *vine* on a western aspect, within seven inches of the ground; the remaining stump had no lateral branches: it was 4 or 5 years old, and ¾ inch diameter. I fixed to the top of the stump, by means of a brass collar, a glass tube seven feet long, and ¼ inch diameter; I secured the joint with stiff cement made of melted beeswax and turpentine, and bound it fast over with several folds of wet bladder and packthread: I then screwed a second tube to the first, and then a third to 25 feet height. (*Plate VII, fig.* 17.) The stem not bleeding into the tube, I filled the tube two feet high with water; the water was imbibed by the stem within 3 inches of the bottom, by 8 o'clock that evening. In the night it rained a small shower. The next morning at 6 and ½, the water was risen three inches above what it was fallen to last night at eight o'clock. The thermometer which hung in my porch was 11 degrees above the freezing point.

March 31 from 6 and $\frac{1}{2}$ a.m. to 10 p.m. the sap rose $8 + \frac{1}{4}$ inches. April 1st, at 6 a.m., thermometer 3 degrees above the freezing point, and a white hoar frost, the sap rose from ten o'clock last night $3 + \frac{1}{4}$ inches more; and so continued rising daily till it was above 21 feet high, and would very probably have risen higher, if the joint had not several times leaked: after stopping of which it would rise sometimes at the rate of an inch in three minutes, so as to rise 10 feet or more in a day. In the chief bleeding season it would continue rising night and day; but much more in the day than night, and most of all in the greatest heat of the day.[1]

In his next experiment, instead of letting the sap pour out into a vertical glass tube 25 ft. high, he employed the modern method of the U-tube mercury manometer (Plate VII, fig. 18), and recorded the enormous pressure of $32\frac{1}{2}$ in. of mercury, equivalent to 43 ft. of water.

This force is near five times greater than the force of the blood in the great crural artery of a horse; seven times greater than the force of the blood in the like artery of a dog; and eight times greater than the blood's force in the same artery of a fallow doe: which different forces I found by tying those several animals down alive upon their backs; and then laying open the great left crural artery, I fixed to it a glass tube: in which tube the blood of one horse rose eight feet three inches, and the blood of another horse eight feet nine inches. The blood of a little dog six feet and a half high: in a large spaniel seven feet high. The blood of the fallow doe mounted five feet seven inches.

From these experiments he concluded that there was "considerable energy in the root to push up the sap in the bleeding season". It was possible, however, that the capillary sap vessels of the stem might play a part, and he therefore connected three different

[1] Hales, *Vegetable Statics*, 4th ed. p. 108.

branches of different ages in the same vine to three separate mercury manometers. The variations in the pressure of the sap in the three branches did not run parallel throughout the day. At the same moment, one branch might be in a state of "pushing sap", and the other two "imbibing"; later this state of affairs might be reversed. "From this experiment we see", he writes, "that this force (protrusion of the sap without the assistance of the leaves) is not from the root only, but must also proceed from some power in the stem and branches".

He now waited until the bleeding season was over. When he came to repeat these experiments in the late summer, he could find no evidence of this remarkable phenomenon. The sap did not rise in his vertical tube, although his earlier experiments on transpiration had shown that, even at this time of year, large quantities of sap are continuously passing up the vine.

Since this flow of sap ceases at once as soon as the vine was cut off the stem, the principal cause of its rise must at the same time be taken away, viz. the great perspiration of the leaves. It seems evident, therefore, that the capillary sap-vessels, out of the bleeding season, have little power to protrude sap in any plenty beyond their orifices; but as any sap is evaporated off, they can by their strong attraction supply the great quantities of sap drawn off by perspiration.

Seven years had now passed since he had first started on this work. In 1725, he read his second paper to the Royal Society:

Jan. 14th. Sir Hans Sloane, Vice-President in the Chair. The Revd. Mr. Hale communicated a Treatise concerning the Power of Vegetation consisting of six heads of experiments delivered in six chapters. Part of the first was read and the rest order'd for the next meeting. And the Society return'd Mr. Hale thanks for communicating the same, desiring him to continue in the prosecution of a designe which seems to promise so fairly for making an advancement in Natural Knowledge.[1]

"I have been careful in making", he said, "and faithful in relating the results of these experiments; and I wish I could be as happy in drawing the proper inferences from them". In this remarkable paper he described the three factors that are still regarded as the most important in promoting the upward flow of sap: transpiration, capillarity, and root pressure. He left root pressure unexplained, but, although theories based on the chemical changes associated with growth have been put forward, it remains largely unexplained to-day. Root pressure is responsible, as he pointed out, for the flow of sap in the young plant in the early spring before the leaves are adequately developed. At other times root pressure ceases, and transpiration and capillarity effect the flow of sap. His theory is still regarded as correct in its main essentials, and when Sachs was at work on his *Pflanzenphysiologie* (1865), he had to go back one hundred and forty years to Hales's experiment on transpiration to find results that he could compare with his own.

"All that was done from Malpighi and Mariotte to Ingen-Houss", writes Sachs, "to advance the knowledge of the nutrition of plants was thrown into the shade by the brilliant investigations of Stephen Hales, in whom we see once more the genius of discovery and the sound original reasoning powers of the great

---

[1] *Royal Society Journal Book*, 1720–1726, XIII, 438.

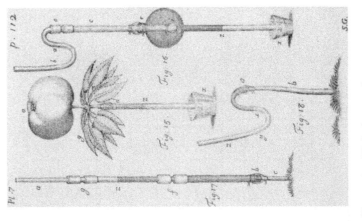

Plate VII. Diagrams from *Vegetable Statics*, illustrating Hales's experiments on "the force with which trees absorb moisture"

explorers of nature in Newton's age. His book was the first work devoted to a complete account of the nutrition of plants and the movements of the sap in them. In it an abundance of new experiments and observations, measurements and calculations, combine to form a living picture of the whole subject. Malpighi had endeavoured to discover the physiological functions of organs by the aid of analogies and a reference to their structure. Mariotte had discovered the main features of the connection between plants and their environment by combining together chemical and physical facts. But Hales may be said to have made his plants speak for themselves. By means of cleverly combined and skilfully managed experiments he compelled them to disclose the forces that were at work in them by effects made apparent to the naked eye, and thus to show that forces of a very peculiar kind are in constant activity in the quiet and apparently passive organs of vegetation. Permeated with the spirit of Newton's age, which, notwithstanding its strictly teleological and even theological conception of nature, did endeavour to explain all the phenomena of life mechanically by the attraction and repulsion of material particles, he was not content with giving a clear idea of the phenomena of vegetation, but sought to trace them back to mechanico-physical laws as then understood. Hales is the last of the great naturalists who laid the foundations of vegetable physiology. Strange as some of their ideas may seem to us, yet they were the first to gain any deep insight into the hidden machinery of vegetable life".[1]

[1] Julius von Sachs, *History of Botany*, translated by Garnsey, and revised by Balfour, Oxford, 1890.

CHAPTER V

Science and Religion. The Growth of Plants. The Ossification of Bone. Marriage. His Wife dies.

ON first thoughts it may seem remarkable that scientific work like this should have been performed by a country parson. In the nineteenth century religion and science became mutually antagonistic, and at the present time it is still uncommon to see them in open association; but in the early years of the eighteenth century the Church looked with success to science for support.

Descartes had based his philosophy more or less on current scientific knowledge. He admitted the real existence of matter, but held that, as knowledge of the external world was entirely limited to the impression that it made upon consciousness, the mind must comprehend and know itself more completely than it could ever understand the physical universe. He therefore postulated two forms of homogeneous substance: one underlying matter, the other the basis of the mind. The metaphysical speculations of Descartes, admitting as they did the existence of God and men's souls, did not contravene to any serious extent the teaching of the Church; but as science progressed, philosophers began to criticise the dogmatic doctrines of religion. Foremost among such advanced thinkers were Hobbes in England and Spinoza in Holland. Hobbes made Bacon's objective realism the starting-point of a systematic materialism. Spinoza attempted to unify the dualism of Descartes into one consistent whole, and in so doing, although he continued to admit the existence of God, he succeeded in denying free will. Such was the sceptical current of the age in which these doctrines were let loose, that by the end of the seventeenth century "Hobbism" had become a cult, and "atheism" fashionable.

By the Church this movement was naturally regarded with abhorrence and alarm. Hobbes was openly an atheist; to him there was nothing in the world but matter, and the physical laws that governed it. Spinoza had professed the existence of God, but by denying free will had made human endeavour appear valueless. Locke argued that, since all experience comes through the senses from the outside world, mind, primarily dependent on the physical universe, must also be material in nature. It is not surprising that divines began to be anxious lest belief in a deity should disappear, and the ethical system on which civilisation was based be left without any religious foundation to support it.

The Hon. Robert Boyle, the founder of modern chemistry, died in the year 1696. During his lifetime he was in the habit of spending a thousand pounds a year in works of charity and the propagation of the gospel. "Wishing that in his death he might promote the cause to which he had devoted his life", he bequeathed in his will a sufficient sum of money to found an annual course of lectures for the purpose of "protecting religion against the infidels". Bentley, Master of Trinity College, and Regius Professor of Divinity in the University, who played an active part in building up the Cambridge school of natural science, was appointed first lecturer under this new foundation. Bentley was a classic rather than a theologian, and in his first series of "Boyle's Lectures", entitled "A Confutation of Atheism", he based his attack against the teaching of Hobbes and Spinoza on the discoveries of modern science, and divided his arguments into "considerations of the faculties of the soul" (Locke), the "structure of human bodies" (Vesalius and Harvey), and the "origin and frame of the world" (Newton). The atheists still made use of the Cartesian system when it proved convenient to support their particular contentions. Bentley therefore seized upon the new and apparently mysterious law of gravitation, and employed it as an effective argument against a purely materialistic conception of the universe. He wrote his lectures with the active co-operation of Newton, and in one of Newton's letters on the subject to the Master of Trinity, is the following passage: "When I wrote my Treatise about our System, I had an eye upon such principles as might work with considering men for the belief of a Deity, and nothing can rejoice me more than to find it useful for that purpose".[1]

This was the University atmosphere in which Hales had been educated, for he had entered Bene't College in the year that Boyle died. He was at Cambridge when Bentley gave his much-discussed lectures, and an undergraduate when Newton was still at Trinity. His own College had brought him up on Locke's famous essay, and on volumes of sermons preached at "Boyle's Lectures". Like all his contemporaries, so at least it must be supposed, he believed that the

---

[1] J. H. Monk, *Life of Richard Bentley, D.D.*, London, 1833.

world had been created by God, more or less as men then knew it. At the beginning the laws of physics and mechanics had been ordained, and there was to be no departure from them: "nature works according to the laws established at her first institution". The animals, and man in particular, had been specially created by God; their minutest parts had actually been designed by the Creator so as to fulfil the particular function that they were intended to serve.

The study of nature will ever yield us fresh matter of entertainment, and we have great reason to bless God for the faculties and abilities he has given us, and the strong desire he has implanted in our minds, to search into and contemplate his works, in which the farther we go, the more we see the signatures of his wisdom and power, everything pleases and instructs us, because in everything we see a wise design. And the farther researches we make into this admirable scene of things, the more beauty and harmony we see in them: and the stronger and clearer convictions they give us, of the being, power and wisdom of the divine Architect, who has made all things to concur with a wonderful conformity, in carrying on, by various and innumerable combinations of matter, such a circulation of causes and effects, as was necessary to the great ends of nature.[1]

His published works abound with such passages. In the complete absence of any conception of evolution, his researches afforded him convincing proof of the existence, and the wisdom and goodness of God:

The animal body in which there is so just a symmetry of parts, such innumerable beauties and harmony in the uniform frame and texture of so vast a variety of solid and fluid parts, as must ever afford room for farther discoveries to the diligent inquirer; and thereby yield fresh instances to illustrate the wisdom of the divine architect, the traces of which are

[1] Hales, *Haemastatics*, Dedication.

so plain to be seen in everything, that the psalmist had good
reason to call him a *fool*, who could be so senseless as to *say
in his heart, that there is no God*; whose masterly hand is so
evident in every part of nature, that if there be any who
pretend that they cannot see it, it can be no breach of charity
to say that they are wilfully blind, and therefore lyars.[1]

Belief of this kind was hardly in accordance with
the critical attitude of philosophers at that time.
Locke had argued that, as matter was only known to
mind through the agency of the special sense organs
in the processes of sensation and perception, mind
itself must be material in nature. Bishop Berkeley
had met this contention by the bold assertion that
Locke's argument really served to show, not, as its
author supposed, that mind was material in nature,
but that matter had no real existence outside the
content of the mind. This thesis remained un-
answered, until David Hume replied that, since
internal perception of ourselves only reveals an ever-
changing stream of ideas, feelings, and associations,
there was no real evidence that any such thing as
unity of mind existed. Metaphysical speculation had
arrived at the ridiculous, and yet apparently logical,
conclusion that neither matter nor mind had any
real existence.

Hales's attitude to this was that of the scientist, and
not that of the philosopher. The experimental method
was the only way in which science could be advanced:

Though we can never hope to attain to the complete knowledge of the texture, or constituent frame and nature of
bodies, yet may we reasonably expect by this method of

[1] Hales, *Haemastatics*, Preface.

experiments, to make farther and farther advances abundantly sufficient to reward our pains. And though the method be tedious, yet our abilities can proceed no faster; for as the learned author of the *Procedure of human Understanding* observes, "All the real true knowledge we have of Nature is intirely experimental, insomuch that, how strange soever the assertion seems, we may lay this down as the first fundamental unerring rule in physics, *That it is not within the compass of human understanding to assign a purely speculative reason for any one phaenomenon in nature*". So that in natural philosophy, we cannot depend on any mere speculations of the mind: we can only with the mathematicians, reason with any tolerable certainty from proper *data*, such as arise from the united testimony of many good and credible experiments. Yet it seems not unreasonable, on the other hand, though not far to indulge, yet to carry our reasonings a little farther than the plain evidence of experiments will warrant; for since at the utmost boundaries of those things which we clearly know, there is a kind of twilight cast from what we know, on the adjoining borders of *Terra incognita*, it seems therefore reasonable in some degree to indulge conjecture there: otherwise we should make but very slow advances in future discoveries, either by experiments or reasoning: for new experiments and discoveries do usually owe their first rise only to lucky guesses and probable conjectures, and even disappointments in these conjectures do often lead to the thing sought for: thus by observing the errors and defects of a first experiment in any researches, we are sometimes carried to such fundamental experiments, as lead to a large series of many other useful experiments and important discoveries. If therefore some may be apt to think that I have sometimes too far indulged conjecture, in the inferences I have drawn from the events of some experiments; they ought to consider that it is from these kind of conjectures that fresh discoveries first take their rise; for though some of them may prove false, yet they often lead to further and new discoveries. It is by the like conjectures that I have been led on step by step, through this long and laborious series of experiments; in any of which I did not certainly know what the event would be, till I had made the trial, which trial often led on to more conjectures, and farther experiments. In which method we may be continually making farther and farther advances in the knowledge of nature, in proportion to the number of observations which we have: but as we can never hope to be furnished with a sufficient number of these, to let us into a thorough knowledge of the great and intricate scheme of nature, so it would be but dry work to be ever laying foundations, but never attempting to build on them. We must be content in this our instant state of knowledge, while we know in part only, to imitate children, who for want of better skill and abilities, and of more proper materials, amuse themselves with flight buildings. The farther advances we make in the knowledge of nature, the more probable and the nearer to truth will our conjectures approach: so that succeeding generations, who shall have the benefit and advantage both of their own observations, and those of preceding generations, may then make considerable advances, when *many shall run to and fro, and knowledge shall be increased.* Dan. XII. 4.[1]

It is clear from this passage that, while he firmly believed the experimental method to be the only way by which science could be advanced, he held that it had very definite limitations: "we can never hope to attain to complete knowledge". On the one hand, he was convinced of divine wisdom and purpose in the creation of man and the animals. On the other hand, he held that their organs so created had to work according to the laws of physics and mechanics established at the first institution of the world. He did not believe that a specific vital force was responsible for the phenomena peculiar to life. Some of

[1] Preface to *Haemastatics.*

the functions of the body would eventually be explained in terms of the laws of chemistry, physics, and mechanics, as then, or subsequently, understood; others belonged to "the great and intricate scheme of nature" into the complete comprehension of which man could never enter. He therefore applied the chemistry and physics, which he had learnt at Cambridge, to the explanation of some of the phenomena of life where there seemed to be some possibility of success, and there is not a single passage in his writings in which he seeks refuge from his difficulties by postulating vital force. With the more difficult subjects he made no attempt to deal. Perhaps he thought that physics and chemistry were not yet sufficiently advanced for the purpose; more likely, he believed that science would never be able to provide their explanation.

When his immediate successors began to push this method further, and endeavoured to explain the more fundamental problems of biology along purely mechanical lines, they soon gave up the attempt as hopeless. Physiologists then got into the way of postulating a vague vital force whenever mechanical explanation seemed inadequate. For a time biological science suffered in consequence, but vitalism of this kind was short-lived, as with the rapid advances that were made in chemistry and physics towards the end of the eighteenth century, the idea of a specific vital force began to wane. Chemists succeeded in synthesising substances hitherto regarded as peculiar to life. Physicists established the laws of the conservation of energy and matter, and physiologists proved them applicable to the animal body. Pasteur had disproved spontaneous generation, but there were many who confidently expected that life would soon be synthesised in the laboratory. Finally Darwin produced a reasoned theory to account for the origin of species based on accidental variation and the perpetuation of favourable, but fortuitous, variations in the universal struggle for existence. Not only could Hales's mechanistic thesis be pushed much further than he himself had ever supposed, but it could be carried to a conclusion which, illogically perhaps, he would never have believed to have been possible. On the other hand, the doctrine of purposive creation, on which he had so largely relied, was completely undermined.

The method that Hales adopted is still generally pursued. Physiologists are attempting to explain the phenomena of life on physical, chemical, and mechanical laws; and at the moment there seems to be little other method of attack. How far can this be carried? Further perhaps than Hales expected, but not so far as scientists confidently believed in the nineteenth century. There are now some who maintain that, in spite of the many striking successes it has achieved, a purely mechanistic biology will always remain inadequate to explain the fundamental phenomena of life: embryonic development from the ovum, heredity, behaviour, adaptation to environment, and protective reaction to disease. It is possible that inorganic nature should be interpreted in terms of life, instead of life in terms of the conventional physical categories, space, time, energy, and matter. The view is gaining ground that the Darwinian theory alone is inadequate to explain organic evolution, and there is a tendency to postulate active adaptation of animals to their environment as the causative force in evolution. Ordered evolution of this kind would be consistent with the teleological point of view which Hales adopted.

An example of his partly mechanistic outlook on the problems of biology is afforded by his work on the growth of plants. He devised a method of making permanent marks on young leaves and shoots, so that the relative positions of their parts could be followed during growth. He drove five pins in a straight line through a piece of thin wood at intervals of a quarter of an inch, dipped their points in an emulsion of red lead and oil, and marked the young shoots and leaves of a vine with a number of equidistant points (Plate VIII, figs. 40, 41, 43, and 44). In the following autumn, when he returned from Farringdon, the marks he had made on the vine were still discernible; they demonstrated clearly the symmetrical inequalities of vegetable growth (Figs. 42, 45):

I found in them all a gradual scale of unequal extensions, those parts extending most which were tenderest. The whole progress of the first joint is very short in comparison of the other joints, because at first setting out its leaves being very small, and the season yet cooler than afterwards, 'tis probable that but little sap is conveyed to it; and therefore it extending but slowly, its fibres are in the meantime grown tough and hard, before it can arrive to any considerable length. But as the season advances, and the leaves inlarge, greater plenty of nourishment being thereby conveyed, the second joint grows longer than the first, and the third and fourth still on gradually longer than the preceding; these do therefore, in equal times, make greater advances than the former.[1]

This was an explanation of the anatomical aspect of growth, but it took no account of the mechanical force responsible for it; it did not explain the shoot of the seed forcing its way up through the soil, or how the sunflower elevated itself high into the air. Borelli in his book, *De Motu Animalium*, had attributed growth to "turgescence", the active absorption of water by the cellular substances of plants. To test the possibilities of this theory, Hales filled an iron pot with dried peas, and covered them over with a loosely fitting cover on the top of which he placed a weight of two hundred pounds. When water was poured in through a hole in the lid, the peas imbibed the water and swelled up, and the force of their expansion lifted up the weight.

We see in this experiment the vast force with which swelling peas expand; and it is doubtless a considerable part of the same force which is exerted, not only in pushing the plume upwards in the air, but also in enabling the first shooting radicle of the pea, and all its subsequent tender fibres, to penetrate and shoot into the earth.

Although he saw a difficulty in a theory which attempted to explain growth in terms of hydrostatic pressure within the cells ("a dilating spongy substance", he said, "would not produce an oblong shoot, but rather a globose one, like an apple"), he accepted Borelli's idea, and argued from it that, when the pith dried up, growth must cease; elongation could then only continue at the soft growing point:

[1] Hales, *Vegetable Statics*, 4th ed. p. 335.

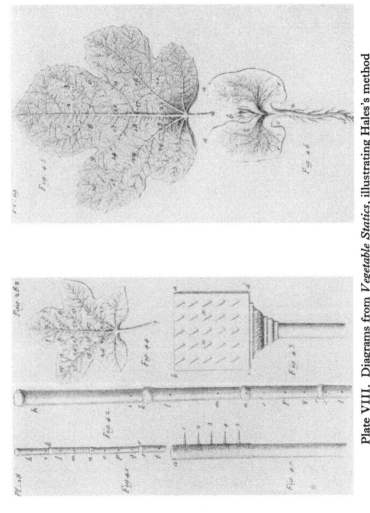

Plate VIII. Diagrams from *Vegetable Statics*, illustrating Hales's method of studying the growth of plants

The wetter the season, the longer and larger shoots do vegetables usually make; because their soft ductile parts do then continue longer in a moist tender state: but in a dry season the fibres soon harden, and stop the further growth of the shoot. And for this reason, beans and many other plants, which stand where they are much shaded, being thereby kept continually moist, do grow to unusual heights, and are drawn up, as they call it, by the over-shadowing trees, their parts being kept long, soft and ductile.

The bones of young animals are soft at first; they only ossify and turn into bone as growth proceeds. The growth of animals was likely to be determined, he thought, by the same kind of factors as regulated that of plants, and he now adapted his method of equidistant marking to find out:

As in vegetables, so doubtless in animals, the tender ductile bones of young animals are gradually increased in every part, that is not hardened and ossified; but since it was inconsistent with the motion of the joints to have the ends of the bones soft and ductile, as in vegetables, therefore nature makes a wonderful provision for this at the glutinous serrated joining of the heads to the shanks of the bones; which joining while it continues ductile, the animal grows; but when it ossifies, then the animal can no longer grow: as I was assured by the following experiment, viz. I took a half-grown *chick*, whose leg-bone was then two inches long; with a sharp-pointed iron, at half an inch distance, I pierced two small holes thro' the middle of the scaly covering of the leg and shin-bone; two months after I killed the *chick*, and upon laying the bone bare, I found on it obscure remains of the two marks I had made at the same distance of half an inch: so that that part of the bone had not at all distended lengthwise, since the time that I marked it; notwithstanding the bone was in that time grown an inch more in length, which growth was mostly at the upper end of the bone, where a wonderful provision is made for its growth at the joining of its head to the shank, called by anatomists *symphysis*.[1]

*   *   *   *   *

He had now reached the fifth decade of life. At the age of forty-three he married Mary Newce, daughter of Dr Richard Newce of the parish of Much Hadham in Hertfordshire, and Rector of Hailsham in Sussex. Of his wife, except that, like his own mother, she was from Hertfordshire, nothing is recorded. The wedding was in St Paul's Cathedral:

> Stephen Hales, B.D., of the Parish of Teddington in the County of Middlesex, and Mary Newce of the Parish of Much Hadham in the County of Hertfordshire, were married by license in the Cathedral on the 26th day of March 1720 by me, William Stanley.[2]

His married life was brief. Just over a year after the wedding his wife died, and left him childless. She was buried in the churchyard at Teddington. He conducted the funeral service himself, and in the parish register he had to write:

> Mary Hales, my dear wife was buried. Oct. 10. 1721.

*   *   *   *   *

Of his character one of his contemporaries wrote: "He was remarkable for social virtue and sweetness of temper; his life was not only blameless but exemplary to a high degree; he was happy in himself, and beneficial to others".[3] Butler writes: "He possessed a native innocence and sim-

---

[1] Hales, *Vegetable Statics*, 4th ed. p. 339. This experiment is usually attributed to John Hunter, but was actually performed by Hales several years before Hunter's birth in 1728.

[2] St Paul's Cathedral Register.

[3] Peter Collinson, *Gentleman's Magazine*, 1764, XXXIV, 273; *Annual Register*, 1764, vol. VII, Characters, 42.

plicity of manners, which the characters of other men, and the customs of the world, could never alter; and though he often met with many unworthy objects of his kind and uncharitable offices, yet they never once lessened his natural and unwearied disposition for doing good and relieving distress. His temper, as well as the powers of his understanding, were happily fitted for the improvement of Natural Philosophy, possessing, as he did, in an uncommon degree, that *industry and patient thinking*, which Sir Isaac Newton used modestly to declare was his own only secret by which he was enabled so fortunately to trace his wonderful analysis of nature. There are two things in his character, which particularly distinguish him from almost every other man: the first was, that his mind was so habitually bent on acquiring knowledge, that, having what he thought an abundant income, he was solicitous to avoid any further preferment in the church, lest his time and attention might thereby be diverted from his other favourite and useful occupations. The other feature of his character was no less singular: he could look even upon wicked men, and those who did him unkind offices, without any emotion of particular indignation; not from want of discernment or sensibility; but he used to consider them only like those experiments which, upon trial, he found could never be applied to any useful purpose, and which he therefore calmly and dispassionately laid aside".[1]

[1] Rev. Weeden Butler, *Memoirs of Mark Hildesley, D.D., Bishop of Sodor and Man*, London, 1799; *Gentleman's Magazine*, 1799, LXIX, 9.

CHAPTER VI

Respiration and Combustion. The Nutrition of Plants. Free and
Fixed Air. The Function of the Leaves. Rebreathing Experiments. Carbon Dioxide. Publishes *Vegetable Statics*.

A DESCRIPTION of Hales's work on plant nutrition
and animal respiration would be meaningless
without some account of the position of
chemical knowledge at that time. Galileo and Newton
had made physics an exact science, but chemistry
remained to a large extent an empirical and speculative study. The mediaeval conception of four
elementary substances, earth, air, fire, and water,
had been modified only in so far as to teach that
"earth", in its different forms, consisted of various
mixtures of three other elemental substances, salt,
mercury, and sulphur. All the common substances
that could be burnt were considered to be "salino-
sulphureous" combinations of various types. Combustion was still regarded as the peculiar property
of sulphur, which held in its pores a subtle spirit
that was thrust out when the substance was heated,
and then became visible as flame.

The foundations of modern chemistry, however,
had been laid in the previous century. In 1660, the
Hon. Robert Boyle had demonstrated that a candle
became extinguished, and that animals died, when
they were placed in an evacuated vessel; air, therefore, was necessary both for life and for combustion.
The next advance was made a few years later by
Robert Hooke, Curator of the Royal Society, whose

duty was to perform experiments before the Fellows
at their meetings. Artificial respiration had been
practised by Vesalius, but Hooke showed that an
animal could be kept alive without any excursion
of the chest, or lungs, provided that small holes were
made in the lung substance, and a rapid current of
air blown through them; the movement of the lungs
in breathing was not a necessary feature of respiration. Hooke, however, failed to provide the explanation of his experiment, and physiologists continued
to think that breathing served to cool the blood over-
heated by friction in the vessels.

Accurate knowledge of the chemistry of respiration
began with the work of Richard Lower and John
Mayow. Lower, of Christ Church, demonstrated that
venous blood changes colour on exposure to air, and
that this change is due to the blood taking up some
of the air. Mayow, a scholar of Wadham and a
Fellow of All Souls', showed that an animal in a
closed vessel died, and that a candle became extinguished, when only a fourteenth part of the air
had been used up; it was not the whole air that was
necessary for respiration and combustion, but a part
of it only. This active principle of the atmosphere he
called the "spiritus nitro-aereus". He then demonstrated that a body gains weight when burnt; he
concluded that the "spiritus nitro-aereus" must
enter into combination with the burning substance.
Combining these discoveries with Lower's observations, he postulated that the "spiritus nitro-aereus"
entered into union with the blood. Identifying
respiration and combustion, he perceived that

the muscles were the chief place where animal heat is produced. Mayow virtually discovered oxygen, laid the foundation of the correct conception of the origin of animal heat, and described the main chemical changes underlying respiration and combustion. He saw that in these processes something entered into combination with the animal or with the burning substance, although he failed to realise that anything was given out in exchange. Had Mayow lived longer, the history of science might read quite differently, but he died in the year 1679 at the age of thirty-five, "having been married a little before not altogether to his content". The result of his premature death was that his work received but scant attention. Soon after, Stahl, failing to make the necessary distinction between energy and matter, adopted the view that in combustion a body was losing something; that which held for energy, he believed to be true for matter, and in so doing put back the study of chemistry by over a hundred years! Within thirty years of Mayow's death "in an apothecaries house bearing the sign of the Blue Anker in Covent Garden", Stahl had introduced his phlogiston theory. According to this conception, which dominated biology and chemistry alike for nearly a century, when a substance was burnt, something material departed from it; the body suffered a loss, it became dephlogisticated. This theory was little more than an old idea in a new dress. Moreover, Stahl, rejecting Mayow's idea that animal heat was due to chemical action, returned to the old view as to its causation, and prided himself as having been the first to show that the lungs, instead of having a cooling effect upon the blood, were the chief place where heat was engendered by friction. Stahl's influence was so great that Haller, a pupil of Boerhaave, writing only a few years before Hales died, expressed similar views. He even denied that air entered into combination with the blood; so completely had the work of Mayow and Lower been forgotten!

Apart from Mayow's work, little progress was made in purely chemical knowledge until the latter part of the eighteenth century. Except in the empirical description of chemical substances, their physical properties, and the different reactions that might occur between them, chemistry advanced but little. During the years in which Hales worked (1710–1727), there was no clear conception of elements, atoms, or molecules; a logical formulation of chemical compounds was not possible, and substances were still classified empirically according to their properties. All gases were called "air"; the existence of different gases was explained by supposing that the element "air" could alter its physical properties. Much attention continued to be paid to the elastic properties of gases; reduction in the volume of a gas was referred to as a decrease in its elasticity. Biochemistry had not originated as a separate science, and of the chemical physiology of digestion, secretion, and metabolism, nothing was known. Science as a whole lacked in an all-important respect: in spite of the rapid rise of exact physics, there was as yet no clear conception of energy, and the laws of the conservation of mass and energy were undiscovered. In England, Mayow's work had been forgotten. On the Continent, Stahl's phlogiston theory dominated chemistry.

This confusion of thought prevented any clear conception of the mechanism of the nutrition of plants. Aristotle had supposed that the food of plants was elaborated beforehand in the earth, and that it was there rendered suitable for the purposes of growth; and not until the latter half of the seventeenth century did botanists break away completely from this idea. Mariotte then showed that plants convert the materials, which they derive from the ground, into entirely new chemical substances; that earth and water supply the essential elements of nutrition for the most diverse forms of vegetable life. Malpighi began to explain the share which belonged to the different organs of the plant in the work of nutrition. He came to the conclusion that the fibrous constituents of the wood conducted the nutrient sap, and that air passed along the vessels. Whether the air entered the plant by the roots or leaves, he was uncertain; he could find no openings in either, but held that it was most probably by the roots. Malpighi attributed special importance to his discovery that plants require air to breathe, like animals, but of the actual part played by air in the internal economy of the plant he remained in doubt. Most important of all, he perceived with remarkable insight that the green leaves must be the organs which prepare the food, and that somehow it must pass thence to all parts of the growing plant. In this country Grew, Secretary of the Royal Society, adopted Malpighi's views in most essentials.

Mariotte, Malpighi, and Grew, were Hales's immediate predecessors in botany, and with their writings he was familiar. In physiology he followed closely on Lower; in chemistry on Mayow. He lived during the years in which Mayow's work was being forgotten, and during the period in which Stahl's phlogiston theory came to dominate physical and biological science throughout Europe. As Hales died in 1761, he did not live to see the great discoveries that were made towards the end of the eighteenth century. Thirteen years later Priestley discovered oxygen, and Lavoisier made this discovery the starting-point of an entirely new view of chemical processes. He showed that "fixed air" (carbon dioxide) was a compound of carbon and "vital air", demonstrated the chemical composition of water, and then proved that the respiration of animals is a process of oxidation which accounts for their internal heat. In 1785, setting himself free from the old notions, he developed his anti-phlogistic system into one connected whole. These discoveries were rapidly turned to account in vegetable physiology. Priestley showed that the green parts of plants exhale oxygen. Ingen-Houss discovered that this only occurs under the influence of sunlight, while at all times every part of a plant is absorbing oxygen and liberating carbon dioxide. In 1796 he came to the conclusion that plants absorb the whole mass of their carbon from the carbon dioxide of the atmosphere, and in 1804 De Saussure proved that they are capable of fixing the elements of water.

The reader should now be in a position to understand Hales's outlook on the problems of animal respiration and plant nutrition. In his first experiment on the bleeding vine he had observed "a continuous series of air bubbles constantly ascending from the stem through the sap in the tube, in so great plenty as to make a large froth at the top of the sap ". This observation suggested that growing plants must draw up air by their roots, and his work on vegetable nutrition began with experiments "whereby to prove that a considerable quantity of air is inspired by plants". He cemented the stems of branches into closed vessels of air fitted with water manometers, and demonstrated that air was drawn up through the plant as water "perspired" off from the leaves. He then subjected the stems of trees to reduced atmosphere by means of an air pump, and showed that air would enter through the cut stem and through the surface of the bark and leaves. He came to the conclusion that "air freely enters plants, not only with the principal fund of nourishment by the roots, but also through the surfaces of their trunks and leaves, especially at night, when they are changed from a perspiring to a strongly imbibing state".[1] These observations, he thought, supported Grew and Malpighi in their idea that the vessels of the wood served the function of air conduction, and that the air taken up in this way was "perspired" off with the sap through the leaves. He also agreed with Malpighi in regarding respiration as one of the

[1] His observations may well have been correct, but his inferences from them were not strictly justifiable. Nevertheless, as is sometimes the case, they led him to more or less correct conclusions.

essential activities of plants, and expressed regret that Malpighi and Grew (who performed few experiments to support their speculations) had not "fortuned to have fallen into his statical way of enquiry". As to the exact part played by air in the internal economy of the plant, Hales still remained uncertain.

In his next series of experiments he subjected miscellaneous substances, animal, vegetable, and mineral, to distillation, fermentation, the action of acids, and other chemical procedures. He collected the gases that were evolved over water (Plate IX, fig. 38), and it is said that he introduced this important and now universal method into chemistry.[1] In other experiments weighed or measured quantities of various substances were subjected to the action of heat, and the volume of gas evolved (or absorbed) determined; the weight of gas was then calculated, and expressed as a fraction of the weight of the substance from which it had been derived.

Some of his results are set out in a table, but it is not worth while to enter into these experiments in detail, or to attempt to interpret them along modern lines. Many of his results must have been vitiated by solution of gas in the water over which his receivers were placed, and of this he knew nothing. He must also have prepared a great variety of different gases; among them hydrogen, carbon dioxide, sulphur dioxide, ammonia, and oxides of nitrogen. The "distilled air" of peas "flashed", and that of

[1] Ernst von Meyer, *History of Chemistry*, translated by George McGowan, London, 1906.

Substance Distilled	Quantity Distilled		Quantity of air Generated		Ratio of Weight of air to weight of substance
	Volume Cub. ins.	Weight grains	Volume Cub. ins.	Weight grains	
Hog's blood	1	—	33	—	—
Tallow	1	—	36	—	—
Horn	1	482	234	66	1/7
Oyster shell	1	532	324	92	1/6
Oak wood	1	270	216	60	1/4
Wheat	—	388	270	79	1/4
Peas	1	318	396	113	1/3
Mustard seed	(1 ounce)	437	270	77	1/6
Amber	1	270	270	76	1/4
Tobacco	—	142	153	44	1/3
Honey	1	359	144	41	1/9
Bees' wax	1	243	54	15	1/16
Sugar	1	373	126	36	1/10
Coal	1	316	360	51	1/3
Sal tartar	1	608	224	64	1/9
Bladder stone	¾	230	516	148	1/2
Gall stone	⅙	52	108	30	1/2
			Absorbed		
Sal ammoniac	1 dram	—	2½	—	—
Phosphorus	—	2	3	—	—

"Newcastle coal" killed a sparrow; but he regarded them all as "true air", and showed by weighing that they were not "mere flatulent vapours". His interest was centred on the gaseous content of solid substances, and not on the properties of different gases. These experiments were crude, but they were good enough to convince him that "air" could exist in two states: an "elastic" or gaseous state in which the particles repelled each other, and a "fixed" or solid state in which the particles were attracted by some other substance. "It is by this amphibious property of air", he said, "that the main and principal operations of nature are carried out". His writings contain a clear account of the existence of gases in both a free and combined state: "by clearly stating this principle he exercised a notable influence on other men's researches, and thus powerfully aided the discoveries that were made by others after him".[1]

He had now shown that air ascended with the sap, and that apparently solid vegetable substances contained air. Was it possible to demonstrate directly that plants actually "fixed" air in the course of their growth?

June 29th, I set a well-rooted plant of *pepper-mint* in a glass cistern full of earth, and then poured in as much water as it would contain: over this glass cistern I placed an inverted glass. At the same time also I placed in this same manner another inverted glass of equal size with the former, but without any plant under it: the capacity of these vessels above the water was equal to 49 cubick inches. In a month's time the *mint* had made several weak slender shoots, and many small hairy roots shot out at the joints that were above water; half the leaves of the old stem were now dead; but the leaves and stem of the young shoots continued green most part of the following winter: the water in the two inverted glasses rose and fell, as it was either affected by the different weight of the atmosphere, or by the dilatation or contraction of the air inside (*with temperature*). But the water in the vessel in which the *pepper-mint* stood, rose so much above the surface of the water in the other vessel, that one-seventh part of that air must have been reduced to a fixed state, by being imbibed into the substance of the plant. This was chiefly done in the two or three summer months; for after that no more air was absorbed. The beginning of April in the following spring, I took out the old *mint*, and put a fresh plant in its place, to try if it would absorb any more of the air; but it faded in four

[1] Sir Michael Foster, *Lectures on the History of Physiology*, Cambridge, 1901.

or five days. Yet a fresh plant put into the other glass, whose air had been confined for nine months, lived near a month, almost as long as another plant did in fresh confined air; for I have found that a tender plant confined in this manner in April, would not live so long, as a stronger grown plant, put in in June. The like plants placed in the same manner separately, in the distilled airs of *tartar* and Newcastle *coal*, soon faded; yet a like plant confined in three pints of air, a quart of which was distilled from an ox's tooth, grew about two inches in height, and had some green leaves on it, after six or seven weeks' confinement.[1]

Mariotte had demonstrated that plants change the crude materials taken up with the sap into chemical substances suitable for growth. Malpighi had perceived that the leaves were concerned with nutrition, and that respiration was an essential activity of vegetable life. Hales supplied the third essential fact on which the modern theory of vegetable nutrition rests, when he showed that plants imbibe and fix " air " in a solid form. Malpighi believed that air passed into plants by their roots. Hales inclined to the view that air was absorbed by the leaves, and he extended his limited conception of their function, as organs designed exclusively for the elevation of the sap, into a more comprehensive whole:

It is very plain from many of the foregoing experiments and observations, that the leaves are very serviceable in this work of vegetation, by being instrumental in bringing nourishment from the lower parts, within the reach of the attraction of the growing fruit; which, like young animals, is furnished with proper instruments to suck it thence. But the leaves seem also designed for many other noble and important services; for nature admirably adapts her instruments

[1] Hales, *Vegetable Statics*, 4th ed. p. 329.

so as to be at the same time serviceable to many good purposes. Thus the leaves, in which are the main excretory ducts in vegetables, separate and carry off the redundant watery fluid, which by being long detained, would turn rancid and prejudicious to the plant, leaving the more nutritive particles to coalesce; part of which nourishment, we have good reason to think, is conveyed into vegetables through the leaves. The new combinations of air, sulphur, and acid spirit, which are constantly forming in the atmosphere, are doubtless very serviceable in promoting the work of vegetation; when being imbibed by the leaves, they may not improbably be the materials out of which the more subtile and refined principles of vegetables are formed. We may reasonably conclude, that one great use of leaves is to perform in some measure the same office for the support of vegetable life, that the lungs of animals do, for the support of animal life; plants very probably drawing through their leaves some part of their nourishment from the air.

A few paragraphs lower he makes the following significant suggestion:

May not light also, by freely entering the expanded surfaces of leaves and flowers, contribute much to the ennobling the principles of vegetables?[1]

From the gaseous metabolism of plants, he turned his attention to the corresponding problem of the respiration of animals. He repeated Mayow's experiments on respiration and combustion. He burnt candles under closed vessels over water, and demonstrated that the volume of air absorbed was more or less proportional to the amount of combustion that had taken place.

I then placed a half-grown *rat* under a vessel, whose capacity above the surface of the water was but 594 cubick

[1] Hales, *Vegetable Statics*, 4th ed. p. 328.

inches, in which it lived 10 hours; the quantity of elastick air which was absorbed, was equal to 45 cubick inches, *viz.* 3/13 part of the whole air, which the *rat* breathed in: a *cat* of three months old lived an hour in the same receiver, and absorbed 16 cubick inches of air, *viz.* 1/30 part of the whole; an allowance being made in this estimate for the bulk of the *cat's* body. A candle in the same vessel continued burning but one minute, and absorbed 54 cubick inches, 1/11 part of the whole air.[1]

These observations were responsible for a remarkable rebreathing experiment which he performed upon himself:

I made a bladder very supple by wetting of it, and then cut off so much of the neck as would make a hole wide enough for the biggest end of the largest fosset to enter, to which the bladder was bound fast. The bladder and fosset contained 74 cubick inches. Having blown up the bladder, I put the small end of the fosset into my mouth: and at the same time pinched my nostrils close, that no air might pass that way, so that I could only breathe to and fro the air contained in the bladder. In less than half a minute I found a considerable difficulty in breathing, and was forced after that to fetch my breath very fast; and at the end of the minute, the suffocating uneasiness was so great, that I was forced to take away the bladder from my mouth. Towards the end of the minute the bladder was become so flaccid, that I could not blow it above half full with the greatest expiration that I could make.[2]

Then, to gain some idea of the quantity of air that was actually taken into the body during breathing, he constructed inspiratory and expiratory valves, and inspired a measured volume of air out of a container; at the same time he collected all his expired air over

[1] Hales, *Vegetable Statics*, 4th ed. p. 237.
[2] *Ibid.* p. 239.

water (Plate IX, fig. *A*). On returning his expired
air back into the container, he found that 1/136th of
its original volume had disappeared. In another experiment he tied a bladder into the trachea of a dog,
and observed the same increase in pulmonary ventilation, as the dog was forced to rebreathe the air in
and out of the bladder; he also found that he had to
keep replenishing the bladder with fresh air, as it
became flaccid, to keep the dog alive. Air therefore
was absorbed during the respiration of animals, just
in the same way as it entered into the substance of
growing plants. This observation supported Lower's
conclusion that some of the inspired air entered into
combination with the blood in the lungs, which "by
a wonderful artifice", Hales said, "are admirably
contrived by the divine Artificer, so as to make
their inward surface to be commensurate to an ex-
panse of air many times greater than the animal's
body".

As a matter of fact, in Hales's and in Mayow's
experiments on respiration and combustion, the reduction in volume of the air inside the containers, in
which their animals or candles were placed, must
have been considerably less than the actual volume of
oxygen absorbed. In the combustion of a candle, and
in the respiration of an animal, a volume of carbon
dioxide is set free which is nearly equal to the
volume of oxygen absorbed. Some of this carbon
dioxide must have dissolved in the water over which
their containers stood. The reduction in volume
of the air inside them that Hales and Mayow
measured was not due so much to the absorption of

oxygen as to the solution of a part of the volume of carbon dioxide which had been evolved.[1] Their experiments were almost identical, but they interpreted them differently. Mayow came to the correct conclusion that the extinction of the candle and the death of the animal were both due to the exhaustion of a specific constituent of the atmosphere. He failed to see that in combustion and respiration anything was given off; this was the weak point of Mayow's system. Hales, on the other hand, realised that something is evolved which vitiates the atmosphere inside the container, as in writing of one of his combustion experiments he says: "The candle cannot be lighted again in the *infected* air by a burning glass: but if I first lighted it, and then put it back into the *infected* air, it was extinguished in 1/5 part of the time". On finding that a candle would burn longer in a closed receiver when the walls were lined with flannel well soaked in a solution of "sal tartar", he concluded that "this must be owing to the *sal tartar* in the flannel lining, which must needs have absorbed one third of the fulginous vapours, which arise from the burning candle". In another place he writes: "It is plain from these effects of the fumes of burning brimstone, lighted candle, and the breath of animals, on the elasticity of the air, that its elasticity in the

[1] It is interesting to remember that had Mayow placed his containers over mercury, instead of over water, he would probably not have made his great discovery. The rapid reduction in the volume of the air inside the bladders, which Hales used in his rebreathing experiments, was probably due to the rapid diffusion of exhaled carbon dioxide through their walls. Of this he knew nothing, but again, although his inferences were not strictly justifiable, his conclusions were more or less correct.

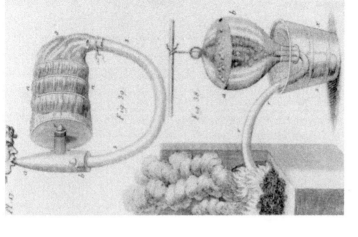

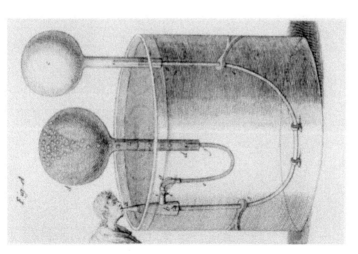

Plate IX. Buffon's diagram of Hales's experiment on the quantity of air destroyed by respiration. Diagrams from *Vegetable Statics*: Hales's "rebreathing" experiment, and his method of collecting gases over water

vesicles of the lungs must be continually decreasing by reason of the vapours it is there loaded with ".

In the interpretation of the results of his experiments he was wrong, however, on two important points where Mayow had reasoned correctly. In the first place, admitting as he did that some of the air entered into combination with the burning body or with the blood of the animal, Hales came to the conclusion that the extinction of the candle and the death of the animal were both due to vitiation of the atmosphere, and not to exhaustion of Mayow's specific constituent:

If the continuance of the burning of the candle be wholly owing to the *vivifying spirit*, then supposing in the case of a receiver, capacious enough for a candle to burn a minute in it, that half the *vivifying spirit* be drawn out with half the air, in ten seconds of time; then the candle would not go out at the end of those ten seconds, but burn twenty seconds more, which it does not; therefore the burning of the candle is not wholly owing to the *vivifying spirit*.

Again, after discussing the poisonous effect of air contaminated by respiration, as revealed to him subjectively by his rebreathing experiments on himself, he writes:

The sudden and fatal effect of these noxious vapours has hitherto been supposed to be wholly owing to the loss and waste of the *vivifying spirit* of air; but may not unreasonably be also attributed to a loss of a considerable part of the air's elasticity, and the grossness and density of the vapours, which the air is charged with.

In the second place, he failed to follow Mayow in his conception of a specific constituent of the atmosphere essential to life, the "spiritus nitro-aereus" or "vivi-fying spirit of the air". He admitted that air entered into combination with the blood, but this was whole air, not a particular part of it. "I made some attempts", he writes, "both by fire and also by fermenting and absorbing mixtures, to try if I could deprive all the particles of any quantity of elastick air of their elasticity (*volume*); but I could not effect it". If he had adhered to the logical inference that he should have drawn from this experiment, he would have arrived at a conclusion in support of Mayow's views. Unfortunately he doubted the validity of his result: "There is therefore no direct proof from any of these experiments, that all the elastick air may be absorbed, tho' it is very probable it may, since we find it in such great plenty generated and absorbed; it may well therefore be all absorbed and changed from an elastick to a fixed state".

He had failed to conceive of a specific constituent of the atmosphere being absorbed in respiration and combustion, but his conception of the vitiation of the air by breathing was sufficiently clear to "put him upon attempting some means to qualify and rebate the deadly noxious quality of these expired vapours". He now constructed a more complicated form of rebreathing apparatus: a bladder fitted with inspiratory and expiratory valves so arranged that his expired air had to pass through diaphragms of cloth before being inspired again (Plate IX, fig. 39).

I could breathe to and fro the air inclosed in this instrument for a minute and a half, when there were no *diaphragms* in it; when the four *diaphragms* were dipped in vinegar, three minutes: when dipped in a strong solution of *sea-salt*, three minutes and a half. In a lixivium of *sal tartar*, three minutes; when the *diaphragms* were dipped in the like lixivium, and then well dried, five minutes; and once $8 + \frac{1}{2}$ minutes with very highly calcined *sal tartar*. Hence *sal tartar* should be the best preservative against noxious vapours, as being a very strong imbiber of sulphureous, acid, and watery vapours, as is sea-salt also: for having carefully weighed the four *diaphragms*, before I fixed them in the instrument, I found that they had increased in weight 30 grains in five minutes; and it was the same in two different trials; so they increased in weight at the rate of 19 ounces in 24 hours. From which deducting 1/6 part of the quantity of moisture, which I found these *diaphragms* attracted in 5 minutes in the open air; there remain $15 + 2/3$ ounces, for the weight of the moisture from the breath in 24 hours.[1]

If Mayow can be said to have discovered oxygen, the first description of carbon dioxide may well be attributed to Hales. He may also have been the first to think of the respirator:

In several unwholesome trades as the smelters of metals, the ceruss-makers, the plumbers etc., it might not unlikely be of good service to them, in preserving them, in some measure at least, from the noxious fumes of the materials they deal in; to prevent which inconvenience the workmen might, while they are at work, make use of pretty broad mufflers, filled with two, four, or more *diaphragms* of flannel or cloth dipped in a solution of *sal tartar* or *pot-ash*, or sea-salt, and then dried. The like mufflers might also be of service in many cases where persons may have urgent occasion to go for a short time into an infectious air: which mufflers might, by an easy contrivance, be so made as to draw in breath thro' the *diaphragms*, and to breathe it out by another vent.[2]

[1] Hales, *Vegetable Statics*, 4th ed. p. 266.
[2] *Ibid.* p. 272.

It is not worth while to follow him far into his speculations on the nature of combustion, as they led to no particular result. On the whole he followed Mayow, with whose work he was familiar, but not as closely as he should. He completely ignored the phlogiston theory, however, as the following quotation shows:

That the sulphureous and aereal particles of the fire are lodged in many of those bodies which it acts upon, and thereby considerably augment their weight, is very evident in minium or red lead, which is observed to increase in weight about 1/20 part in undergoing the action of fire. And that there is a good store of air added to the minium, I found by distilling first 1922 grains of lead, from whence I obtained only seven cubick inches of air; but from 1922 grains which was a cubick inch of red lead, there arose in the like space of time thirty-four cubick inches of air. It was therefore doubtless this quantity of air in minium, which burst the hermetically sealed glasses of the excellent Mr. Boyle, when he heated the minium contained in them by a burning glass; but the pious and learned Dr. Nieuwentyt attributes this effect wholly to the expansion of the fire-particles lodged in the minium, "he supposing fire to be a particular fluid matter, which maintains its own essence and figure, remaining always fire, though not always burning!" *Religious Philosopher*, p. 310.[1]

It is difficult to imagine the perspective of Hales's outlook on these problems. If he had followed Mayow more literally, he would have conceived of different kinds of gases, instead of one air with variable properties. Had he done this, and then combined his own observation on the vitiation of the atmosphere by respiration and combustion with

[1] Hales, *Vegetable Statics*, 4th ed. p. 289.

Mayow's discovery, he might well have arrived at the true conception of the nature of these processes. Be this as it may, his experiments on respiration had a great practical outcome in his work on ventilation. On February 2nd, 1727, he communicated to the Royal Society an account of "An Attempt to analyse the Air by a great Variety of Chymio-Statical Experiments". The first half of this paper was read the following week, and the second on February 16th, the last occasion but one on which Sir Isaac Newton occupied the Presidential Chair. At this meeting "Mr. Hales had thanks for communicating these curious experiments", the President ordered that his papers should be printed, and in 1727 his first book appeared under the following title:

VEGETABLE STATICS; Or, An Account of some Statical Experiments on the Sap in Vegetables. Being an Essay towards a Natural History of Vegetation: Of Use to those who are curious in the Culture and Improvement of Gardening, etc. Also a Specimen of an Attempt to analyse the Air, by a great Variety of Chymio-Statical Experiments, which were read at several Meetings before the Royal Society.

Feb. 16. 1726–7. *Imprimatur* Isaac Newton. Pr. Reg. Soc.

It was the custom of the day for scientists and authors to dedicate their books to one of the nobility, or to a member of the Royal Family. Hales solicited royal patronage for his work by dedicating his first book to the Prince of Wales (afterwards George II):

To His Royal Highness George, Prince of Wales. May it please your Royal Highness, I Humbly offer the following Experiments to your Highness's patronage, to protect them from the reproaches that the ignorant are apt unreasonably to cast on researches of this kind, notwithstanding that they are the only solid and rational means whereby we may ever hope to make any real advance in the knowledge of nature: a knowledge worthy the attainment of princes. And as Solomon, the greatest and wisest of men, disdained not to inquire into the nature of plants, *from the cedar in Lebanon, to the hyssop that springeth out of the wall*: so it will not, I presume, be an unacceptable entertainment to your royal highness, at least at your leisure hours. The searching into the works of nature, while it delights and inlarges the mind, and strikes us with the strongest assurance of the wisdom and power of the divine Architect, in framing for us so beautiful and well-regulated a world, it does at the same time convince us of his constant benevolence and goodness towards us. That this great Author of nature may shower down on your royal highness an abundance of his blessings, both spiritual and temporal, is the sincere prayer of Your Royal Highness's Most Obedient Humble Servant, Stephen Hales.

In the year in which *Vegetable Statics* was published, he was elected a member of the Council of the Royal Society.

CHAPTER VII

The Distemper of the Stone. Publishes *Haemastatics*. The Gin Laws. Mrs Stephens's Medicines. The Copley Medal.

THE brief account of his work, which has been given in previous chapters, can have given the reader, who is not familiar with science, little idea of the time and labour that he had devoted to these experiments. In any research, the number of successful experiments is small in comparison with the number of failures. As often as not, some line of reasoning is followed up which eventually proves abortive, and a whole series of carefully planned experiments proves valueless. Many of his experiments were of much greater technical difficulty than might at first sight be supposed; of his failures there is, of course, no record. His work did not afford any particular exception to these general rules, and the time passed quickly by. In the year that *Vegetable Statics* was published, he entered the sixth decade of life.

At about this time his outlook on science began to change. Hitherto he had paid little attention to the practical application of his physiological discoveries to medicine. This is not surprising, as he had been educated in an atmosphere of pure science. His work on the blood pressure of animals had been the outcome of an attempt to discover the cause of muscular movement: an academic problem. He had no medical degree, and no particular knowledge of physic; he did not appreciate the possible clinical significance of these experiments. His more recent work on the respiration of man had, however, taken him very near medicine, and in the circle of the Royal Society he came into close contact with medical science. Sir Hans Sloane, the veteran physician, had succeeded Newton as President, and many of the Fellows were also physicians. Considerable interest was taken in his experiments, and from Stukeley and others, Hales learnt much of the problems of pathology and physic.

In the eighteenth century, renal and vesical calculus, "the distemper of the stone", was an exceedingly prevalent disease, and he knew that many fruitless attempts had already been made to find a cure:

> I am sensible that some may be apt to think it favours too much of vanity and presumption, for any one, after such innumerable fruitless researches of the ablest chymists, to attempt to find out a safe dissolvent of the stone in the *bladder*. Yet in a matter of so great importance to the ease and welfare of a considerable part of mankind, we ought not wholly to despair.

Sir Hans Sloane and Mr Ranby, F.R.S., Surgeon to the Royal Household, readily supplied him with different varieties of human calculi for his experiments, and he proceeded to subject them to the action of various solvents, and other chemical procedures. His work, which was extensive, may have thrown a little new light on the chemical nature of animal concretions, but his experiments failed completely for the purpose for which they had been primarily intended. He was unable to discover any chemical solvent, sufficiently strong to dissolve calculi *in vitro*, which could be administered to man. His first endeavour in applied science was certainly unfortunate. A therapeutic solvent for the stone is still undiscovered, and the only practical outcome of his work was an ingenious surgical instrument:

> I cut off the lower end of a strait *catheter*, which made it a proper *canula* for a stillet or *forceps* to pass through; the lower end of the *forceps* was divided into two springs, like tweezers, whose ends were turned a little inwards: these springs were made of such a degree of tenderness and pliancy, as not to bear too hard against the sides of the *urethra*, by their dilatation. When this instrument is used, the springs are drawn up within the *canula*; which being passed into the *urethra* as far as to the stone, the *canula* must then be drawn back, so far as to give room for the *forceps* to dilate; which dilated *forceps* being then thrust down a little further, so as to embrace the stone, then the *canula* must again be slid down, to make the *forceps* take fast hold of the stone, so as to draw it out. I sent this instrument to Mr. Ranby, to have his opinion of it, who tells me, that upon repeated trials he found it extracts these stones with great ease and readiness: and that it is so well approved by other surgeons, that many of them make use of it.[1]

When he had finished his experiments on calculi, he wrote an account of his work on the blood pressure of animals, which had recently attracted so much attention. Remarkable to relate, at that time it still remained unpublished.

HAEMASTATICS; Or, an Account of some Hydraulic and Hydrostatical Experiments made on the Blood and Blood-Vessels of Animals.

---

[1] Hales, *Haemastatics*, 3rd ed. p. 248. He also invented an instrument for "conveying liquors into the abdomen during the operation of tapping"; *Phil. Trans. Roy. Soc.* XLIII, 20 and 502.

To this account he added some experiments that he had recently performed on the perfusion of the arteries and veins of animals with the production of oedema and anasarca. He also wrote:

An Account of some Experiments on Stones in the Kidneys and Bladder; with an Enquiry into the Nature of those Anomalous Concretions.

The former is one of the classics of physiology, but the latter a hundred worthless pages.

When he had completed these papers, he went to Kent to see his brother, Sir Thomas Hales, who was ill. Their father had died in their childhood; their mother and old Sir Robert were long since dead, and the family home at Bekesbourne had been given up. His brother, who had inherited the family title at his grandfather's death, now lived at "Howletts", near Canterbury, and was Member of Parliament for the county; with him lived his two unmarried sisters, Catherine and Anne. Of the others, Margaret had died a child; Mary had married the Hon. William Booth, D.D., Dean of Bristol and Archdeacon of Durham, and his youngest sister, Elizabeth, the Rev. John Metcalfe, Vicar of Sunbury.[1] His next eldest brother, Robert, was Clerk to the Privy Council. His youngest brother, William, "a citizen and a goldsmith", had been committed to Newgate for some crime, which is not recorded, and had died there of the gaol distemper on February 18th, 1729.[2]

[1] "Rev. John Metcalfe, Vicar of Sunbury, was married to Elizabeth, the sister of Sir Thomas Hales of Bekesbourne, at Somerset House by Stephen Hales, B.D., Feb. 11th, 1717" (Sunbury Parish Register).
[2] Hovenden's genealogy of the Hales family; *vide* Preface to this book.

While down in Kent he wrote the following letter to the President of the Royal Society:

To Sir Hans Sloane Bart. in Bloomsbury Square.

Howletts near Canterbury
July 15. 1732.

Sir,

I received your favour of ye 10th with the enclosed yesterday, which I have this post sent to Mrs. Hales. I am very sorry to find Mr. Hodges so very unkind to his poor grandchildren who have never offended him; one would think the notorious injury he did their Parents in not settling the promised £500 per annum on them should move him to small amends at least; but it too often happens that those who have greatly injured others rarely forgive the injured. I should have waited on you to thank you for your good offices in the affair, if I had not been prevented by this journey.

I sent for my Haemastatical papers designing to make some few additions and alterations; but will return them to you before the 26th of October, that you may if you approve of it finish the reading of them before the Society: Do not think of printing them till some time after the reading is over; for I am desirous to have them impartially examined that I may not be guilty of any heresies either in Philosophy or Physick.

I beg my service to Dr. Mortimer whose letter I answer in this. Sir Thomas Hales who is now very well gives his Service to you.

I am, Sir, your obliged humble Servant,

STEPHEN HALES.[1]

Early in the following year his "Haemastatical papers" were read before the Royal Society—twenty-two years after his first experiment on blood pressure had been performed!

[1] British Museum, Sloane MSS, f. 4052, page 147.

At a Meeting of the Council of the Royal Society, Feb. 28. 1732–3. The greatest part of this second Volume of Statical Essays, by Stephen Hales, B.D., F.R.S., having been read at several meetings of the Royal Society, for which he had their thanks, it is ordered, that he be desired to print the same. Hans Sloane, P.R.S.

When, a few months later, this book was published, he dedicated it to the King (George II), and on the title-page is printed:

"Desideratur Philosophia Naturalis vera et activa, cui Medicinae Scientia inaedificetur." Fran. de Verul. Instaur. Magna.

To the King's Most Excellent Majesty. Sir, Your Majesty's gracious acceptance of my former Volume of Experiments, has encouraged me, both further to pursue these natural researches, and also to lay the result of them at your feet. Your Majesty's subjects of Great Britain are allowed, by the candid confession of other nations, to excel in experimental philosophy, which has long been found to be most beneficial to mankind. As the advancement of arts and sciences much depends upon the protection of princes, whose patronage they are well worthy of; so we have a pleasing prospect of their flourishing under your Majesty's auspicious favour, whose care and concern for the welfare and prosperity of his people, is in every respect most extensive. That Your Majesty, after having long continued a blessing to your subjects in a prosperous reign here on earth, may hereafter enjoy a happy immortality in heaven, is the sincere prayer of, may it please your Majesty, Your Majesty's most humble and Dutiful subject, Stephen Hales.

He had now gained a considerable reputation as a scientist, and in the year in which *Haemastatics* was published, he was honoured by the University of

Oxford. The Chancellor, the Earl of Arran, sent the following letter to Convocation:[1]

Grosvenor Street,
May 29, 1733.

Mr. Vice-Chancellor and Gentlemen,

The Revd. Mr. Stephen Hales is recommended to me as a person deserving some mark of favour from the University on account of his excellent performances so justly esteemed in the learned world, and the virtues which adorn the character of a clergyman. I think it therefore an act worthy of the University to give that testimony of such singular merit that he cannot receive from the University of Cambridge by conferring on him the degree of Doctor in Divinity by Diploma.

I am, Mr. Vice-Chancellor and Gentlemen,

Your affectionate friend and servant,

(Signed) ARRAN.

Accordingly, on July 5th, 1733, the University conferred upon him the Degree of Doctor of Divinity:

Cancellarius, Magistri, & Scholares Universitatis *Oxon.* omnibus ad quos praesentes hae Literae pervenerint salutem in Domino sempiternam. Cum eum in finem Gradus Academici a Majoribus nostris prudenter instituti fuerint, ut Viri de Re Literaria optime meriti istis Insignibus a Literatorum Vulgo secernerentur, Cumque Nobis compertum sit Reverendum Virum *Stephanum Hales* sacrae Theologiae Baccalaurum Ingenio atque Scriptis de materia recondita pariter ac curiosa inter hujusce saeculi Philosophos merito inclamisse, iisque porro quae hominis Clerici famam commendant Virtutibus inter primos eximium extitisse, aequum judicavimus & Academiae nostrae consentaneum venerabilem hunc virum in Republica Literaria pariter & Ecclesia tanta

---

[1] University of Oxford, Convocation Register. Hales had incorporated at the University of Oxford two years previously (June 1st, 1731).

cum laude versatum, Testimonio nostro publico cohonestare;
idcirco in solenni Convocatione Doctorum, Magistrorum,
Regentium & non Regentium vicesimo primo die mensis
Junii Anno Domini Millesimo septingentesimo tricesimo tertio
habita (conspirantibus omnium Suffragiis) Reverendum &
Egregium Virum *Stephanum Hales* Doctorem in Sacra
Theologia renunciavimus & constituimus; Eumque: virtute
praesentis Diplomatis singulis Juribus, Privilegiis & Honori-
bus Gradui isto quaqua pertinentibus frui & gaudere jussimus.
In cujus Rei Testimonium Sigillum Universitatis *Oxon*:
Commune (quo hac in parte utimur) Praesentibus apponi
fecimus. Dat. in Domo nostrae Congregationis quinto Die
mensis *Julii* Anno Domini praedicto.[1]

Not only had he gained a reputation as a scientist,
but he was also becoming well known in the outside
world. His attendance at meetings of the Royal
Society was regular; he was a member of the Council,
and was personally acquainted with many of its prominent members, Hans Sloane, Cromwell Mortimer,
and a number of the leading physicians and surgeons
of the day. He had begun to interest himself in works
of charity outside his own parish, and in missionary
work abroad. With James Oglethorpe and Viscount
Percival, he was a Trustee of Dalone's Trust "for
Converting the Negroes in the British Plantations to
Christianity", and also of Dr Bray's Legacy "for
Establishing Parochial Libraries in the American
Colonies". He may have visited his brother in
Newgate, and when Oglethorpe started his scheme
for a new settlement in America, to serve as an asylum
for the debtors liberated from prison under the new
Act, he became one of the Trustees for the colony of

[1] Robert Masters, *The History of Corpus Christi College, Cambridge*, Cambridge, 1753.

Georgia. Most important of all, he played an active part in promoting the Gin Act of 1736.

In 1689, the Government had prohibited the importation of all spirits from abroad. This measure had started a great extension of the manufacture of spirits throughout the country, but it was not until about the year 1724 that "the passion for gin drinking appears to have infected the masses of the population, and spread with the rapidity and violence of an epidemic".[1] The Middlesex magistrates insisted on the necessity for legislation, and the first Gin Act was passed in 1729. By this measure an excise duty of five shillings per gallon was imposed upon gin, the retailer had to pay £20 a year for a license to sell it, and hawking it about the streets was prohibited. Although the law was largely evaded, and led to the invention of new forms of spirit, one of these being called in derision "Parliament Brandy", it was not altogether ineffectual. When, in 1733, the Act was repealed on the plea that, while it did no good, it interfered with trade by checking the sale of home-grown barley to the distillers, the consequences were disastrous, and the universal orgy that followed is said to have been terrible.[2] In the streets of London gin shops now invited passers-by to get "drunk for a penny or dead drunk for two pence", and advertised "clean straw for nothing", on which to sleep off the effects of the debauch (Plate X). The Grand Jury of the Tower-Hamlets wrote in their report:

It is with great Trouble that we observe the number of

[1] W. E. H. Lecky, *History of England in the XVIIIth Century.*
[2] H. B. Wheatley, *Hogarth's London*, 1909.

Gin-Shops not only to multiply in every street, but also that we find in many places it is privately sold, and that every separate room in some Houses is becoming a place for vending *Distilled Liquors*; for that (if not timely restrained) we fear the number of Sellers will soon be near equal to the Drinkers of the *General Poison*. The Effects of these pernicious *Liquors* are to all sober Christians a matter of the highest Abomination; for how often do we hear the name of the *Great God* profaned by these intoxicated drinkers, while they are swallowing down their own Destruction? How often are the Publick Streets infested with these abominable Wretches, whose wicked Oaths and Imprecations would endanger the drawing down God's Vengeance on this Kingdom, were it not for his infinite Mercy? How often do we see Women as well as Men, lying in the very Channels and Corners of Streets like dead Carcases, generally without Cloathes to protect them from the inclemency of the Weather, or cover their Nakedness and Shame? How many Breaches of the Peace, dangerous Assaults and often Murders have been occasioned by this Deluge of Debauchery?

Hales himself saw the same thing everywhere, in the streets of London, in the towns and villages through which he passed, even in his own parish of Teddington. Many of his parishioners had become drunkards, crime had increased, pauperism abounded, and he was powerless to control it. In 1734, he wrote and published an anonymous tract entitled:

A Friendly Admonition to the Drinkers of Brandy and other Distilled Spirituous Liquors.[1]

Two years later he followed this up with another anonymous tract. He addressed himself directly to

[1] This tract passed through no less than six editions; the last was published by the Society for the Promotion of Christian Knowledge in 1807.

the House of Commons, and implored the Government to take vigorous steps to exterminate a vice, which was rapidly undermining the morals and constitutions of the "common people":

DISTILLED SPIRITUOUS LIQUORS, THE BANE OF THE NATION: Being some Considerations Humbly offered to the *Hon. the House of Commons.*

By which it will appear,

  I. That the Landed Interest suffers greatly by the Distilling of Spirituous Liquors.

 II. From a Physical Account of the Nature of all Spirituous Distilled Liquors, and the Malignant Effects they have upon Human Bodies.

III. From the several Disorders and Immoralities occasioned by This Sort of Excess,—That all Ranks and Orders of Men are concerned in using their utmost Endeavours to put an immediate Stop to it.

To which is added, an Appendix, containing the late Presentments of the Grand Juries of *London, Middlesex*, and the *Tower-Hamlets*: Together with a Report made by His Majesty's Justices of the Peace at Hick's Hall, Jan. 1735–6.

He claimed that the social disorder occasioned by the unrestricted sale and consumption of gin had reached such a pass that the civil magistrates were unable to cope with the situation. He therefore called upon the Government to take drastic and immediate action, and urged that the financial interests of the distillers should be completely subordinated to considerations relating to the welfare of the community as a whole; it should be made impossible by law for a small group of people to corrupt the lives and ruin the health of the multitude in this wholesale way. He advocated the complete suppression of the distillation of spirits in the country, and a prohibitive tax on spirits imported from abroad. To arouse the interest of the landed gentry in his campaign, he pointed out that the loss of appetite and general deterioration of health, from which "dram drinkers" suffered, caused an enormous decrease in the total consumption of food-stuffs; he estimated the loss occasioned to the land-owning classes, by the distillers of London alone, at the sum of six million pounds per annum! The financial loss to the community caused by the prohibitive taxation of imported gin, would be more than balanced, he said, by the increased revenue, which could then be drawn from the moderate taxation of wine, and the increased agricultural prosperity of the country that would result, if the distillation of spirits was completely prohibited. He concluded:

The Short Question, with the utmost Submission to the Honourable House of Commons, seems to be,—Whether the Distillation of Spirituous Liquors, big with so many Mischiefs, should be allowed at all.

A little later in the same year, Sir Joseph Jekyll, Master of the Rolls, brought in and carried through Parliament a measure to which Robert Walpole was forced to submit. "This day (*March 8th*)", wrote Lord Egmont in his diary, "the Gin Bill was treated in the House of Commons, and a resolution came in to lay a duty of 20 shillings a gallon on spirituous liquors, and all who sell it to pay £50 per annum for a license to sell it. Dr Hales, Minister of Teddington, who dined with me, had tears in his

Plate X. *Gin Lane*. William Hogarth

eyes for joy. He had wrote last year an excellent treatise on the poisonous quality of spirituous liquors".[1] In one of his letters, Gilbert White of Selborne writes:

> Under the patronage of Sir Joseph Jeckyll, Dr. Hales was instrumental in procuring the Gin Act, and stopping that profusion of spirituous liquors which threatened to ruin the morals and the constitutions of the common people.[2]

The reason why Dr Hales published his tracts anonymously is obvious enough. As he had anticipated, the prohibition of gin under the new Act led to serious riots:

> "*Mother Gin* lay in state yesterday at a distiller's shop in Swallow Street near St. James's Church; but to prevent the ill consequences from such a funeral, a neighbouring justice took the undertaker, his men and all the mourners into custody" (*Grub Street Journal*)...."Yesterday morning double guard mounted at Kensington; at noon the guards at St. James's, the Horse Guards, and Whitehall, were reinforced, and last night about 300 life guards and horse-grenadier guards paraded in Covent Garden, in order to suppress any tumult that might arise at the going down of Gin" (*London Daily Post*)...."A party of foot-guards was posted at the house of Sir Joseph Jeckyll, Master of the Rolls. Two soldiers with their bayonets fixed were planted at the little door next Chancery Lane in case any persons should offer to attack the house which the mob had tumultuously surrounded" (*Daily Advertiser*)...."Several persons were committed, some to prison and some to hard labour, for publickly and riotously publishing, No Gin, No King!" (*Daily Journal*).[3]

[1] *Diary of Viscount Percival, first Lord Egmont*, Historical Manuscripts Commission, vol. II, London, 1923.

[2] J. E. Harting, *Gilbert White's Natural History of Selborne*, 2nd ed. with letters not included in any previous edition of the work, London, 1876.

[3] *British Museum Catalogue of Satires*, III, 192.

He had now gained his object; even if the new law could not be enforced strictly, it remained on the Statute Book until it was repealed in 1743. In the meanwhile, he was free to turn his attention to other things, and it was at about this time that his earlier work on the calculus had an interesting sequel.

A certain Mrs Joanna Stephens, "the daughter of a gentleman of good estate and family in Berkshire", discovered a method of dissolving the stone by means of medicines administered by the mouth. Dr Hales was appointed one of the "Trustees" to conduct an investigation into their reputed efficiency:[1]

In the year 1735, the Hon. Edward Carteret, Esq., *Postmaster General*, began Mrs. *Stephens's* Medicines, and received great Benefit from them. This engaged the attention of the Public, and more particularly of such as were afflicted with Gravel or Stone, so that the number of Persons that took them increased every day. In the Year 1737, the Cures performed by these Medicines were so many, and so well attested, that the speedy Publication of them was judged to be of great Importance to Mankind. And accordingly in the Year 1738, a Proposal for raising £5000 by Contribution, as a Reward to Mrs. *Stephens* for discovering her Medicines, was made to the Public with her Consent. But as this Proposal did not meet with Success, she was advised in the Beginning of the Year 1739 to apply to the House of Commons by Petition for the above-mentioned Reward, submitting her Medicines when discovered to such Examination as the House should think fit, before the Payment of the Reward. This she did, and a Bill was brought in for that

[1] *A Supplement to a Pamphlet intitled, A view of the Present Evidence for and against Mrs. Stephens's Medicines etc., being a collection of some Particulars relating to the Discovery of these Medicines, their Publication, Use and Efficacy.* By David Hartley, M.A., F.R.S. London, 1742.

purpose, which passed both Houses, and received the Royal Assent at the Conclusion of the Session, *June* 14.

The text of the Bill was as follows:

An Act for providing a Reward to JOANNA STEPHENS, upon a proper Discovery to be made by her, for the Use of the Publick, of the Medicines prepared by her for the Cure of the Stone.

Whereas *Joanna Stephens* of the City of *Westminster*, Spinster, hath acquired the Knowledge of Medicines, and the Skill of preparing them, which by a dissolving Power seem capable of removing the Cause of the painful Distemper of the Stone, and may be improved, and more successfully applied, when the same shall be discovered to Persons learned in the Science of Physick; now for encouraging the said *Joanna Stephens* to make a Discovery thereof, and for providing her a Recompence, in case the said Medicines shall be submitted to the Examination of proper Judges, and by them be found worthy of the Reward hereby provided; may it please Your Majesty that it may be enacted, and be it enacted by the King's most excellent Majesty, by and with the Advice and Consent of the Lords Spiritual and Temporal, and Commons, in this present Parliament assembled, and by the Authority of the same, That out of all or any of the Aids or Supplies granted to His Majesty for the Service of the Year One thousand seven hundred and thirty nine, there may, and shall be applied and paid to the said *Joanna Stephens*, or her Executors, Administrators, or Assigns, the Sum of Five thousand Pounds, upon Condition that she shall, with all convenient Speed, after the passing of this Act, make such Discovery for the Use of the Publick of the Said Medicines, and her Method of preparing the same, in such manner as his Grace *John* Lord Archbishop of *Canterbury*, the Right Honourable *Philip* Lord *Hardwick*, Lord High Chancellor of *Great Britain*, the Right Honourable *Spencer* Earl of *Wilmington*, Lord President of the Council, the Right Honourable *Francis* Earl *Godolphin*, Lord Privy Seal, his

Grace *Lionel* Duke of *Dorset*, Lord Steward of His Majesty's Household, his Grace *Charles* Duke of *Grafton*, Lord Chamberlain of His Majesty's Household, his Grace *Charles* Duke of *Richmond* and *Lennox*, his Grace *John* Duke of *Montagu*, the Right Honourable *Henry* Earl of *Pembroke* and *Montgomery*, the Right Honourable *Richard* Earl of *Scarborough*, the Right Honourable *Henry* Lord Viscount *Lonsdale*, the Right Reverend *Martin* Lord Bishop of *Gloucester*, the Right Reverend *Thomas* Lord Bishop of *Oxford*, the Right Honourable *Arthur Onslow* Esquire, Speaker of the Honourable House of Commons, the Right Honourable *Henry Hyde* Esquire, commonly called Lord Viscount *Cornbury*, the Right Honourable *Charles* Lord *Baltimore* in the Kingdom of *Ireland*, the Right Honourable Sir *Robert Walpole* Knight of the most noble Order of the Garter, and Chancellor of the Exchequer, the Right Honourable *Stephen Poyntz* Esquire, the Honourable *Thomas Townshend*, Esquire, the Reverend Doctor *Stephen Hales*, Doctor *Thomas Pellet*, President of the Royal College of Physicians, Doctor *John Gardiner*, Doctor *Robert Nesbitt*, Doctor *Simon Burton*, and Doctor *William Whitaker*, Censors of the Royal College of Physicians, Doctor *Peter Shaw*, *David Hartley* Master of Arts, *William Cheselden*, Esquire, Surgeon to *Chelsea* Hospital, *Caesar Hawkins* Esquire, Surgeon to his Royal Highness the Prince of *Wales*, Master *Samuel Sharp* Surgeon to Guy's Hospital, or the Survivors of them, or the major Part of them, or of the Survivors of them shall direct or approve; and upon this further Condition, that the said medicines so discovered, shall be examined and approved by the said Lord Archbishop of *Canterbury*, etc. or the Survivors of them, or the major part of them, or of the Survivors of them: And the Commissioners of His Majesty's Treasury, or any Three or more of them, or the Lord High Treasurer, or any Three or more of the Commissioners of the Treasury for the time being, are hereby authorized and required to direct the Payment of, and issue the said Sum of Five Thousand Pounds to the said *Joanna Stephens*, her Executors, Administrators, or assigns, upon her or their producing a Certificate under the Hands of the said *John* Lord Archbishop of *Canterbury*, etc. or the Survivors of them, or the major part of them, or of the Survivors of them; expressing that the said *Joanna Stephens* did, with all convenient Speed after the passing of this Act, make a Discovery, to their Satisfaction, for the Use of the Publick, of the said medicines, and of her Method of preparing the same; and that they have examined the said Medicines, and are convinced by Experiment of the Utility, Efficacy, and dissolving Power thereof.

With the anticipation of receiving such an enormous reward, it is not surprising that Mrs Stephens was only too ready to "discover", or reveal, to the Archbishop the nature of her remedy. The powder consisted of egg shells and garden snails, "well calcined until the snails had done smoking". The decoction was made by boiling various herbs with soap, honey, and "swines-cresses burnt to a blackness". The pills were composed of "calcined snails, wild carrot seeds, burdock seeds, ashen keys, hips and haws", all "burnt to a blackness", soap and honey!

On March 5th, 1740, the trustees appointed by the Act met in the Prince's Chamber adjoining the House of Lords. There were only eight absentees out of the thirty: the Duke of Grafton, the Duke of Richmond and Lennox, the Earl of Scarborough, the Viscount Lonsdale, Sir Robert Walpole, the Right Honourable Arthur Onslow, the Honourable Thomas Townshend, and Dr Whitaker. Four persons who had been cured of the stone by taking Mrs Stephens's medicines appeared before them, and, in one case, no less than thirteen physicians testified to the completeness with which the distemper of the stone had been eradicated.

Twenty out of the twenty-two trustees present signed the certificate required by Act of Parliament:

> That the said *Joanna Stephens* did, with all convenient Speed after the passing of the said Act, make a Discovery to our Satisfaction, for the Use of the Public, of the said Medicines, and of her Method of preparing the same; and that we have examined the said Medicines, and are convinced by Experiment of the Utility, Efficacy and dissolving Power thereof.

Only two of the trustees, Drs Nesbitt and Pellet, made reservations; having some doubt as to the words "dissolving power", they chose to give separate certificates which were annexed to the official document. On March 18th, 1740, at Whitehall, Mrs Joanna Stephens duly received the reward of £5000 assigned to her by Act of Parliament!

Hales himself put Mrs Stephens's medicines to some sort of experimental test, and published a pamphlet entitled:

> An Account of some Experiments and Observations on Mrs. Stephens's Medicines for dissolving the Stone, wherein their Dissolving Power is inquired into, and shown. By Stephen Hales, D.D., F.R.S. Published by T. Woodward, at the Half-Moon between the Temple Gates in Fleet Street, Printer to the Royal Society. 1740.[1]

He attributed no particular potency to the herbs, snails, and "swines-cresses", but on very slender evidence succeeded in persuading himself that the

---

[1] So great was the interest taken in Mrs Stephens's medicines on the Continent that this pamphlet was translated into French: *Etat de la Médecine etc. par M. Clifton* (translated by M. l'Abbé des Fontaines): *Avec les expériences sur le Remède de Mlle. Stephens, faites par M. Hales*, translated by M. Cantwell of the Royal Society, Doctor of the faculty of Montpellier, Paris, 1742.

medicines, by virtue of the "soap-lees and lime of egg-shells" they contained, were a powerful solvent for the stone outside the body. When, therefore, they maintained that the stones had disappeared, he was prepared to accept the testimony of the "men of physick", in whose province, as he so often said, "it was not for him to meddle".

All perpetrators of quack medicines did not get off as lightly at his hands as Mrs Stephens. In October, 1746, he wrote anonymously to the editor of the *Gentleman's Magazine*:

Mr. Urban. If you please to put the following Remarks on the *Liquid Shell* into your next magazine, you will do good service to the Public.

Some remarks on the boasted *Liquid Shell*. The newspapers having frequently repeated a long advertisement in praise of the *Liquid Shell* as a powerful dissolvent for the stone and gravel, I thought it of importance to enquire, by proper trials, whether it had that boasted efficacy or not; and, if not, to caution people against throwing away their money, and hazarding their lives, by the use of an un-efficacious medicine. Having therefore procured some of the *Liquid Shell*, which is a clear transparent liquor, I put into it a human stone formed in the urinary passages, upon which a fine white sediment precipitated; and there was a like white sediment when a few drops of spirit of hartshorn were dropped into some of the same liquor; which fully proves that it was in both cases the lime of burnt shell, and not the parts of the dissolved stone as is pretended; for there was no stone put in with the spirit of hartshorn. Whereas it is stated in the advertisement "that, if the stone be put into a vial of the *Liquid Shell*, in a moderate sand heat, it will in a few hours be dissolved or broken to pieces": On the contrary, it has been found, that, on putting human stones of different degrees of hardness, into a vial of the *Liquid Shell*, they have *not* been dissolved, *nor* broken to pieces, tho' they continued in that state, not a few hours only, but many days; the last four hours of which time, the vial of *Liquid Shell* was put into scalding water. Hence we see how improbable it is that this *Liquid Shell*, "given every four hours in the quantity of 70 drops in a dose", should have any efficacy to dissolve stones in the body.[1]

Among the book notices for the following year is an anonymous *Dissertation on the Liquid Shell, Price 6d.*[2]

In 1739, he was awarded the Copley Medal of the Royal Society. There is no mention of the particular work for which this was given, but Peter Collinson, his contemporary and a Fellow of the Royal Society at the time, states that it was for his experiments on the calculus. He therefore received this high award of the Royal Society, not for his best researches in physiology, but for the least successful and least creditable part of all his scientific work.

[1] *Gentleman's Magazine,* 1746, XVI, 520.
[2] *Ibid.* 1747, XVII, 548.

CHAPTER VIII

A Trustee of the Colony of Georgia. *Philosophical Experiments.* Purification of Water. Disinfection with Sulphur. Preservation of Meat. A Sea-Gauge.

IN 1729, James Oglethorpe had been appointed chairman of a committee to investigate and report upon the condition of debtors' prisons. The knowledge of social conditions that he had gained in this capacity led him to think of founding a new colony in North America to serve as an asylum for the paupers and debtors, who crowded the Fleet and other London prisons, and as a refuge for the persecuted Protestants of Europe. Oglethorpe himself was the promoter of the scheme, but the enterprise was launched in connection with two charities already in existence: Mr Dalone's Trust for converting the negroes in the British plantations to Christianity, and Dr Bray's Legacy for establishing parochial libraries in the American colonies. Hales, Oglethorpe, and Egmont, were already trustees of these bequests. (I, 119 and 273.)[1] On April 1st, 1730, Lord Egmont wrote in his diary:

I called on Mr. Oglethorpe, who kept me three hours and more in explaining his project of sending a colony of poor and honest industrious debtors to the West Indies by means of a charitable legacy left by one King, a haberdasher, to be disposed of as his executors should please. Those executors have agreed that five thousand pounds of the money shall be

[1] The numbers throughout the text in this chapter refer to Lord Egmont's diary published by the Historical Manuscripts Commission in three volumes, London, 1920–1923.

employed to such a purpose, and our business is to get a Patent or Charter for incorporating a number of honest and reputable persons to pursue this good work, and as those executors desired the persons entrusted with that sum might be annexed to some Trust already in being, I am desired to consent to admit such as are to manage that money into my trust for disposing of the legacy left by Mr. Dalone for converting negroes to Christianity, to which I very readily have consented. (1, 90.)

And again a few days later (April 30th):

Went down to the Society of Associates for Mr. Dalone's Legacy to convert blacks in America, and settle a colony in America. There were present Mr. Oglethorpe, myself, Mr. Anderson, Mr. Hucks junior, Captain Coram, the Rev. Mr. Smith, and the Rev. Mr. Hales. We agreed on a petition to the King and Council for obtaining a grant of lands on the south-west of Carolina for settling poor persons of London, and having ordered it to be engrossed fair, we signed it, all who were present, and the other Associates were to be spoke also to sign it before delivered. (1, 99.)

The motive of the petitioners was essentially philanthropic: the relief of pauperism by emigration. The Government saw an additional advantage in the scheme, for the territory in southern Carolina was in dispute with Spain, and the establishment of a new colony on the Savannah would provide a barrier against Spanish aggression from the south and west. Parliament readily voted the sum of £10,000 for the initial expenses of the new settlement, and on June 9th, 1732, the King granted a Charter for the foundation of the colony of Georgia:

His Majesty having taken into Consideration the miserable Circumstances of many of his own poor Subjects, as likewise the Distress of many Foreigners, who would take Refuge from Persecution; and having a Princely regard to the great Danger the Southern Frontiers of South Carolina are expos'd to, by Reason of the small Number of white Inhabitants there, hath granted a Charter for incorporating a Number of Gentlemen by the Name of, *The Trustees for establishing the Colony of Georgia in America*. They are impower'd to collect Benefactions, and lay them out in cloathing, arming, sending over, and supporting Colonies of the Poor, whether Subjects or Foreigners, till they can build Houses and clear Lands. And His Majesty farther grants all his Lands between the Rivers *Savanah* and *Alatamahah*, which he erects into a Province by the Name of Georgia. At the Desire of the Gentlemen there are Clauses in the Charter restraining them and their Successors from receiving any Salary, Fee, Perquisite or Profit whatsoever, by or from this Undertaking; and also from receiving any Grants of these Lands.[1]

By the terms of the Charter, the twenty-one associates, who had signed the original petition, were now incorporated into a Board of Trustees, and became the proprietors and virtual governors of Georgia for twenty-one years. At the end of this period the colony was to revert to the Crown. Provision was made for their original number to be maintained by election among themselves of others to fill any vacancies caused by resignation or death. The Government demanded an annual statement of accounts, and a yearly report to the Secretary of State and the Board of Trade. The Crown reserved the right to appoint officials to collect the King's revenue within the colony. All laws passed by the Board for the government of the new province had to receive the Royal Assent before being put into execution. Apart from these restrictions, the Trustees

[1] *Gentleman's Magazine*, 1732, II, 894.

were free to govern Georgia as they thought fit. They were empowered to raise money, send out emigrants, establish settlements, appoint magistrates, set up courts, and provide for the defence of the colony against attack. To facilitate the discharge of their duties, there was a provision in the Charter for a Common Council, with a quorum of eight members, in addition to the Board of Trustees; the chairmanship of both these bodies was to be held in rotation by all members. It was the intention of the Government, as well as of the Trustees, that the colony should be kept under strict control from home, so the Crown appointed no governor, and the Board made no provision for local government. Georgia was almost unique among the American settlements yet founded. The other colonies had been commercial enterprises or the result of religious differences; some began as means to provide escape from control, and were steps towards independence. The new colony had its origin in an attempt to remedy the social conditions of England by extending the British Empire beyond the seas. Georgia was both a philanthropic and an imperialistic enterprise.

The first meeting of the Common Council was held on June 22nd, 1732, under the chairmanship of Lord Egmont:

We met in our new house, taken for a year certain, with liberty to continue it if we like. We pay only £30 a year, and no manner of taxes. It stands in a lane that goes out of that street that leads from Palace Yard to Milbank Ferry. I found there James Vernon Esq., Mr. Oglethorpe, Mr. Hales the clergyman, Mr. Heathcot, Mr. Roger Holland, Mr. La Roche, Captain Coram. They were busy setting down the names of the Aldermen of London in order to apply to them for subscriptions to promote the colony. (I, 282.)

A month later, the Board of Trustees met for the first time, and Lord Egmont, as first chairman, was empowered by the Lord Chancellor to administer the oath to his colleagues.[1] After this, meetings of the Trustee Board were held fortnightly, and Common Councils almost every week. To begin with the attendance was excellent; but later, some members began to lose interest, the numbers at meetings fell off, and frequently the Common Council could not act because it was without its statutory quorum of eight. Of the Trustees, Egmont was the most influential, and Vernon, perhaps, worked the hardest. Dr Hales was very regular in his attendance, except during the summer months when he was at Farringdon. "To make the board this day Dr. Hales came out of the country fourteen miles"; most of the other Trustees lived in London, but Hales had to come up from Teddington on each occasion. After meetings, Hales and Vernon often returned to dinner with Lord Egmont, while at other times the Trustees dined together at the Horn Tavern or Cider House.

The newly constituted Georgia Society began its work by printing a letter in which they set forth the charitable and religious objects of the enterprise. This was sent out to all persons from whom subscriptions might be expected. The money raised in this way, supplemented by the grant from the Government, soon made it possible for the Trustees to announce

[1] *Gentleman's Magazine*, 1732, II, 874.

that they were prepared to finance and send over the first part of emigrants. Some of the applicants, mostly persons recently discharged from prison under the new debtors' Act, were selected, and Oglethorpe volunteered to go with them to start the colony. He accompanied the expedition, paying his own expenses, and took with him no definite official commission. He was empowered by the Trustees, however, to distribute the land among the settlers on arrival, and to swear the new magistrates into office. He was also instructed to lay out the town of Savannah, and to establish friendly relations with the Indians. By October 30th, 1732, the first party was ready to sail:

> The *Ann* Galley, of about 200 Tons, is on the point of sailing from *Deptford* for the New Colony of *Georgia*, with 35 Families, consisting of Carpenters, Bricklayers, Farmers, etc. who take all proper Instruments. The Men were learning Military Discipline of the Guards, as must all that go thither, and to carry Musquets, Bayonets, and Swords, to defend the Colony in case of an Attack from the *Indians*. She has on board 10 Ton of Alderman *Parson's* best Beer, and will take in at the *Madeiras* 5 Ton of Wine, for the Service of the Colony. *James Oglethorpe*, Esq., one of the Trustees, goes with them to see them settled.[1]

A few days later, many of the Trustees went on board to see that all was in order, and to take leave of Oglethorpe:

> Nov. 17th. 1732. Set sail from *Gravesend*, the *Ann* Frigate, having on board 116 People design'd for the first Settlement in *Georgia*. They are already under a regular Government, by Constables and Peace Officers, attended by the Rev. *Henry*

[1] *Gentleman's Magazine*, 1732, II, 1029.

Herbert. On the 12th they went on Shoar to *Milton* Church, and behaved with admirable Decency and Devotion. On the 17th many of the Trustees were on board to see nothing was wanting, and to take leave of a worthy Gentleman of their own Body who goes with them, to direct in laying out the Lands and forming a Town. An elderly Man came on board just before they sail'd, and would have persuaded a sober well-bred young Woman, his Cousin, to return with him to *London*, promising to take care of her; her Father and Mother, with whom she was going to *Georgia*, gave their consent, but she would not leave them; which rejoiced all the Company, she having promised to stand Godmother to a Male Child born under the Protection of the Trustees. Thus they begin already to increase, and five Couple have promised Marriages to each other: So that the Rev. Dr. will not be without Employment.[1]

The journey was accomplished without serious mishap. "They wrote us they were safely arrived at Georgia, none dead but two children under three months old; all in good health and spirits, except ten, who were down of the bloody flux, occasioned, as they believe, by the cold and lying under tents". (1,364.) On Thursday, March 15th, 1733, the Trustees celebrated their first anniversary in London:

We met in the vestry of Bow Church, and after sermon preached by Mr. Burton, by ballot elected nine new Common Councillors and a tenth in the room of Mr. Belitha, who resigned. Of these ten were elected, the Earl of Shaftesbury, the Earl of Tyrconnel, Lord Viscount Limerick, and of the Trustees, the Earl of Derby. We then dined at the King's Arms in St. Paul's Churchyard, at a crown a head, and were with friends about thirty in number, after which I went to the Royal Society, and then returned home. (1, 343.)

[1] *Gentleman's Magazine*, 1732, II, 1079.

At their second anniversary meeting, Dr Hales preached the sermon at the church of St Bride's, Fleet Street. It is interesting, in view of the peculiarly charitable nature of the enterprise, that on this occasion he should have confidently justified negro slavery as being in accordance with the teaching of Christianity![1]

A full account of the work carried out by the Trustees in London, and of the progress of the colony in America, is beyond the scope of these pages. As, however, Hales played a prominent part in the work both of the Trustee Board and the Common Council, the early history of Georgia must be told in brief. The Board rendered yearly petitions to the Government for financial aid, and, up to the beginning of the war with Spain in 1739, received annual grants from the Exchequer ranging from £2,500 to £26,000. They also collected subscriptions from private sources. The object of the scheme was the relief of pauperism in the home country, so the destitute emigrants were granted fifty acres of land each, free from all rent for the first ten years. They were provided with the necessary arms and tools, conveyed free across the Atlantic, and supported at the expense of the colony during their first year. A provision was made that no grant of land to any one individual should exceed 500 acres, in order to prevent the growth of large estates, which had become such a prominent feature in the other colonies. The Trustees held it to be

[1] *A Sermon on Galatians, vi. 2: Preached before the Trustees for establishing the Colony of Georgia in America. To which is annexed the general account for one whole year.* London, 1734.

essential that every estate in a border province such as Georgia, always open to the possibility of attack, should have a man to defend it; they therefore passed a law by which land could only be inherited by males. The Common Council carried on the more detailed work of administration. They organised the transportation of emigrants across the Atlantic; they interviewed applicants, and gave grants of land to deserving persons; they sent out cattle and horses, and an "ingenious person" to search out medicinal plants and roots, and instruct the colony in agriculture. As the colony grew, and particularly as war with Spain became increasingly more likely, arrangements had to be made for stores, food, arms, and ammunition, to be sent out at regular intervals. Deserving cases always received their personal attention. When, on one occasion, a widow, who had gone over in the ship with Oglethorpe and lost her husband and two sons in Georgia, came home to be cured of a "flux", the Council ordered that she should appear before them. She told them that she had recently married a man who had been pressed on board a man-of-war at Portsmouth. The Trustees at once ordered that his release should be obtained: "We then clubbed most of us our guineas apiece, which rose to eleven or twelve pounds, and ordered her to come from time to time to us until she shipped herself off."

The Trustees were zealous in the religious service of the colony. Money was raised to build a church at Savannah. Mr Quincy, a minister, was sent out to take the place of Dr Herbert, who had volunteered his services temporarily. They opened a subscription list for the persecuted Protestants of Austria and Germany, and raised £4000 for the purpose of shipping a party of Swiss over to Georgia:

> The Leader, Minister, and others of the Congregation of *Swiss* Protestants, who are going to establish a Town upon the River *Savanah*, attended the Trustees, who order'd a Library of Books to be given the Minister, for him and his Successors, and a handsome Sum of Money, to subsist 'em on their Voyage and their first Arrival.[1]

The first serious difference of opinion on the Trustee Board arose on the question of the Established Church in Georgia. Heathcote, White, Towers, Hucks, and Moore, who "seemed to be carrying on some particular schemes, and on that account to neglect the general good of the colony, and also to have too little regard to the religious part of our designs, leaning to the new opinions that are unorthodox", succeeded in gaining the separation of the affairs of the colony from Dalone's Trust and Dr Bray's Legacy with which they had been originally associated. "I perceive a division growing up among the Trustees of Georgia", wrote Egmont, "which I must labour to stifle, or our affairs will go on very heavily". Oglethorpe, Vernon, Bedford, Hales, Smith, Egmont, Anderson, and Coram, however, remained the Trustees of these charities. "Dr. Bray's Associates" now met every month, and one of their first acts was to appoint Hales, Bedford, and Smith, to go into and report upon the best possible use that could be made of the books left by Dr Bray for parochial libraries in America, "there

---

[1] *Gentleman's Magazine*, 1732, II, 874.

being few of one sort and hundreds of another". Dalone's legacy was a small one, amounting to about £40 a year, but, anxious to promote missionary work in America, they sent Dr Hales and four others to wait on the Bishop of London, and persuaded him to engage the co-operation of the Society for the Propagation of the Gospel in Foreign Parts in sending out catechists to the plantations to convert the negroes to Christianity. The Bishop replied that he feared considerable opposition on the part of some of the merchants of the City, and when he communicated the scheme to the Society, they sent a very unsatisfactory reply to Dr Bray's Associates. "The whole board was offended", says Egmont, "with the little concern that the Society shows for the conversion of negroes. It only says that if the Assembly of Carolina will settle catechists it is a thing desirable, but there is no promise to concur with us, not even conditionally". (II, 182.) They therefore collected subscriptions to augment the legacy, and to extend the purpose of the original bequest: "in the evening Dr. Hales came to us, and brought £100 from a gentlewoman unknown to be applied to the support of a Missioner to the Indians". (II, 370.)

A few years later, when the question arose of the use to be made of money subscribed for religious purposes within the colony, there was an actual split on the Board of Trustees. On February 4th, 1736, a proposal, that three hundred acres of land in Georgia should be handed over as an endowment to the church at Savannah, was outvoted. It was then agreed that this land should be assigned to religious purposes, and the following resolution was passed: "That the 300 acres being cultivated with money given for religious uses, the proceeds should, when the salary for a minister and schoolmaster, together with the repairs of the church were answered, be offered to such other *religious* uses as the Trustees should think proper". White, however, abetted by Heathcote and Towers, seized his opportunity as chairman to cut out the word *religious* from the resolution as recorded in the minute. (II, 231.) When this was discovered at the next meeting, a stormy debate arose on the question of replacing it, as Vernon, Egmont, Tyrconnell, and Hales, claimed that it was a plain breach of faith to apply money given for religious purposes to secular use. Mr White, "apperceiving himself publickly taxed with playing a trick", maintained that he had expressed the wishes of the meeting in the wording of the minute; in this contention he was supported by La Roche and Towers. After a heated discussion the matter was adjourned to a full meeting of the Common Council to be specially summoned for the purpose. Lord Egmont wrote in his diary that night:

It gave me much trouble to see so little concern for the religious concerns of the colony, but if we lose our point next meeting, I shall be obliged to protest, and so Mr. Vernon designs likewise. He told me also that he would withdraw from the trust, which I said I also would do, but I begged him not to do it till Mr. Oglethorpe should be returned to England, for it would be a great shock and discouragement to him to see himself deserted by those who hitherto had shown the greatest zeal and been of most advantage to the success of the colony. The weight of the thing will, I suppose, carry the question on our side, although the greater number are in their minds contrary, among whom are Mr. White a professed dissenter, Mr. Towers, Mr. La Roche, Lord Shaftesbury, Mr. Moore, Mr. Heathcote, and Mr. Hucks. (ii, 233.)

Eventually, largely due to the labours of Towers, the lawyer, who "in this affair sought to please both parties", a compromise was arrived at, and it was agreed to draft a new minute to take the place of the controversial one. This provided that proceeds, arising out of money given specifically for religious uses, should be applied solely to that end, without specifying the particular purposes to which they were to be applied. By this means an alteration was made in the controversial minute by the whole body, and no aspersion was cast on Mr White, which would have been the case if the word *religious* had been restored to the original. At the meeting at which the revised order was formally agreed to, White, La Roche, Heathcote, and Moore, absented themselves in protest. An open split had been avoided, but the breach was never healed, and six of the Trustees remained definitely hostile to the Established Church. At the next anniversary meeting White resigned his seat on the Common Council, "because", says Egmont, "he could not induce us to leave room for public encouragement to set up Dissenting congregations in Georgia, so that he had no zeal for the colony except under that condition". On that day only nine Trustees attended the sermon: Tyrconnell, Carpenter, Egmont, Holland, Vernon, Hucks, Bundy, Hales, and White.

After which Mr. White withdrew, and did not dine

with us, being exasperated at the letter written him by the Bishop of Durham, wherein he chid him for altering the minute in disfavour to religious uses. This letter, they tell me, he answered sharply (for a token of his displeasure at some of us, who were offended at that alteration). He this day (instead of attending the Trustees dinner) invited company at his own home, which were I suppose, Mr. Moore, Alderman Heathcote, Mr. Hucks, and Lord Shaftesbury, for none of them dined with us, though Heathcote and Hucks were for a time present with us in the vestry to assist in making a Board. Mr. La Roche had been invited by Mr. White, but he chose to dine with us. (II, 246.)

"I observe", wrote Lord Egmont a few months later, "that since the opposition made to granting the 300 acres to religious uses, neither Mr. White nor Mr. Moore has attended the board, and Mr. La Roche, Alderman Heathcot, Mr. Hucks and Lord Shaftesbury, but rarely". (II, 252.) Mr Hucks and Mr Moore also withdrew from the Common Council:

It is unfortunate that Mr. White was ever among us, for by what appears he is no friend to Church Establishment, and being of a busy working temper he has been doubtless prejudicial to us with the Episcopal people, and by his persuasion has wrought on Mr. Moore and Mr. Hucks to desert the Common Council, and with him act in concert Mr. La Roche, Alderman Heathcote, and the Earl of Shaftesbury, who yet remain among us. I can perceive a manifest coolness in all these gentlemen towards our proceedings, and where they are active it is to guard against any resolutions we may take in favour of the Established Church and particularly the persons of our missioners. Moreover, they use little artful managements to carry their points (of which I and Mr. Vernon and Dr. Hales take no public notice) to carry matters their own way, caballing together and not communicating their thoughts to us. This morning Hucks and

White whispered to me that they hoped we did not design to elect any more clergymen to be new Trustees. (II, 373.)

Such controversies did the reputation of the Trustees no good in the eyes of the outside world. When they refused to hand over three hundred acres of land unconditionally to the Church, the Society for Propagating the Gospel withdrew the fifty pounds a year, which they had voted towards the salary of the minister at Savannah. Dr Bearcroft, one of their members, told Egmont that the Society had formed a very bad opinion of the Georgia Board, and that, speaking for himself, he knew only Egmont and Vernon, who were not enemies of the Church. "I replied that they injured our gentlemen extremely, and named Mr. Digby, Lord Tyrconnell, Mr. Oglethorpe and Dr. Hales who were as zealous as any for the Established Church". (II, 350.)

His duties as a Trustee, and a member of the Common Council for the new colony, brought Hales into close association with the sea-faring fraternity. Among others, he became acquainted with Captain Thomson, of the frigate "Success", and Captain Henry Ellis, of a slave ship, "The Earl of Halifax". They sent him accounts of their voyages, and from them he learnt something of the conditions of life at sea in those days. The ships were over-crowded; the men had no proper kit, and seldom any change of clothing. The scanty supply of fresh water was often contaminated, and the odour of the bilge pervaded the whole ship. To ensure a supply of fresh meat at sea, cattle and other live stock were sometimes carried between decks; they encroached on valuable space already over-crowded, contaminated the decks, and added to the offensive odour of the bilge water. The men themselves, recruited from gaols and prisons, or press-ganged from the lowest haunts on shore, were brought on board without any medical inspection or attempt at disinfection. The conditions of life on ships were just such as to spread disease, and the British Empire was being built up at a great cost of men.

In 1740, Hales published a book entitled:

PHILOSOPHICAL EXPERIMENTS: containing Useful, and Necessary Instructions for such as undertake long Voyages at Sea. Shewing how Sea-Water may be made Fresh and Wholesome; And how Fresh-Water may be preserv'd Sweet. How Biscuit, Corn, etc., may be secured from the Weevel, Meggots, and other Insects. And Flesh preserv'd in hot climates, by Salting Animals whole. Which were read before the Royal Society, at several of their Meetings. Imprimatur, Hans Sloane, Pr. Reg. Soc., March 29, 1739.

This was dedicated to the Lords Commissioners of the Admiralty, and in the Preface he writes:

The particular occasion of my ingaging in this Attempt to make distilled Sea-Water wholesome, was from a Conversation I had with some seafaring Persons, who were giving an account of the very bad stinking Water, they were obliged often to make use of at Sea, and of the great hardships they sometimes underwent for want of enough of that bad Water. And a Person told me, that on board an *East-India* ship, in which he was; for want of fresh Water, the Ship's Crew was sustained fourteen Days, with distilled Sea-Water, which they distilled off at the rate of ten Gallons in a Day. The Instances of being brought to a very short Allowance of Water, are, as I find upon Inquiry, very frequent: I am informed also that many perish at Sea for want of fresh Water to drink.

Philosophical Experiments, in spite of its attractive title, is dull reading, and calls for little comment. The greater part is devoted to an account of his attempts to make contaminated distilled sea water wholesome, but his only important suggestion was that acid should be added to fresh water, or distilled sea water, to prevent putrefaction. The rest is largely devoted to instructions for disinfection with sulphur, which had been in use for centuries for this purpose; even in his own College at Cambridge, sulphur and charcoal had been kept burning in the porter's lodge during the visitation of the plague. He now advocated its use to kill off "weevel and meggots" in bread and biscuit. He also suggested that ships might be fumigated with burning brimstone to cure them of "pestilential infections"; the ship's company might be disinfected at the same time, if they covered their faces with respirators consisting of folds of cloth dipped in potash.[1]

To preserve meat on board ship during long voyages, he suggested that better results might be obtained by injecting brine along the arteries, than by soaking the flesh in salt water:

When I reflect on the great Number of Experiments of this kind, which I had made several Years before on Animals, it seems very natural thence to have fallen on this Method of salting Animals whole; yet I did not think of it, till several Years after; when upon a sea-faring Man's telling me, of the very bad stinking Flesh, they were sometimes obliged to eat at Sea; it presently occurred to my thoughts, that Flesh might be made to take Salt in hot

---

[1] *Gentleman's Magazine*, 1754, XXIV, 243.

Climates, by thus infusing Salt Pickle through its whole Substance.

On April 17th, 1736, he gave a demonstration of his method of salting animals to the Lords Commissioners of the Admiralty at the Victualling Office. On one occasion, at least, this method was actually put into practice:

> Having furnished my parishioner, Mr. Macpherson, then Purser to the Honourable Admiral Boscawen, in his expedition to the East Indies, with a brass cock proper to fasten to the great descending artery on the left side of the back bone at the small of the back; he made trial at Madagascar on four oxen in the mid-day heat, by injecting brine thus for four or five minutes only; for it immediately flows to the extremest parts and pervades all the flesh to such a degree as to make it readily taste salt, when cut in proper pieces to be salted and barreled. This they fed upon for two months on the voyage home till it was all eaten; it continued good till the last. This method of preserving flesh in hot climates will therefore be doubtless of service especially to sea-farers.[1]

Captain Henry Ellis of "The Earl of Halifax" was a Fellow of the Royal Society, and had accompanied an expedition in search of the north-west passage in the capacity of hydrographer. Conversation with Ellis suggested to Hales the construction of an ingenious machine, a sea-gauge to measure "the Unfathomable Depths of the Sea" with, he said, "great Expedition and Certainty". This consisted of a large hollow copper sphere attached to a long metal tube with a central metal rod. It was dropped to the bottom by means of a sinking weight, attached to it by a "catch hook", which

[1] Hales, *Treatise on Ventilators*, 1758.

then mechanically let go its hold, and allowed the sea-gauge to float to the surface. Internally it was so constructed that, as the external pressure rose and forced water up the tube compressing the air within the copper sphere, "tingid unctuous matter" of low specific gravity floated up on top of the entering water. When the pressure fell in the upward return of the apparatus, the height to which the water had ascended inside the tube could be seen by the mark of the unctuous matter on the central rod. The depth to which the instrument had descended (ignoring the complicating factor of change of temperature) could be calculated from the change of volume of the air inside the copper sphere.[1]

This machine was constructed with the assistance of Mr Desaguliers, and Hales demonstrated its action in a cylinder of water to the Royal Society.[2] In 1739, a rather simpler form of the apparatus was tried at sea by Mr Erasmus King, when in attendance on the Earl of Baltimore, one of the Lords of the Admiralty, on a voyage to St Petersburg. The machine registered the depth of the Baltic at a certain point to be 288 ft., which corresponded very nearly with a determination made in the ordinary way with the lead. Some years later the complete machine was tried in mid-ocean:

The late *Colin Campbell*, Esq., who employed the ingenious Mr. *Francis Hawksbee* to make the machine, which, tried in various depths of the *Thames*, answered very well, and

[1] Hales, *Statical Essays*, vol. II, 3rd ed. 1769, p. 327; *Gentleman's Magazine*, 1754, XXIV, 215.
[2] *Phil. Trans. Roy. Soc.* XXXV, 559. He also invented a "bucket sea-gauge" with which to obtain samples of sea water from different depths, *Phil. Trans. Roy. Soc.* 1751, XLVII, 214.

always returned, leaving the ballast behind. It was soon after put aboard the ship in which Mr. *Campbell* sailed for *Jamaica*; and in a clear calm day was by him let down into the sea, not many leagues from *Bermudas*, several other ships being in company, and a good look out ordered from them all; yet it was not seen to return, though they waited for it between three and four hours. This account, and the paper, the Communicator had from Mr. *Campbell* himself before his last departure, with his desire, that it should be published some time or other.[1]

To what extent Dr Hales's various suggestions were officially adopted is uncertain. Some, like disinfection with sulphur, were not original. Others, like the ingenious machine which was to determine the unfathomable depths of the sea with "great expedition and certainty" (and yet failed to reappear), were hardly practical. As scientific achievements they were nothing much, but he was continually bringing scientific methods to the notice of the Government, and this in itself was valuable. The Admiralty, to their credit, gave him some encouragement, and these endeavours prepared the way for the acceptance of his more important invention that was to follow.

[1] *Gentleman's Magazine*, 1754, XXIV, 215.

CHAPTER IX

The Ventilation of Ships. The Slave Trade. Experiments by the Admiralty.

IN the year 1740, troops under the command of Lord Cathcart lay embarked off Spithead for an expedition to America. When Hales heard that an epidemic had broken out among the soldiers, he conceived the idea that large wooden bellows might be installed in ships to make the air on board more wholesome. These bellows, or ventilators, were to be worked by hand, and so arranged that, by sucking the foul air out from between the decks, they would cause fresh air to enter through the port holes and hatches:

It may not be improper to give an Account how I, who am neither concerned nor skilled in naval Affairs, came first to think of these Ventilators; viz. In the beginning of *September* in the Year 1740, I wrote to Dr. *Martin*, Physician to Lord *Cathcart*, General of the Forces which lay imbarked at *Spithead*, for an Expedition in *America*, to propose (besides the usual sprinkling between Decks with Vinegar), the hanging up very many Cloths dipped in Vinegar, in proper Places between Decks, in order to make the Air more wholesome: And in case an infectious Distemper should be in any Ship, to cure the Infection with the Fumes of burning Brimstone. It was from these Considerations, which often recurred to my Thoughts, that it occurred to me the *March* following, that large Ventilators would be very serviceable, in making the Air in Ships more wholesome; this I was so fully satisfied of, that I immediately drew up an Account of it; several Copies of which were communicated, both by myself and others, to many Persons of Distinction, and Members of the

Royal Society: Before whom I laid a large Account of it, which was read in their Presence the *May* following, as appears by the Minutes of the Society.[1]

At about the same time, Mr Samuel Sutton, variously described as a brewer and a coffee-house keeper in Aldersgate Street, was informed by a friend that some of the sailors on board the Fleet at Spithead were dangerously ill for want of fresh air; many had to be put on shore to recover their health. After performing a number of experiments, Sutton found that, if he stopped up all the windows of a room in which there were two chimneys and lighted a fire under one, the air was drawn down the other with sufficient velocity to extinguish a candle placed in the grate. He therefore concluded that, if a pipe was fixed into the hold of a ship and a section of it kept heated by the cook-house fire, the bad air would be drawn up through it out of the hold, and replaced by fresh air which would enter from above.

In the spring of the following year, 1741, Martin Triewald, Captain of Mechanics and Military Architect to the King of Sweden, devised a machine, identical apparently with Hales's simultaneous and independent invention, for use on board the Swedish men-of-war which were sent in the summer to blockade St Petersburg. It was, as Hales said, "a very extraordinary Circumstance that two Persons at so great a Distance from each other, without getting a Hint of it, one from the other, should happen to hit on inventing a like very useful Engine". It proved "a sickly summer" in all the vessels of the Swedish

---

[1] Hales, *A Description of Ventilators*, London, 1743, Preface.

fleet, with the exception of the few that had already been fitted with Triewald's ventilators, and their success prompted Triewald to write a *Deduction on the Usefulness of his Engine*. This paper was read before the Royal Academy of Sciences of Sweden on April 3rd, 1742, "which noble work", it is said, "the Academy wished to see soon printed". The Academy's wish was quickly gratified, for the King ordered printed copies of Triewald's *Deduction* to be circulated to his naval officers, and commanded that Triewald's ventilators should be installed without delay on board all his ships. For this service to his country, Triewald was rewarded by being granted a "Privilege", or patent, on his invention for life by the King and Senate of Sweden. He forwarded a copy of his *Deduction* to Dr Cromwell Mortimer, Secretary of the Royal Society,[1] and in a letter to Baron Wafenburg, Envoy from the King of Sweden in London, told how he had sent one of his "engines", calculated for a sixty-gun man-of-war, to France, where, after it had been approved by the Royal Academy of Sciences in Paris, Louis XV had ordered similar ventilators to be installed in all his ships.

Hales lost no time in putting his own idea into practice, and for this purpose obtained the use of a large granary at Teddington. He constructed two pairs of large wooden bellows worked by a horizontal lever turning on a central pivot. These were provided with

---

[1] This document is preserved in the Royal Society's library at Burlington House, and shows Triewald's "Privilege" printed at the end of his *Deduction*.

inlet and outlet valves, arranged so that, as the lever was raised at one end, air was drawn out of the large room of the granary, and forced into the small room when the lever was depressed:

By alternate raising and pressing down of the Lever, the Midriffs (*diaphragms*) were also alternately raised and depressed, whereby those double Bellows were, at the same time, both drawing in Air and pouring it out; one of each Pair of Bellows, being in a dilating state, drew in the Air; while the other two, which were at the same time in a compressing state, blew it out.

In the meanwhile, Sutton had succeeded in obtaining an introduction to Sir Charles Wager, who sent him with a letter of recommendation to Sir Jacob Ackworth, the Surveyor of the Navy. After listening impatiently to Sutton's explanation of his scheme, Sir Jacob cut him short with the curt reply that no experiment should be performed if *he* could prevent it. Undismayed by this rebuff, Sutton petitioned the Lords of the Admiralty, who at length agreed that an experiment should be tried on board the "Greenwich", a man-of-war then lying at Woolwich:

I forthwith carried their lordships order to *Woolwich*, and pursuant thereto, to the satisfaction of myself, and all on board the *Greenwich*, I placed the pipes, and all things necessary for my experiment, except the soldering of two pipes: but, whilst the solder was hot, and the plumber in readiness to solder them, a messenger from the builder of his majesty's yard came to order the workmen ashore.[1]

The "Greenwich" was ordered out to sea, and the experiment had to be abandoned. Disgusted with

[1] Samuel Sutton, *An Historical Account of a new Method for extracting the foul air out of Ships*, London, 1745; 2nd ed. 1749.

the treatment he had received at the hands of the Admiralty, Sutton now approached Dr Mead, Physician to the King's Household, who brought his invention to the notice of the Royal Society, and constructed a model to demonstrate its action.[1] With the assistance of the President, Martin Folkes, he then succeeded in persuading the Admiralty to order another trial; Sutton installed his pipes on board the hulk at Deptford, and an official test was carried out in the September of 1741:

> This arrangement being put in execution at Deptford before the Lords of the Admiralty and the Commissioners of the Navy, our very learned and ingenious President Mr. Folkes Esq., Dr. Mead, etc. performed to their satisfaction in bringing air up from the bread-room, orlop and well of the ship at the same time in such quantity, that large lighted candles being put to the end of the tube, the flame was immediately sucked out as fast as applied, though the end of one of the tubes was 20 yds distant from the fire.[2]

Sutton's invention had now received provisional approval; but it had still to be tried out at sea. In the following November (1741), he was requested to proceed to Portsmouth, and install his pipes on board the "Norwich", a ship about to set off on a voyage to Guinea and the West Indies. Sutton was then told that he would have to wait until the Captain of the "Norwich" should report on his return to England.

The "Norwich" was away on her voyage for nearly two years, and in the meanwhile Hales's ventilator began to engage the attention of the Admiralty:

[1] *Phil. Trans. Roy. Soc.* 1742, XLII, 42.
[2] William Watson, F.R.S., *Phil. Trans. Roy. Soc.* 1742–3, XLVII, 62.

Dr. *Lee* having heard of them, he first, and then the rest of the *Right Honourable the Lords Commissioners of the Admiralty*, were pleased to send for me, to be further informed about them; and thereupon were pleased to order, the Master Ship-Wrights, and other Officers of *Woolwich* and *Deptford* Yards, to consider of the most commodious Place where to fix them in a Ship. Which was judged to be under the fore Part of the *Orlop* or lowest Deck, next to the Carpenter's Room. And accordingly they were fixed there, between the main Beams of the *Orlop*, on board his *Majesty*'s Ship *Captain*, a seventy Gun Ship; with their Valve-end and Nose next to the side of the ship....They are worked by a Lever twelve Feet long, by two Men standing upon the Orlop. And being each ten Feet long, four Feet three Inches wide, and thirteen Inches deep, throw out at the Rate of a Tun of Air at each stroke, sixty Tuns in a Minute; three thousand six hundred in an Hour; which passing off thro' a Trunk a Foot square, the Air rushes out with a Velocity of twenty five Miles in an Hour.[1]

Before any definite conclusion had been arrived at as to the practical merits of Dr Hales's invention, the "Norwich" arrived home. The Captain reported half-heartedly on the merits of Sutton's scheme:

As to the air-pipes which were put on board of me, I was obliged to stop up two of them, by reason the fire came down between decks: the other to the well was kept open, but the ship making water enough to keep her sweet, I was not able to judge of their use, having been so healthy as to bury only two men all the time I was on the coast.

Sutton was disgusted: "This Gentleman it seems lost so few men, that he could not discover the usefulness of my pipes; but, had he lost the greatest part of his crew, I dare say that he would have been able

---

[1] Hales, *A Description of Ventilators*, London, 1743, p. 25.

Plate XI. Ships in harbour, 1747

(From a print in the British Museum)

to judge, that my pipes were of no service at all."
He therefore proceeded to bombard the Admiralty
with a series of petitions, demanding recognition and
adequate payment. These at length produced a curt
reply, and an order for a hundred pounds:

In pursuance of an order from the right honourable the
lords commissioners of the admiralty, dated 22 *October* 1743,
signifying that, whereas Mr. *Samuel Sutton* did, some time
since, propose to that board an invention of his, for extracting
the foul air out of ships by fire, and letting in fresh air, an
experiment of which was ordered to be made on board his
majesty's ship *Norwich*, bound to the coast of *Africa*; and
captain *Gregory*, who commanded the said ship, having since
his return made a report thereof, a copy of which their lordships sent us therewith, whereby it appears that it does not,
in all respects come up to the expectation, and that the use
thereof is dangerous, and liable to accidents by fire: yet, as
the said Mr. *Sutton* has employed a great deal of pains and
time about the said invention, for the benefit of the navy, and
had encouragement from their lordships to do so; and their
lordships being desirous to give encouragement to persons
who shall turn their thoughts to any inventions, that may tend
to the advantage of the navy, do thereby desire and direct
us to cause a bill of one hundred pounds to be made out to
the said *Samuel Sutton*, as a reward for the loss of time and
expences he has been at about the said invention.

We pray you to pay unto Mr. *Samuel Sutton* accordingly,
the sum of one hundred pounds, dated 22 *Oct.* 1743.

This was the year in which Sir Robert Walpole's
long term of office came to an end. It is possible that
the reason why the Admiralty took up Hales's ventilators, and treated Sutton with his simpler invention
in this shabby way, was that some of Hales's influential friends had risen to political and administrative power. Sutton writes:

I am persuaded that if the usefulness of my scheme had appeared in the most demonstrative light, I should, after all, have fallen short of a suitable reward; and indeed this is the truth of the case. Dr. *Hales's* Ventilators, which were designed to answer the same purpose as my pipes, had, by some means or other, got such an ascendancy in the esteem and regard of some leading persons in the affairs of the navy, as, in spite of conviction itself, to admit of nothing to come in competition with them. I think it incumbent on me to observe, how much I was surprised to find no mention made by the candid author of the *Description of Ventilators*, of my invention: whereas he himself saw an experiment made before the royal society with a model of it, and heard Dr. *Mead's* account of it read to that learned body; which account was published in the *Philosophical Transactions* some time before the book of Ventilators was printed.

This accusation was certainly just. Hales may have honestly thought that his invention was superior in all respects to Sutton's ingenious device, but to ignore Sutton, in the way he did, was quite unfair.

In spite of influence, Dr Hales's ventilators did not meet with the immediate approval of the Admiralty. "They were received with coolness by some", he says, "and contempt by others, as is usual in the case of new things". The men no doubt regarded it as too much trouble to work them; the officers of His Majesty's ships regarded this troublesome and persistent parson with his many fads as an intolerable nuisance. In one of his letters Gilbert White writes:

He once told my father with some degree of emotion, that the first time he went on board a ship in harbour at Portsmouth the officers were rude to him; and that he verily believed he should never have prevailed to have seen his ventilators in use in the Royal Navy, had not Lord

Sandwich, the First Lord of the Admiralty, abetted his pursuits in a liberal manner, and sent him down to the Commissioners of the Dock with letters of recommendation.

More important was the fact that Sir Jacob Ackworth, Surveyor of the Navy, was himself sceptical. On April 6th, 1744, Lord Egmont wrote in his diary:

I went to the Hospital at Hide Park Corner where we agreed some matters for building a chapel and enlarging the house, and in my return visited my brother Percival who is still laid up with the gout. At the Hospital, I saw Dr. Hale's ventilator, or engine for recruiting the sick persons' apartments with fresh air, for he had fixt one there, which on occasion will draw the tainted air of three stories out in the space of half an hour, and supply its place with fresh air. A noble and salutary invention, which would be of great use at sea for hospital ships, transport vessels and men-of-war, after sea fights or long voyages when the seamen fall sick; but Sir Jacob laughs at it and will not suffer the use of it in the King's ships, which astonishes me.

Having rejected Hales's scheme, Sir Jacob and his colleagues reverted in favour of Sutton's simpler and less expensive device. In the year 1744, Sutton was granted Royal Letters Patent on his invention for a period of fourteen years in "England, Wales, the town of Berwick upon Tweed, and our plantations in America"; his pipes were fitted on board the "Namur", the "Warwick", the "Sandwich", and the "Vigilant", and were reported on favourably by Admiral Boscawen and others (1749). Sutton now wrote to his champion, Dr Mead:

I have the satisfaction to inform you that my invention has at length surmounted all obstacles through the wisdom and zeal of the present right honourable the lords of the admiralty, and the right honourable the principal officers and commissioners of his majesty's navy, who having taken the whole affair into their serious consideration, were so thoroughly satisfied of the great advantages that must accrue to the nation from the faithful execution of my scheme; that the said principal officers and commissioners of his majesty's navy have contracted with me for fixing my engine on board his majesty's ships, whether laid up or in commission.

Sutton was triumphant over Dr Hales:

His darling scheme is now out of date and exploded. Far be it from me, to insult and triumph over a conquered adversary; and it is needless, as well as cruel, to spend much time in confuting a scheme, that experience has abundantly shown to be absurd and ridiculous. His ventilators· are cumbersome machines, taking up more room than can conveniently be spared, and require many hands to work them: my pipes take up no room, and stand in no need of manual labour at all. His ventilators have only a casual and uncertain action, but my pipes a certain and uninterrupted effect. His ventilators cannot extract the air from the well at the bottom of the ship; but mine do this. His ventilators, he tells us, will keep a prison sweet; but my pipes will sweeten even a boghouse. My scheme in all these respects surpasses his; for his is dead and buried, without any hope of resurrection whilst mine rises in its reputation daily: and the report of Captain *Comyns*, commander of the *Fame* privateer, which I fitted up some months ago, and which is returned to *Lisbon* with his crew in health and vigour, will give such an ample and satisfactory attestation of the safety and usefulness of my pipes, as will be sufficient to dispel the doubts and suspicions of the most incredulous.

His scheme rejected by the Admiralty, Hales sought to convince the public by publishing a book in which he set out all the possible useful purposes to which his ventilators might be profitably applied; it was in this that he ignored Sutton's invention completely:

A DESCRIPTION OF VENTILATORS: Whereby Great Quantities of Fresh Air may with Ease be conveyed into Mines, Gaols, Hospitals, Work-Houses and Ships, in Exchange for their *Noxious Air*. An Account also of their Great Usefulness in many other Respects: As in Preserving all Sorts of Grain Dry, Sweet, and free from being Destroyed by Weevels, both in Grainaries and Ships: And in Preserving many other Sorts of Goods. As also in drying Corn, Malt, Hops, Gun-Powder, etc., and for many other useful Purposes. Which was read before the Royal Society in May 1741.

At a Meeting of the Royal Society, *June* 9. 1743. Imprimatur. M. Folkes. Pr. R.S.

The Royal Navy had rejected them; but, in his capacity as Trustee for the colony of Georgia, he was able to get them extensively adopted in the merchant service, where they proved of particular value on board emigrant and slave ships. Some idea of the slave trade is given by an account which Dr Garden wrote to Hales from Charlestown in South Carolina:

There are few Ships that come here from *Africa* but have had many of their Cargoes thrown overboard; some one-fourth, some one-third, some lose half; and I have seen some that have lost two-thirds of their Slaves. I have often gone to visit those Vessels on their first Arrival, in order to make a Report of their State of Health to the Governor and Council, but I have never yet been on-board one, that did not smell most offensive and noisome; what for Filth, putrid Air, putrid Dysenteries, (which is their common Disorder) it is a wonder any escape with Life.

In 1742, ventilators were fixed on board the 20-gun Guinea slave ship "Blandford", and into Mr Reid's "felon ships" which carried convicts to the American plantations. They proved so successful that Mr Crammond put them into all the slave traders in his service. One was carrying 392 slaves, and twelve of these had been taken on board just before leaving Guinea "ill of a flux"; in spite of this, all the rest arrived safe and well at Buenos Ayres, an almost unprecedented experience, it was then thought, once an "infectious distemper" had been introduced on board. On a Liverpool slave ship, which carried eight hundred slaves, there was an average mortality of fifty on each voyage across the Atlantic; but, after ventilators had been installed, not a single slave died with the exception of one child born at sea. The Board of Trade and Plantations now adopted them officially. In 1749, the Earl of Halifax ordered ventilators to be constructed in five Nova Scotia slave ships, and to every slave who died on board these vessels, twelve or more died on those that had not been fitted with ventilators. Impressed with their economic value, the Lords of the Board of Trade and Plantations sent Mr Yeoman across to Rotterdam with orders to fix ventilators on board the other slave and transport ships in the Nova Scotia service. When Mr Yeoman had executed his commission, he left a model of Hales's ventilator at Rotterdam with instructions how it should be used.

Hales received a number of letters testifying to the value of his invention:

In the Year 1753 Ventilators were put into the Vessels in the Slave-trade, at *Bordeaux*, and in other Ports of *France*; the happy Effect of which was, that instead of the Loss of one fourth of those valuable Cargoes, in long Passages from *Africa* to the *French* Plantations, the Loss seldom exceeded a twentieth. And since my return to *England*, I have been informed of a *French* Vessel, which by this self evidently reasonable Precaution, saved 308 out of 312 Slaves, spite of most tedious Calms, and a long Passage.[1]

In a letter dated September 25th, 1749, Captain Thomson, of the frigate "Success", wrote:

During the Ventilation, the Lower-deck Hatches were commonly kept close shut; by which means the Air was drawn down into the Hold, from between Decks, through the Seams of the Ceiling, among the Timbers of the Ship; by which means we found the foul Air soon drawn off from between Decks. Our Rule for ventilating was for half an Hour every four Hours; but when the ventilating was sometimes neglected for eight Hours together, then we could perceive, especially in hot Weather, a very sensible Difference by that short Neglect of it; for it would then take a longer Time to draw off the foul Air. Our general Rule was, to work the ventilators till we found the Air from them sweet. We all agreed that they were of great Service, the Men being so sensible of the Benefit of them, that they required *no driving* to work that which they received so much Benefit by. We found this good Effect from Ventilation, that though there were near 200 Men on board, for almost a Year, yet I landed them all well in *Georgia*, notwithstanding they were pressed Men, and delivered me out of Gaols, with Distempers upon them. This is what I believe but few Transports, or any other Ships, can brag of; nor did I ever meet the like Good-luck before; which, next to *Providence*, I impute to the Benefit received by Ventilators. It is to be remarked, that we who lay wind-bound, for four Months, with our Expedition-Fleet, which soon after invaded *France*, were healthy all the Time,

---

[1] Dr Demembray to Dr Hales. Hales, *Treatise on Ventilators*, London, 1758.

when they were sickly in all the other Ships of that Expedition.[1]

Captain Ellis, F.R.S., of "The Earl of Halifax", wrote:

Sir,

Could anything increase the Pleasure I have in literary Intercourse with you, it would be, to find that it answered your End in promoting the public Good. The *Vis inertiae* of Mankind, is not the only Difficulty you have had to encounter, but their Ignorance and Prejudices, which are almost insuperable. It is to your Perseverance and Resolution, that the little Progress you have made is due: Indeed I ought not to say little, for it is a great Step to have found the few that have Hearts good enough to relish your Plan, and Heads sufficiently clear to discern the most effectual Method of advancing it. It does Honour to those noble and worthy Personages, that join you in Acts of such extensive Humanity, as the Introduction of Ventilators to Hospitals, Prisons, Ships of War and Transports etc., as they must necessarily render the Miseries of the first more supportable, and the close and constant Confinement of the others less prejudicial and fatal to Health and Life. It is to be lamented that they are not more generally made use of; for, notwithstanding their Advantage is apparent and incontestable, it is scarce credible how few make use of Ventilators among the vast Number of Ships daily employed in carrying Passengers, Slaves, Cattle, and other perishable Commodities. Those of your Invention, which I had, were of singular Service to us; they kept the Inside of the Ship cool, sweet, dry, and healthy: The Number of Slaves I buried was only six, and not one white Man of our Crew, (which was thirty-four) during a Voyage of 15 Months; an Instance very uncommon. The 340 Negroes were very sensible of the Benefits of constant Ventilation, and were always displeased when it was omitted: Even the Exercise had Advantages not to be despised among People so much confined. I must not, however, forget that Venti-

[1] Hales, *Treatise on Ventilators*, 1758, p. 89.

lation alone is insufficient to keep Disorders out of Ships; for often Infections are brought abroad by the Slaves, or others; and frequently Diseases are produced by feeding on bad or decayed Food; but oftener still by Insobriety....Could I but see the immoderate Use of spirituous Liquors less general, and the Benefits of Ventilators more known and experienced, I might then hope to see Mankind better and happier. I am,

SIR,

Your most obedient Servant,

Bristol,   HENRY ELLIS.[1]
Dec. 26, 1753.

Altogether so many passengers and slaves continued to die on board unventilated ships arriving at the American ports, while the mortality was so much less in ships provided with Hales's ventilators, that Mr Penn proposed to the Assembly of Pennsylvania "the Making of a Law, to lay a great Penalty on every Ship which has not Ventilators on-board, and does not work them frequently".

The Board of Trade had now set the example, and the Admiralty began to reconsider the merits of Dr Hales's ventilators. One of the most difficult problems with which the naval authorities had to contend was the prevention of the decay of the timbers of ships. The organic nature of dry rot was not realised at the time; but, if the air in ships could be kept dry by proper ventilation, it was thought that it might do much to prevent decay:

One of these useful machines (*ventilators*) is also fixing in each of the transport ships, which are to carry 500 *Germans*

---

[1] Hales, *Treatise on Ventilators*, London, 1758, p. 91, and *Gentleman's Magazine*, 1754, XXIV, 114. See also *Phil. Trans. Roy. Soc.* 1751, XLVII, 211, and 1755, XLIX, 332.

to the *British* plantations: so that 'tis not questioned but this invention will be brought into general use in the Navy. Foul damp air will rot the timbers in a very short time. And as ship timber grows very scarce and dear, this cheap method of preserving ships, perhaps for a double term, will be an acceptable article of œconomy to the nation, without taking into account the still greater expense of building: for that ships decay, even without going to sea, appears by the condition of the *London*, a first rate, now lying in *Chatham* yard.[1]

In 1751, the Admiralty ordered a further trial to be made of Dr Hales's ventilator to see if it would serve this particular purpose, and he was asked to proceed to Deptford, where the officers were instructed to give him every facility for fixing up one of his machines on board the "Sheerness", a 20-gun ship, laid up in the royal dockyard. Continuous ventilation of the kind that he considered necessary for the prevention of dry rot, would involve a considerable amount of manual labour and corresponding expense; he therefore arranged for it to be worked by a windmill erected on the deck. The Commissioners of the dockyard then instructed the officers of the ship "to report to them the utility of the said Machine, and to send a very particular and accurate account of their observations thereon, and to keep a journal to show the times of its workings and the effect it has on board the said ship". When the Commissioners, having received this report, came to express their opinion on the usefulness of Dr Hales's engine to the Lords of the Admiralty, they said: "We are of the Opinion it will not Answer the Purposes intended". Later, when the Lords of the

---

[1] *Gentleman's Magazine*, June 29th, 1749, XIX, 282.

Admiralty asked them to give their opinion "on the Reasonableness of the charge of the Bill delivered by Mr. Stibbs for fixing a Ventilator on board His Majesty's Ship *Sheerness* and by whom it ought to be defrayed", they wrote:

> We are of Opinion that Dr. Hales ought to be at the Expence, especially as their Lordships by their Order of the 20th December last directed that the alterations made in the Doctor's Machine and the manner of laying his Experiments as he shall judge proper shall not be attended with any Expence to His Majesty.[1]

Three years afterwards, another trial of the method was ordered at Chatham dockyard: the Admiralty directed "one of Dr. Hales's Windmill Ventilators to be fitted on board His Majesty's Ship *The Prince* in order to make a further trial of its Usefulness". Again, the experiment was not considered satisfactory, and when Hales proposed that the number of ventilators on board the "Prince" should be doubled, the Admiralty ordered that further expensive experiments of this kind should cease.[2] His disappointment was great, and on July 11th, 1757, he wrote bitterly to Mr Alderman Janssen:

> I have not yet given the French a particular Account, of what I have done on board the *Sheerness Man of War*, towards preserving the Timbers of Ships layed up in ordinary, because I was desirous we should have the Credit of first doing the Thing. But as the Commissioners of the Navy, to avoid a trifling Expence (which would most assuredly save Millions to the Nation), have put a Stop to my Proceedings, when I was got only to the Threshold of the Ex-

---

[1] Record Office, Admiralty Navy Board Out Letters, 2185, p. 427.
[2] Record Office, Admiralty Navy Board Out Letters (1754), 2187, pp. 133, 174, 200.

perimental Research, and had as yet tried only the fourteenth Part of the Air that could be conveyed among the Timbers of a Ship; For in new Researches we are under a Necessity of feeling out our Way Step by Step.—Since I am thus stopped short in this important Research, I intend, before *Christmas*, to publish the second Volume of my Book upon Ventilators, in which, among other things, both in Justice to the Public, and in Vindication of the Reasonableness of my Proposals, I will give a full Account of it, and of the high Probability, I will say Certainty, of Success, in preserving the Timber of Ships many Years the longer from decaying. This will probably put the *French* upon doing the thing, and then we shall have the Disgrace of copying after them.[1]

It is evident that the Admiralty were losing faith in Sutton's invention, or they would hardly have ordered a second trial of Dr Hales's method. Mr Yeoman was now sent down to supervise the installation of Hales's ventilators at Haslar Hospital, the prison at Porchester Castle, and in other hospitals and gaols at the important naval bases.[2] For this work Hales received the official thanks of the Navy: "The Commissioners of the sick and wounded Seamen wrote me word, that they find most beneficial good Effects from these several Methods, which were put in practice by the Direction of Mr. *Yeoman*, in the Hospitals at *Portsmouth*, *Gosport* and *Plymouth*". Dr Hales's method eventually triumphed: on September 4th, 1756, an order was given "to fit ventilators into all His Majesty's Ships".[3] "They are now

---

[1] Sir Stephen Theodore Janssen, Bart., *A Letter to the Lord Mayor, the Aldermen, the Recorder and the Gentlemen of the Committee appointed for the rebuilding of Newgate. With an appendix*, London, 1767.

[2] Record Office, Admiralty Medical Dept. Out Letters, 5, p. 328.

[3] Record Office, Admiralty Navy Board Out Letters, 2188, p. 452.

come into general Esteem", he wrote, "from the apparent salutary good Effects of them in our Fleets, Hospitals, etc. In the Beginning of the Year 1756, the Lords Commissioners of the Admiralty ordered them to be put on-board the *Royal George*, our largest Ship: In which the Honourable Admiral *Boscawen*, taking care to have them properly worked, they were found to have the desired good Effect, so to refresh the whole Air in the Ship, as to preserve in good Health 850 people; which happy Event occasioned their being ordered to be put into the whole Fleet".[1]

NOTE TO CHAPTER IX

This account of the history of the ventilation of the ships of the Royal Navy has been drawn from Hales's two books, *A Description of Ventilators* (1743) and *A Treatise on Ventilators* (1758), Sutton's book, papers in the *Transactions of the Royal Society*, and the Admiralty Records at the Record Office in Chancery Lane. I have searched the Admiralty records for the years 1740–1760, but they are unfortunately very incomplete, and, in addition, almost all the original enclosures, reports, letters, bills, etc. are missing. I have therefore been unable to fathom completely the inner history of this subject. Why Sutton's invention lapsed is not clear, nor is it at all apparent why Hales's ventilators came to be accepted so suddenly. The Admiralty records, however, confirm the written statements made both by Hales and Sutton. The general order of 1756 does not specify the actual type of ventilator to be installed in all H.M. ships; but it would appear fairly certain that it must have been Hales's and not Sutton's. Sir William Berry, K.C.B., Director of Naval Construction, kindly looked up the matter for me at the Admiralty, and discovered that Mr Yeoman, who specialised in the construction of Hales's invention, was appointed in charge of the ventilation arrangements of all H.M. ships on August 17th, 1756. The Admiralty also possesses a diagram of a windmill ventilator by Mr Yeoman, which was sent to Portsmouth on March 29th, 1765 (four years after Hales died), for guidance in fitting the system into the *Sandwich* and *Arrogant*; this system consisted of bellows operated by wind vanes, and the *Sandwich* was also a ship in which Sutton's pipes had previously been installed. To what extent the general order of 1756 was actually carried into effect is uncertain.

[1] Hales, *Treatise on Ventilators*, 1758.

CHAPTER X

The Progress of Georgia. Prohibition of Rum and Slavery. Financial Difficulties. To be surrendered to the Spaniards? The Trustees relinquish the Charter.

IN 1734, Oglethorpe returned to England bringing some of the Indians from Georgia with him. The party consisted of Toma-chiki, King of the Yamacrees, his wife, Serawli, his nephew, Tonoway, two warriors, and Mr John Musgrave, an interpreter. They were lodged in the garret over the Georgia office, where the porter had special instructions, "not to let the mob in to see them". On July 3rd, they were officially received by the Trustees (II, 114),[1] and, at their request, Mr Verelst, accountant to the Society, painted a picture of the scene for presentation to Lord Shaftesbury. (In Plate XII Dr Hales is seen on the extreme left of the picture standing behind the chair on which one of the Trustees is seated.) Later, when Verelst had to go to Mr White to ask him to pay his share of the expense, White replied: "Yes, if you will cut out my face". "Thus may be seen", wrote Egmont, "the hatred he bears to us, that even to be seen in our company in a picture displeases him".

A few days later, the Indians travelled to the Palace in one of the royal coaches.

The Queen called for the chief's nephew, after the audience she gave them all was over, stroked his face, and told him he must come again to see her, for she had a present for him.

[1] The numbers throughout this chapter refer to Lord Egmont's diary published by the Historical Manuscripts Commission in three volumes, London, 1920–1923.

Plate XII. The Trustees of the colony of Georgia receiving the Indians

(From the painting by Verelst in possession of the Earl of Shaftesbury)

He answered her in English, for he is forward in his learning, Mr. Smith, of our Society, coming three times a week to instruct him in the principles of Christianity. He can say the Lord's Prayer, Belief, and Ten Commandments, but I fear all this will be lost on his return. (II, 120.)

On another occasion they visited the Primate.

They had apprehensions that he was a conjurer, but the kind reception he gave them altered that imagination. The Archbishop would have put some questions to them concerning their notions of religion, but they have a superstition that it is unfortunate to disclose their thoughts of those matters, and refused to answer. They attributed the death of their companion (*who had died in London of the Small Pox*) to having too freely spoke thereof since they came over. Nevertheless the King was so taken with the Archbishop that he must come again alone to talk with him. At coming away he said he now really believed they should have some good man sent them to instruct them and their children. (II, 121.)

When the Trustees first set about negotiating a trade agreement with the Indians, the interpreter turned out to be drunk: "Hereupon we desired Mr Oglethorpe to see what he could settle when Musgrave should be sober".

It was during Oglethorpe's first return visit to England, that, with his full approval and partly due to his influence, the Trustees passed laws which prohibited the introduction of rum into Georgia, and completely suppressed negro slavery in the colony. Their reasons for introducing these measures were quite definite. The consumption of alcohol, if allowed in the form of spirits, would be excessive among settlers recently liberated from debtors' prisons, and would have a debasing effect, not only on the colonists, but also on the Indians with whom it was essential that they should trade. Their objection to slavery was not based on any abstract principle. The law was passed on grounds of expediency. They held that blacks, if introduced, would increase and multiply much faster than the whites, and, by displacing the settlers from their occupations, eventually defeat the original purpose for which the colony had been founded. They were also influenced by the consideration that the presence of a large number of negroes in the colony would constitute a potential danger to a border community always exposed to the possibility of an attack by the Spaniards from the south.

Meanwhile, in Oglethorpe's absence, affairs in Georgia were going on none too smoothly. The Trustees heard a very indifferent account of the Rev. Mr Quincy (whom they had sent out to take the place of Herbert as minister at Savannah), and of the religious disposition of the colonists: "There being some Sundays not ten at church!" On July 2nd, Egmont wrote in his diary:

> We are all of a mind to dismiss our Minister at Georgia, who appears for a long time to be unfit for his employment, and is now gone to Charlestown. He is in league with the malcontents of our Province, and has never writ to us any account of himself, the place, or the performance of his duty, though required both when he first went over and since frequently by letter; so that he seems both to slight us and not to value his place. Dr. Hales proposed enquiring at Lincoln College for a proper man to send in his room, there being several pupils of Dr. West who have been educated with great care. (II, 184.)

It was indirectly due to Dr Hales that the brothers John and Charles Wesley volunteered for service in the colony. They went out to Georgia with Oglethorpe and 280 emigrants on his return in the autumn of 1735. On Tuesday, October 14th, Egmont, Towers, and Hales, went down to Gravesend to see the party off.

After dinner (*at the "Fauchon"*) we went at 5 o'clock on board and were taken up in business until ten, when we returned on shore. We mustered the passengers on board the *Symonds*, Captain Cornish, commander, a ship of about 250 tons, and 19 sailors. On board this ship goes Mr. Oglethorpe, Mr. Johnson, son of the late Governor of Carolina, and the two Wesleys, brothers, both clergymen. The youngest is to be private secretary to Mr. Oglethorpe, as also Secretary to the Indian trade, and to act as minister of the new settlement at Frederica. The elder goes with design to penetrate into the Indian country and try to convert them. A third clergyman was to have gone but he has failed us. His name is Hall; he was ordained for the very purpose to go to Georgia a few weeks ago, in order to succeed Mr. Quincy, who was last Friday removed by a Board of Trustees, and this Hall was designed to succeed him. The Captain has on board Mr. Vanreck's Germans and divers English. (II, 200.)

As the colony was now rapidly increasing in size, the Trustees had planned that a new town, to be called Frederica, should be started on the Ogeechee River. War was impending with Spain, however, and Oglethorpe, influenced by strategical considerations, planted the new settlement at the mouth of the Alatamahah, contrary to the wishes of the Trustees. In addition he proceeded to fortify the whole line of the river by throwing out a series of posts to the south, outside the chartered limits of the colony. His action dismayed the Trustees, as they felt that this, more than anything else, was likely to provoke hostilities with Spain. Accordingly, they informed Oglethorpe that they could not sanction expenditure outside the legal boundaries of Georgia, and that he must apply to the Government, and not to them, for support. This was the beginning of dissensions between Oglethorpe and some of the Trustees, and, in 1736, he was recalled home, nominally to report about a dispute with South Carolina over traffic in rum. When he landed in England on January 2nd in the following year, Egmont went to meet him:

> His account of affairs in Georgia and of his own behaviour and conduct there was very satisfactory to me, and has cleared up divers matters whereof the Trustees were in doubt, and at which they were very uneasy for want of proper lights; the treaty he concluded with the Spaniards is honourable and advantageous to England. (II, 326.)

It was during Oglethorpe's second absence from Georgia, that things began to go really badly in the colony. Unity was essential, but the colonists, drawn from debtors' prisons and the lowest haunts of London, had no sense of discipline. Discontent soon began to grow, and was further promoted by the actions of Causton and John Wesley. Causton, the Trustees' chief bailiff at Savannah, had been appointed storekeeper by Oglethorpe; now, in Oglethorpe's absence, he was in uncontrolled power, and had the full responsibility of distributing the stores sent out by the Trustees. Wesley, as Hall had failed, had been appointed minister at Savannah to take the place of Quincy. Causton started to sell the Trustees' stores

at exorbitant prices, and showed preferential treatment to his friends. Wesley adopted a highly pro-
vocative and intolerant attitude to the different religious sects in the community. The situation was
soon complicated by an unfortunate love affair
between Wesley and Causton's niece. When the lady
suddenly broke off the engagement in order to marry
someone else, Wesley found occasion to rebuke her
publicly for some slight misconduct, and then prohibited her from attending Communion at the church.
This high-handed and uncalled-for action so enraged
Causton and the lady's husband, that they brought
an action against him for damages amounting to
£1000, and a large jury in a secular court found him
guilty on six charges: refusing to christen except by
dipping, reading the Litany at six instead of ten,
refusing to bury an Anabaptist, being a Jesuit, a
spiritual tyrant, and a mover of sedition. Wesley now
demanded a fair trial and an opportunity to justify
his conduct before the Trustees, and, though his
enemies tried to prevent it, set sail for England.
Egmont was unable to attend the meeting, at which
he appeared before the Trustees, and made counter-
accusations against Causton:

Confined at home by a cold, whereby I could not attend
the Georgia Board, where the day's business was to receive
Mr. Wesley's complaints of the usage he received at Georgia,
and which obliged him to come to England. He gave the
Trustees that met several papers and certificates for his
justification, whereby it appeared indeed that he was guilty
of indiscretion, but that Causton our head bailiff was much
more to blame, and he charged upon him many particulars
of gross mis-administration which must be enquired into.

Mr. Vernon took him home to dinner, and in company of Mr. Hales examined him more particularly as to Causton's bad behaviour as a magistrate, which they took down in writing in order to be discoursed at the Board. (II, 467.)

A few days later, the Trustees passed their judgment on Wesley:

Mr. John Wesley, our minister at Savannah, left with us his license for performing ecclesiastical service at Savannah, which we took for a resignation, and therefore resolved to revoke his commission. In truth the board did it with great pleasure, he appearing to us to be a very odd mixture of a man, an enthusiast and at the same time a hypocrite, wholly distasteful to the greater part of the inhabitants, and an incendiary of the people against the magistracy. (II, 481.)

Wesley was succeeded at Savannah by Whitfield. When the latter came home in the autumn of 1738 to take priest's orders, he gave the Trustees an unfavourable account of the condition of people in Georgia:

He acquainted us briefly with the state of the colony, which did not give us entire satisfaction, for he told us the people are many of them lewd, drinkers of rum in spite of our law against it, even to the killing themselves and are very lazy; that most of them alleged the cause of their not improving the lands granted to them was the barrenness thereof, and the not allowing females to inherit, and that the disappointment of last year's crop by the want of rain had discouraged many who are industrious. That, nevertheless, some are industrious, and very many religiously disposed, he having had at Savannah crowded churches, and at morning and evening prayers near two hundred persons. That the children's schools are well frequented and carefully conducted by the schoolmasters. He then told us of the admirable harmony, industry, neatness and piety of the Saltsburgers at Ebenezer. (II, 512.)

Of the laws that had been passed, and of the provisions which had been made by the Trustees for the government of the colony, three regulations were largely responsible for provoking the rapidly growing discontent: the prohibition of rum and other spirits, the law of "tail male", and the suppression of negro slavery. Of these, the first mattered least; rum was freely smuggled into Georgia from the neighbouring colonies, the colonists started their own distilleries, and the Trustees in England were powerless to enforce the regulation they had made. The law relating to the inheritance of land, by males only, caused much dissatisfaction. The Trustees themselves were not completely agreed as to the wisdom of this measure, which, in 1735, had caused an open split on the Board, resulting in the resignation of Captain Coram from the Common Council:

Mr. Sterling, who with a party of Scots are settled in Savannah County, having received a letter full of invectives against the Trustees, accusing us of pursuing our private interests at the expense of those we send, that our constitution is military, arbitrary, and tyrannical, and that in a little time we shall by our management destroy the colony; he honestly gave it to our bailiffs to peruse, who sent us a copy of it, but the name of the writer being scratched out, we can only guess the man; and him we believe to be Captain Coram, our fellow Trustee, who, on account of our not suffering females to inherit, left our Board in disgust, and prates against us. We believe it to be him the rather because mention is made in that letter of a new settlement in another place, which the King and Council have been applied to grant, and all the steps of that application related, as far as it has proceeded, which none but Captain Coram could tell, he being the person who proposes to make a new settlement far from us and absolutely distinct from Georgia. Thus I perceive that enemies are gathering against us, but our integrity will, I trust, weather all storms. (II, 200.)

The most unpopular law was the prohibition of negro slavery. Much of the land in the colony had turned out to be swamp, incapable of cultivation and production, and the labour of clearing the forest areas had proved too great for handfuls of emigrants drawn from debtors' prisons; storms, droughts, and epidemics, had added to their difficulties. The inhabitants claimed that, in consequence of the Trustees' restriction, production was cheaper in South Carolina than in Georgia, and that they therefore suffered from unfair competition. The settlers were soon expressing their grievances in a flood of letters, pamphlets, and petitions, and to Georgia, with all this discontent, there was the ever present danger of war with Spain.

Altogether the affairs of the colony were none too prosperous, and the difficulties of the Trustees were becoming greater every day. The colony had much increased in size, and the expense of running it had become correspondingly large. Oglethorpe had indulged in considerable expenditure which had not been authorised by the Trustees. The question of the defence of the colony was becoming daily more urgent. While in England, Oglethorpe, foreseeing that war with Spain was inevitable, persuaded Sir Robert Walpole to raise a British regiment, returning to Georgia at its head with the rank and pay of a colonel in the regular army. This had an unexpected and unforeseen result. The grant from the Government for the year was reduced on this account, but the sailing of the regiment was for some reason delayed for over twelve months, and during this period the Trustees were compelled to continue to provide for the defence of the colony. In addition, they had gained for themselves a reputation for mismanagement of their own affairs, and private subscriptions were falling off. The finances of the colony were getting into a serious state, and on March 23rd, 1738, the Trustee Board, determined to make a serious effort to put their own house in order, appointed "a Committee of Correspondence" consisting of Vernon, Towers, Hales, Egmont, Lapotre, and Sloper. They were instructed to draw up recommendations for the remedy of abuses, and the prevention of unnecessary expenditure; the establishment of the colony was to be reduced to within the £8000 voted by Parliament that session.

We could not but observe that Mr. Oglethorpe has been very careless of attending the Board of late, that is, since he knew the Gentlemen were resolved to reduce the Colony's expenses, in which he told Mr. Verelst he desired to have no hand. He sees how cool many of the Trust are grown to the work, and that there is only one set who remain to carry it on, whom if he should disgust, the charter might fall for want of a sufficient number to support it, and therefore since he is not thoroughly pleased with our proceedings, he chooses to be absent as often as he can with decency, without falling out with us. The Lord Talbot, Alderman Heathcote, Alderman Kendall, Lord Carpenter and Dr. Bundy have withdrawn this year. Captain Eyles and Mr. Frederick never attend. Lord Limerick and Mr. La Roche but seldom. This is observed in town, and creates a report that our affairs are under bad management. If a few more should withdraw, that report would be too truly confirmed. On the other hand Mr. Vernon, Mr. Towers, myself, Mr. Lapotre, Dr. Hales, Mr. Archer and Mr. Smith continue their zeal, and Sir William Heathcote, the Earl of Shaftesbury and Mr. Sloper act tolerably well,—when a house is falling, the rats leave it. (II, 474.)

Soon after his arrival in Georgia in the October of 1738, Oglethorpe himself sent the Trustees a melancholy account of the condition of their colony. Causton had abused his trust; of the vast collection of stores carefully laid in by the Trustees practically nothing remained. The settlement at Frederica had nearly starved on account of the drought. The colony as a whole had contracted enormous debts, and most of the settlers had lost all their savings. The hogs and steers, sent out by the Trustees, had run wild. On account of the Spanish alarms many of the colonists had failed to cultivate their lands, and numbers had actually migrated away to the neighbouring colonies. Oglethorpe's demand for money was urgent, as the £8000 voted for the previous year had proved quite insufficient. On receipt of this news, the Trustees sent out orders that Causton should be arrested, and set about drawing up a petition to Parliament for increased financial aid.

In 1739, the affairs of Georgia came to a sudden crisis. The territory in Florida was in dispute; Spain claimed Georgia, and Walpole regarded their claim as a matter for negotiation:

Mr. Towers acquainted the Board that he had lately had discourse with Sir Robert Walpole concerning the Spanish claim to Georgia, who told him that by the Convention our

Minister at Madrid is to settle with that Court the limits of Carolina and Florida. That they claimed Georgia to be part of Florida, and he was surprised that His Majesty's grant to us of Georgia should have passed the approbation of the Board of Trade and the Attorney General before they were satisfied that Georgia was no part of Florida. But the matter was to be determined in nine months. Mr. Towers was therefore of opinion we should defer our petition (*for financial aid*) as long as we could to see what would be done with us, and whether we should not ask for money to dislodge the colony and bring the people home, but he did not offer this as his proposal. Mr. La Roche agreed with him. But the other gentlemen present were surprised at his discourse. Alderman Heathcote made a long speech against it and said, whether Mr. Towers was in earnest or jest he knew not, nor could he understand his meaning. For his part, the honour of the Trustees and of Parliament and the interest of the nation and the safety of the colony and Col. Oglethorpe's life were so much concerned, and depended so much on our vigorous appearance on this occasion, that he never would give up the colony, or endanger the want of an immediate support by delaying the petition, for the drawing up of which he had already sufficient light and grounds. (III, 9.)

For a long while Walpole's real attitude towards Georgia remained in doubt, and the enemies of the colony made the most of the uncertain situation. "It is in everybody's mouth", wrote Egmont bitterly, "that Georgia is to be given to the Spaniards". Meanwhile, the situation in which the Trustees found themselves placed was exceedingly delicate. If they pressed their petition for increased financial aid at the moment, the whole question of Georgia would come up for discussion in the House, and the condition of the colony was not one such as would encourage Walpole and his friends to go to any particular length to keep it, if the surrender of the colony would serve to avoid an open breach with Spain. On the other hand, Georgia was in urgent need of funds, and the Trustees could ill afford to wait. When they approached the minority leaders in Parliament, they were told that, if the members of the Board, who were in the House, would back the general attack on Walpole, the Opposition would oppose the colony being given up; but, failing their support, the Trustees "would not get a shilling that year". After much discussion the Trustees adopted the braver course. They drew up a petition for the previous year's grant to be increased from eight to twenty thousand pounds, caused it to be "engrossed fair", and sent it in. A few days later, Sloper, Towers, Vernon, Hales, and Egmont, dined together at the Cider House: "We drew up the forms of two papers to be shown to our friends in the House of Commons particularising the sums we want to put us out of debt, and for carrying on the cost of the affairs of the colony from Lady Day 1739 to 1740".

At this point the unexpected happened. Walpole's majority in the House was dwindling, and, afraid of losing the Trustees' votes in Parliament, he suddenly came down to them, and suggested that they themselves should draw up the title of the right of the King of England to Georgia, thus passing over for this purpose all the proper officers of the Crown. He said that he was amazed how it could be believed that Georgia was to be given up under the Treaty, that there was no such design, and that he was sorry that the gentlemen of Georgia were his enemies.

The Trustees refused this task, as they considered it to be entirely outside their province:

> We were in a difficult situation, the minority threatening to be against supporting us unless we joined with them *tête baissée* against the ministry, and inflamed the House, and on the other hand no money to be expected if Sir Robert were disobliged; but since we find ourselves courted by both sides, it would become us to stand on our own legs, and make no strong professions to either. (III, 15.)

Eventually the terms of the Convention with Spain relating to trading rights in North America were made public: Georgia was not to be surrendered entire, but its southern boundary was to be settled by plenipotentiaries appointed by England and Spain. "I tell you", said Walpole in response to the Trustees' inquiries, "Georgia is not intended to be given up, and although we call the commissaries plenipotentiaries, they are to receive instructions from hence for everything they sign". The Board was not entirely satisfied, and at a meeting on February 21st, 1739, Egmont proposed that Parliament should be petitioned to interpose a clause into the Convention providing that Georgia should be left intact when the boundary between Florida and Carolina came to be settled. The motion was agreed to without dissent; but when the petition was presented to Parliament, White, Hucks, and Wollaston, three Trustees, immediately got up and left the House. "This", wrote Egmont, "was very surprising to the rest of our body".

On Thursday, March 8th, 1739, the Convention

was debated in the Commons. Walpole was still for peace at almost any price, but the minority, desiring war with Spain and, therefore, an aggressive policy in North America, opposed it. Most of the Trustees, wishing to ensure the safety of Georgia, for which the Convention now provided, and anxious in the interests of the colony to maintain peace, voted on the ministerial side; they also wanted to keep in with Walpole who had promised further financial aid. Some, to the great disgust of the minority, sank their private political feelings in the interest of the colony. Only five voted against the Convention. After twelve hours debate it was carried by 260 to 232: a majority of 28! Keene in Madrid was now instructed to insist that the St John's river should be the boundary between Georgia and Florida. Thus Georgia was assured for the British nation, and for the moment war with Spain averted.

The Convention through the House, the Trustees were free to press on with their petition to the Government for further funds:

A committee was appointed for to prepare directions to take account of the stores; to appoint commissioners to state and examine upon oath the debts upon the Trust; to consider of the resumption of lands deserted by the owners, and forfeited by the tenure of their grants, and to prepare an estimate at the most frugal rate for the year's expenses from midsummer 1739 to midsummer 1740. This committee agreed to meet after dinner, and accordingly Mr. Towers, Mr. Vernon, Dr. Hales, Mr. Sloper and I dined together, and finished the instructions relating to the debts and stores, as also relating to the vacant Trust lots; but we had not time to make an estimate of the year's expenses ending 1740. It was much concern to us to find in the gross by Mr. Oglethorpe's letters, that the debts contracted in Georgia, together with the necessary expenses of the Colony to midsummer 1739, will amount to nearly £12,000. (III, 46.)

A few months later, war broke out with Spain. The prosecution of the campaign was taken over by the Government, but the civil affairs of Georgia during the hostilities remained the province of the Trustees. The Committee of Accounts, of which "only Mr. Vernon, Mr. Holland, Mr. Towers, Dr. Hales and I (Lord Egmont) remained", continued their labours. In 1740, Walpole was given to understand by some of his friends among the Trustees that no grant was needed for that year. Egmont and his party, knowing well that further financial assistance was really necessary, now decided to make an attempt to escape from complete dependence on the minister by laying an account of the needs and the condition of Georgia before the House. They courted a full Parliamentary inquiry. Walpole avoided it by consenting to a grant of £4000.

Meanwhile attacks accusing them of incompetence and mismanagement continued to be levelled at the Trustees. In 1741, therefore, the Board drew up a pamphlet entitled, *An Account of the Progress of the Colony of Georgia from its first Foundation*, which was circulated among all members of both houses. It was met by a more virulent attack than ever on the part of Thomas Stephens, son of the Stephens whom the Trustees had appointed their secretary in Georgia. Meanwhile, Walpole had been defeated in the House, and the minority which had succeeded him under the nominal control of Lord Wilmington were even less friendly to the Georgia Society than Walpole himself had been. Stephens's allegations had been brought to the notice of the Commons, and, to the astonishment and dismay of the Trustees, a motion to refer their application for a grant to the Committee of Supply was defeated. The Board therefore insisted on the hearing of their case before the whole House, with the result that Parliament expressed their opinion that Georgia as a colony was of such value to England that it should receive the support of the nation. Stephens's accusations against the Trustees were declared scandalous and malicious, and he was compelled to kneel in the presence of the House, and receive the reprimand of the Speaker. Their victory was decisive. During the remaining years of its existence as a proprietary province, Georgia received from Parliament such sums as the budget made possible.

During these later years the Trustees found it necessary to modify some of the original provisions they had made for the government of the colony. On the law relating to the inheritance of land they were forced to give way, and unable to prevent the importation of rum, they left the law to be openly disobeyed. To the prohibition of negro slavery they held fast, but eventually the opinion was expressed at a meeting of the Trustees that "they must come into a scheme of admitting negroes, or they would get no money". Egmont now resigned his seat on the Common Council, nominally on grounds of ill health. At the close of the war with Spain, the

Board again reaffirmed its opposition to negro slavery; but, during the years which had intervened, slaves had found their way in. All efforts to drive them out had proved ineffectual, and Stephens now wrote that any further attempt to do so would depopulate the colony. When, in 1749, the colonists petitioned the Trustees to sanction negro slavery, the Board approached Parliament, and the slave exclusion law of 1735 was repealed.

The twenty-one years' period of the Trustees' proprietorship of Georgia was now drawing near its end, and they were about to surrender their powers under the Charter to the Crown. They had expended £150,000 in the service of the colony; of this £130,000 had been voted by Parliament. They had made the mistake of holding the reins of government too tightly in their own hands, and of administering the colony too much from home. Suspicious of the powers that a government, which was not actuated by the same ideals, might hold over his appointment and dismissal, the Trustees had never appointed a governor in their colony. They had made no provision for local government in Georgia; but, as taxes had never been collected in the colony, it had not been demanded by the inhabitants as a means of redress for their grievances. Now, in view of the impending transition, the Committee of Correspondence, fearing that without it Georgia would cease to exist as an independent province and become a part of Carolina, recommended the calling of a representative body. Electoral law was drawn up, and the first assembly met at Savannah in 1757.

Two years later the Trustees surrendered their powers to the Crown.

Georgia had been started by Oglethorpe and others for philanthropic and religious purposes. As an imperialistic enterprise, it stands almost unique in the history of the British settlements in North America. The Trustees can be accused of administrative incapacity, and many of them were admittedly idealists, or amateurs who lacked completely in the necessary experience. But it is difficult to find reflections to cast on the sincerity of their motives, and, after all, their work must be judged by its results. They had carried the Trust through to its completion, without a deadlock among themselves, and without an open quarrel with the Government or the Board of Trade. As a result of private effort, territory, which would otherwise have been seized by Spain, was appropriated for the British Empire as it then was. It is perhaps significant of the important but quiet and unobtrusive part that Dr Hales played in the government of Georgia, that one of the first and most successful governors appointed by the Crown was his friend and admirer, Captain Henry Ellis, commander of the slave ship, "The Earl of Halifax".

CHAPTER XI

The Ventilation of Prisons. The Gaol Distemper. Newgate and the Savoy.

WHEN, in 1744, his ventilators were rejected by the Admiralty, Hales at once set out to find other uses to which they might be profitably applied. In those days debt was punished by imprisonment, and theft by death. Executions were frequent, and the gaols throughout the country were crowded with debtors, felons, trivial offenders, and hardened criminals, while in military prisons men, "pressed" into the service of their country, were kept in confinement until they were drafted on board ship, or sent out as recruits to reinforce regiments on service abroad. These institutions were swept by frequent terrible epidemics of the "gaol distemper",[1] and seemed obvious places where his ventilators might prove useful. They were first put into practice for prison use at Winchester, where he was Proctor for the clergy of the diocese, and could bring pressure to bear on the authorities. Ventilators were installed in the "Debtors' Room" and in the "Criminal Dungeon" of the County gaol.

In the eighteenth century the area between the river bank and the Strand, near Charing Cross, was occupied by the Savoy Palace. It served a number of useful and miscellaneous purposes:

---

[1] This disease, typhus, is now unknown in this country. The nature of the organism which causes it is uncertain, but the infection is conveyed from man to man by lice.

This *Savoy* House is a very great and at this present a very ruinous Building. In the midst of its Buildings, is a very spacious Hall, the Walls three Foot broad at least, of Stone without and Brick and Stone inward. This large Hall is now divided into several Apartments. A cooper hath a Part of it for stowing of his Hoops, and for his Work. Other Parts of it serve for two Marshalseas for keeping Prisoners, as Deserters, Men prest for military Service, *Dutch* Recruits, etc. In this *Savoy*, how ruinous soever it is, are divers good Houses. First, the King's Printing Press for Proclamations, Acts of Parliament, Gazets, and such like public Papers; Next, a Prison; Thirdly, a Parish Church, (St. Mary-le-Savoy) and three or four other Churches and Places for Religious Assemblies, *viz.* For the *French*, for *Dutch*, for High *Germans*, and *Lutherans*, and Lastly, for the Protestant Dissenters. Here be also Harbours for many Refugees, and poor People.[1]

The Savoy prison had an evil reputation for the gaol distemper. Regiments on service were afraid of receiving drafts of recruits from the Savoy; they so often brought infection with them. When the Secretary of State for War, the Right Honourable Henry Fox, came to hear of his ventilators, and their success on slave ships, convict ships, and in the prison at Winchester, Dr Hales was asked to pay a visit to the Savoy. On Thursday, June 29th, 1749, the following item of news appeared in the *Historical Chronicle*, of the *Gentleman's Magazine*:[2]

The good Doctor, by desire of the Secretary at War, was to-day at the Savoy Prison, to direct a proper place for the erection of a large Ventilator.

---

[1] J. Strype, *A Survey of the Cities of London and Westminster*, London, 1720.
[2] 1749, XIX, 282.

According to his own account at least, the result of the ventilation of the Savoy prison was eminently successful:

In the Year 1749, of 200 Men but one died, and he of the Small-Pox. And in the Year 1750, of 240 which were there three months, but two died. In the Year 1751, none died; And, in the Year 1752, only one old Person died. Whereas, before the Ventilators were put up, there often died 50 or 100 of the infectious Gaol-Distemper. And what contributes the more to the present Healthiness of the Place, is that Mr. *Hayward*, the Master of the Prison, continues with the same Care and Zeal to keep it clean. And, the more effectually to cure the Wards of any Infection, he burns, as I desired him, every six Weeks two Pounds of Brimstone in the larger Wards, and a Pound in the smaller Wards.

Soon after this, ventilators were constructed for the "dungeon" at Northampton gaol, and the County prisons at Shrewsbury, Maidstone, Bedford, and Aylesbury. They were then introduced into St George's Hospital in London (where they were worked by a windmill on the roof of the old building), and into the County Hospitals at Winchester, Durham, Bristol, and Northampton. They were even adopted on the Continent, for they are said to have been installed in a hospital at Naples "through the influence of Prince Santo Severino". Dr Hales was one of its Vice-Presidents, and, in 1752, they were installed in the Middlesex smallpox hospital at "Sir John Oldcastle's".[1] In the same year they were introduced into Newgate, the chief civilian prison of the City.

Newgate, partly destroyed in the Great Fire of 1666, had been rebuilt with great magnificence. It now

[1] *Gentleman's Magazine*, 1747, XVII, 270.

consisted of a massive and ornate stone building with a carriage archway in the centre which divided Newgate St. from Giltspur St. Above the portal on the east side stood emblematical figures of "Justice", "Mercy", and "Truth"; on the west, "Liberty" (with Dick Whittington's cat at her feet), "Peace", "Plenty", and "Concord".[1]

On the side, the footpath was continued through it, which supplied a shelter for two or three old women, who fried small sausages for sale: and in the centre of it was an entry to the then chief prison of the city; the mendicant prisoners for debt stood within the iron-grated door, vociferating their constant supplication for benefactions to a leathern bag, which they drew in as often as it was touched; the upper chambers of the building constituted the prison for felons, for whom a door was opened on the south side adjoining the old wall which still abuts upon the street by the ordinary's house, and it was from this door that the malefactors were received into the cart for their last journey to Tyburn. Upon the summit was a machine for air invented by Dr. Hales.[2]

Ventilators were first installed in some of the wards of Newgate by order of the Lord Mayor, Sir Richard

[1] A Roman gateway once existed on the same site, but Newgate, so called, was first built in the reign of Henry I, and is mentioned in the Pipe Roll as a prison. Sir Richard Whittington, "thrice Lord Mayor of London", is said to have expressed a desire that Newgate should be rebuilt, and in 1425, a few years after his death, this wish was carried into effect by his executors. Whittington's gate escaped complete destruction in the Great Fire of 1666, and ten days later, when the ruins of the greater part of the City of London were still smouldering, the order was given for Newgate to be repaired at once, as the demand for prison accommodation was very urgent. It was not, however, completed in the form described until the year 1672. (R. S. Sharpe, *Memories of Newgate Gaol*, London, 1907; Arthur Griffiths, *Chronicles of Newgate*, London, 1884.)

[2] G. L. Gomme, *The Gentleman's Magazine* Library, *English Topography*, Part xv, London, vol. 1, London, 1904.

Hoare. They were operated by manual labour, and an ingenious device was employed to encourage those whose laborious duty was to keep them working:

The Velocity with which the wind rushes into the Trunk is so great, as to twirl fast round a little Wind-mill placed at the Mouth of the Trunk. And in Cases where such a Windmill cannot be seen by the Workers of the Ventilators, then the Wind-mill may be made to make a very small tinkling Bell to sound as was done at *Newgate*. This is found to be of considerable Use in diverting, and thereby encouraging those who work the Ventilators to persist in working; without which sensible Amusement they are apt to be discouraged from working the Ventilators; because, as it has been found by Experience, they are apt to look upon it as working to no Purpose, since they can see no visible Effect that it has on the invisible Air. It is found to be of use, not only to divert and amuse those who work the Ventilators, but also to let the patients in each Ward know that they have their due proportion of Ventilation.

In spite of this device, the use of the ventilators was soon neglected, and the gaol distemper continued prevalent in all the wards of Newgate. In the spring of 1750, a tragedy occurred during the trial of malefactors at the Old Bailey:

A fatality happened at the *Old Bailey* in *May* sessions, by the infectious disorder among the prisoners brought from *Newgate* to take their tryals, whereby 64 persons then in court lost their lives; (among whom were Sir *Samuel Pennant*, Lord Mayor, Sir *Thomas Abney*, and Baron *Clarke*, Judges, Sir *Daniel Lambert*, Alderman, several Counsellors, one of the Under Sheriffs, and five of the *Middlesex* Jury.) The number of prisoners tried that sessions being remarkably great, and some of the trials being interesting to the public (particularly the trial of Capt. *Clarke* for killing Capt. Innes in a duel in Hyde Park) the court was unusually crowded, and became so hot, that it was necessary to let down the right hand sash, facing the bench, through which the wind, then at North East, blew directly upon them who sat on the South and South West parts of the court; and here indeed the great mortality fell: for it was observed, that on the opposite part of the court, not above 2 or 3 of the above number died of the fatal malignity.[1]

Mr Alderman Janssen, one of the Sheriffs at the time, took immediate action:

He began by consulting that excellent pattern of humanity, the late Dr. S. Hales; in consequence of which, the following steps were successively taken. Mr. *Ackerman*, the keeper of *Newgate*, had directions to have the *jail* cleansed thoroughly: three cartloads of the most abominable filth were carried away, but lest the *effluvia* of such poisons should infect the air, the Sheriff had it carried a considerable distance from town, and there buried ten feet under ground. After this, he went into the dismal jail himself, and ordered it to be washed with vinegar, and likewise that the prisoners, a day or two before their being brought down to the *Old Bailey* to take their trials, should undergo the same operation; all which was done. He then went to the *Gate-House* Prison, *Westminster*, which he found in a most noisom state; this prison he ordered also to be thoroughly cleansed and washed with vinegar, and the prisoners to be washed likewise, before they were removed to *Newgate*, against the approaching sessions. He also went to *New Prison* and *Clerkenwell, Bridewell*, where the same orders were put in execution, although these *jails* were cleanliness itself, when compared with the two former. While these measures were carrying on, the court in the *Old Bailey*, and the whole house from top to bottom (to which nothing had been done in 30 years before) were scraped, cleansed and washed with vinegar, and the worthy Dr. Hales had certain herbs burnt in the court for some days before the sessions began to obstruct any infection from taking place again.[1]

[1] *Gentleman's Magazine*, 1764, XXXIV, 17.

These measures, however, were not considered sufficient, and in the following October a Committee of the Court of Aldermen was appointed:

To enquire into the best Means for procuring in *Newgate* such a Purity of Air, as might prevent the Rise of those infectious Distempers, which had not only been destructive to the Prisoners themselves, but dangerous to others, who had any Communication with them, and particularly to the Courts of Justice upon the Trial of Malefactors, whereof a fatal Instance had occurred that Year at the Sessions held in the *Old Bailey*.

This Committee consulted the Rev. Stephen Hales and Dr Pringle,[1] and arranged to make a tour of inspection of Newgate.

Some idea of the condition of the interior of Newgate at the time can be gained from a book entitled: *An Accurate Description of Newgate; Written for the Public Good*, by "B.L. of Twickenham", and published in 1724. Things may have improved a little in the thirty years that had intervened. Parliament had appointed a Commission to investigate some of the scandals associated with debtors' prisons, and this body, under the chairmanship of Oglethorpe, had reported on the Fleet. But the first half of the eighteenth century was not conspicuous for active social legislation, and it is not likely that the condition of Newgate had changed much.[2] Nor can this anonymous author, although he had

---

[1] Later Sir John Pringle (1707–1782), the army surgeon and the reformer of military sanitation and hygiene, who, by his book *Observations on the Diseases of the Army*, laid the foundation of modern military medicine.

[2] This was before Howard, the pioneer of prison reform, had begun his work. Howard visited, reported on, and condemned the new prison which was built after the old one had been pulled down. He never visited the old Newgate.

been confined there as a debtor, be accused of prejudice against Newgate as a prison. His object was to draw a parallel between the "Master Debtors' Side" of Newgate and the several "Sponging-Houses in the County of Middlesex", of which he had also intimate knowledge; to set forth "the Cheapness of Living, Civility, Sobriety, Tranquility, Liberty of Conversation, and Diversions" of the former, in comparison with "the Expensive Living, Incivility, Extortions, Close Confinement, and Abuses" of the latter. His account is therefore sufficiently reliable to give an idea of what Hales, Pringle, and the Aldermen of the City of London, saw when they made their tour of inspection of the prison.[1]

Newgate at that time consisted of the original gateway and a block of buildings stretching down the south side of Newgate St. in the direction of the Sessions House. It is said to have been "a structure of more cost and beauty than was necessary, because the sumptuousness of the outside but aggravated the misery of the wretches within". Under the arch of the gateway close to the main entrance of the prison was the "Condemned Hold". This was a room half underground, and completely devoid of furniture except for a "bed", to which, it is said, "the disorderly were fixed". Newgate was fed by an incessant stream of the worst criminals in London, and they were lodged here pending their execution at Tyburn or on the gallows outside the "Debtors' Door".

The treatment which prisoners received depended

[1] The account of Newgate which follows is based on this tract (1724), *Chronicles of Newgate* (Arthur Griffiths, London, 1884), and the *History of the Press Yard* (Anonymous, 1717).

largely on their ability to pay certain prison fees. The Press-Yard, a separate building, was kept for the wealthy and aristocratic. The "Master Side" of Newgate was set aside for those who could afford to pay a moderate sum. Here, there was one ward for debtors, another for felons, and a third for women. Some comforts were allowed; wines and spirits were to be had at all hours on payment, beds were available for half-a-crown a week, and sheets for two shillings a month. Adjoining was a room called the "Gigger", on account of an iron grating, or "gigger", in the wall, through which, on payment of one and sixpence, prisoners were allowed to converse with friends who came to see them.

The large majority of the inmates of Newgate could not afford to pay these prison fees; they were therefore relegated to the "Common Side", where all the prisoners were kept in fetters, unless they could scrape together enough money to purchase "easement" of their warders. There were three wards set aside for debtors: the "Stone Hall", the "Tangier", and the "Debtors' Hall". Out of the "Stone Hall" opened three smaller rooms: the "Iron Hold", where the fetters were kept; the "Partners' Room" (the "partners" were certain prisoners entrusted with the maintenance of discipline); and the "Taphouse", where unlimited drinking was allowed, and of which the anonymous author of *An Accurate Description of Newgate* gives some account:

'Tis a great Pity that a better *Decorum* is not maintained among the Prisoners of this *Common Side*, especially in this Taphouse; for therein, by Connivance, the Felons are permitted to converse and drink with the Debtors; by which Means, such Wickedness abounds therein, that that Place seems to have the exact Aspect of Hell itself; and by this Means 'tis much to be questioned, whether one Debtor in Ten, who enters therein an Honest Man, comes the same out, the Wickedness of the Place is so great.

From the "Taphouse" a low and dark passage led to the "Tangier": "a large dark stinking ward occasion'd so by the Multitude of the Prisoners in it, and the Filthiness of their Lodging". In contrast to the "Tangier", the "Debtors' Hall" was lighted by a large window, but this was unglazed, and the wind and rain blew straight in. On the floor above there was a ward for female debtors; "their Conversation", it is said, "was very profligate being perpetually Drinking and Cursing with the Felons".

The "common felons", who could pay no prison fees at all, were confined in the "Stone Hold": "a most terrible, stinking, dark, and dismal Place, situated Underground, in which no Daylight can come". Adjacent to this was a similar dungeon, the "Lower Ward", reserved for those unable to pay fines imposed upon them. On the floor above was the "Middle Ward", for felons who could pay a small fee, and the "Waterman's Hall" for females, another "terrible, dark and stinking Place". From the "Waterman's Hall" a door led into the "Condemned Hold for Women". Women in prison are well known to those with prison experience to sink lower than the men. "It is with no small Concern", wrote the anonymous B.L. of Twickenham, "that I am obliged to observe, that the Women in every Ward of this Prison, are exceedingly worse than the worst of the Men, not only in respect to Nastiness and Indecency of living, but more-especially as to their Conversation, which, to their great Shame, is as profane and wicked, as Hell itself can possibly be."

On the top floor of the prison was the Chapel, where on Sundays before executions the Ordinary preached the "condemned sermons" to the male-factors under sentence of death. The Chapel was open to the public, and London society flocked to see this sight. Next door to the Chapel was a special room for those under sentence of transportation:

Knowing their Time to be short here, rather than bestow one Minute towards cleaning the same, they suffer themselves to lie far worse than Swine; and to speak the Truth, the *Augean* Stable could bear no Comparison to it, for they are almost poisoned with their own Filth, and their Conversation is nothing but one continued Course of Swearing, Cursing, and Debauchery, insomuch that it surpasses all Description and Belief.

When they had completed their tour of inspection with Dr Hales and Dr Pringle, the Committee rendered a report on Newgate to the Court of Aldermen. This report was probably not unanimous. Many were sceptical that ventilation by Dr Hales's method would accomplish much, and were in favour of pulling Newgate down. Nevertheless, at the next meeting of the Aldermen the following resolution was passed in respect of Newgate:

That considering the Smallness of the Place, in proportion to the Number of Prisoners, it would be proper to make a farther trial of the Ventilator, and to have it worked by a Machine in the Manner of a Windmill, to be erected for that Purpose upon the Leads of Newgate.

On account of the agitation to rebuild the prison,

there was a delay of two years before this decision was put into execution. On July 11th, 1751, Hales wrote from Teddington to Mr Alderman Janssen:

Sir,

Not having Time, when I was with you t'other Day at *Richmond*, to talk to you fully of the Affair I came about, I shall do it fully in this Letter, *viz.*, Last Year, when many died of the pestilential infectious Jail Distemper, which they got in the *Old Bailey* Court, there was, on that Occasion, a Probability, that large Ventilators would be fixed in *Newgate*, to be worked by a Windmill, as you saw was done on board a *Man of War* at *Deptford*, which would effectually preserve all the Wards in *Newgate* in a sweet healthy State. I am sensible that the Deliberations, whether *Newgate* should be pulled down and new built, have with good Reason delayed the fixing of Ventilators there.—But if it is, or shall soon be resolved, that *Newgate* shall not be pulled down; then, I could wish, if it is at all to be done, that it might be done before next Winter; that I may be able to give an Account of its being done, in my second Volume on Ventilators. I am the more desirous to have it done in *Newgate*, not only for the Sake of the Prisoners there, but also as a laudable Pattern, not only for the rest of the Nation, but for the Benefit of the world.

Of what importance will this be to the Nation, when we engage in War, to have our brave, undaunted Sailors and Soldiers, when Prisoners of War, preserved from being poisoned and rotting in Jails? For it is highly probable, that three in four of those who die in War, loose their Lives by the Stench of Jails, and Hospitals.

I have several Years since wrote to Mons. *Du Hamel*, to propose the Ventilating the Prisons of Prisoners of War, and if the Example were set at *Newgate*, the good Effect of it would probably induce the several warring Nations, on both Sides, to do so great an Act of Humanity.

Thus you see, Sir, that what I am so desirous of having done in *Newgate*, is an Affair of the greatest Importance, not only to this Nation, but to the whole World. I am therefore persuaded, that the opulent and renowned City of *London* will not long hesitate about it. When you and several other Aldermen, with Dr. *Pringle* and myself, went in *October* last into *Newgate*, we were but too sensible of the Stench of several of the principal Wards, a Stench so very offensive, that it would be a great Act of Humanity to deliver, not only unhappy Debtors, but even the vilest Criminals from it; even though it occasioned neither the Sickness nor the Death of any. But when, withal, we are assured, it causes the Sickness and Death of many, can anyone hesitate, whether an effectual Means shall be made use of to cure so destructive a Pest?

I am, Sir,

Your obliged, humble Servant,

STEPHEN HALES.[1]

Eventually conservative counsels prevailed, and it was decided to give Newgate a further lease of life by proceeding forthwith with the construction of the ventilator, and the erection of the windmill on the leads. The work was carried out under the general direction of Dr Hales. Mr Stibbs, the carpenter, of Fore Street, London Wall, made the ventilators and the main shafts and pipes communicating with the various wards. Mr Cowper, of Penny Fields, Poplar, constructed the windmill which was erected on the top of the tower above the gateway (Plate XIII):[2]

[1] Sir Stephen Theodore Janssen, Bart., *A Letter to the Lord Mayor, the Aldermen, the Recorder and the Gentlemen of the Committee appointed for the rebuilding of Newgate. With an appendix,* London, 1767.

[2] I have been unable to trace the origin of this print which is in the possession of the British Museum. The windmill over the gateway is also figured in the frontispiece to William Maitland's *History of London* (1775). Both prints are engraved on eighteenth-century penny tokens (Dalton and Hamer, *The Provincial Token Coinage of the Eighteenth Century*, vol. I, Nos. 659 and 80).

The Ventilators were fixed in an upper room of *Newgate*, in order to be near the Windmill on the Leads, which works them. From each of the outer Nostrils there goes a Trunk, which is 12 Inches in the Clear within-side; these Trunks pass along on each Side of the open Area over the gate-way, but at some Distance from the Sides of the Area, and then descend through all the Floors as far as a little below the Ceiling of the Ground-Rooms; and are covered with plate Iron within the Reach of the Prisoners. From these descending Trunks, lesser Trunks, six Inches square within, branch off near the Ceiling of every Room. These branching Trunks extend more or less into the several Wards, in such manner, that when the foul Air is drawn out of any Ward, the fresh Air enters on the opposite Side; and by that means drives all the foul Air out before it. And that many Wards may be ventilated at the same Time, there are sliding Shutters with long Handles, which slide up and down in Staples; in order not only to ventilate several Wards at a Time by partly closing the side Trunks; but also wholly to shut up the Trunks of some Wards, while others are ventilating. By this means, all the Wards may be ventilated in their Turns, in such Proportion as shall by Experience be found most convenient. The tubes from the several wards all unite in one great trunk, conveying all the putrid streams into the atmosphere through a vent made in the Leads of Newgate.[1]

During the construction of the ventilators there was a curious outbreak of gaol distemper. Seven of the eleven workmen employed by Mr Stibbs were suddenly taken ill, and when Pringle heard about it, he tried to discover what had become of them. He found Clayton Hand in St Thomas's Hospital, and William Thompson and Adam Chaddocks in St Bartholomew's; all three had typhus. He then visited the

---

[1] Hales, *Treatise on Ventilators*, 1758. See also his account in the *Gentleman's Magazine*, 1752, XXII, 179 and 182.

Plate XIII. Newgate in 1752, showing Dr Hales's windmill ventilator
(From a print in the British Museum)

homes of Thomas Wilmot and Michael Sewell, who both had the disease; the former had infected his wife, and the latter his wife and family. When he went in search of John Dobie, a lad of fifteen, he heard a curious story. The boy, his mother said, had been forced by the other journeymen working in Newgate "to go down into the great Trunk of the Ventilator, in order to bring up a Wig one of them had thrown into it". As the machine was working at the time, he had almost "died of the Stink before they could get him up", and had been taken ill of the gaol distemper that night.[1]

On February 11th, 1752, after the machine had been working about six weeks, Dr Hales, Dr Pringle, and Dr Knight, accompanied by Mr Stibbs, the carpenter, made another tour of inspection of Newgate. A few months later, Hales paid a second visit in order to render an official report on his work to the Aldermen of the City of London. The following day he wrote to Janssen, and enclosed a copy of his report:

Teddington,
June 10th, 1752.

Dear Sir,

Happening Yesterday to be in Town I find your's at my Lodging, but please to direct to me here, till the Princess returns to reside at *Leicester-House*.

It will be absolutely necessary to have a Man to furl and unfurl the sails of the mill, as Occasion shall require; and also to open and shut the sliding Shutters of the several Trunks daily, that all the foul Wards may be refreshed in their Turns. It is probable that about eight or ten Wards may be aired at

---

[1] Pringle communicated an account of this epidemic to the Royal Society, which Hales caused to be published in the *Gentleman's Magazine*, 1753, XXIII, 71.

a Time. I was at *London* Yesterday, purposely to view the Ventilators and Windmill at *Newgate*, in order to give a written Report to the Lord Mayor and Aldermen, one of which I sent to the Lord Mayor and two Sheriffs, and one I have here inclosed for your Perusal. It is great Pleasure to me, Dr. *Pringle* and Dr. *Knight*, two Physicians, to see the Ventilators worked by a Windmill, drawing, like large heavy Lungs, at the Rate of 7000 Tuns of foul Air *per* Hour, out of several Wards at the same time, which were thereby sensibly sweetened, to the great Comfort of the Prisoners, who informed us with Pleasure, that they thereby enjoyed much the better Health. I think it will be very requisite to have the Mill go as much as it can every Day: And even in Winter to change the Air daily to such a Degree, as it shall be found the Prisoners can bear without Inconvenience. For foul Air long confined, will putrefy in Winter, though not so soon as in Summer. There are some Rooms that have little Passage for Air to pass in or out, which ought more especially to be daily ventilated. If it shall be thought proper, to make it the Business of him who has the Care of the Mill, to clear the Wards frequently, by scraping and sweeping, it would contribute to the Healthiness of the Prison. I make no Doubt but the happy Event will show the Reasonableness of this Humane, laudable Example of the City of *London*; and it will be a great Pleasure to me, to have been in any Degree serviceable in doing them so acceptable a Service.

I am, Sir,

Your obliged, humble Servant,

STEPHEN HALES.

His report contains no other feature of particular interest beyond a recommendation that Mr Cowper, who had rashly undertaken to keep the windmill in repair and well greased for the next three years for the sum of fifty guineas, should be relieved of an unprofitable contract.

The yearly mortality from the gaol distemper in Newgate is said to have been considerably reduced, and had Dr Hales's ventilator been given a better trial, it might have done more towards reducing the death-rate from typhus by improving the general health of the inmates. A few years later, Pringle complained to Janssen that he often passed the prison to observe that the windmill was not working, although there was ample wind to turn the sails; this, he said, must continue unless one man was specially detailed to superintend it. Nevertheless, the windmill continued to function intermittently over the gateway for some time, while the view gradually gained ground that Newgate must be pulled down. In 1755, the "Common Council" declared the prison to be habitually over-crowded with "victims of public justice, under the complicated distress of poverty, nastiness, and disease"; the prisoners "had neither water, nor air, nor light, in sufficient quantities, and the buildings were old and ruinous, and incapable of any improvement or tolerable repairs". Janssen termed it "an abominable sink of beastliness and corruption". Then a virulent outbreak of the gaol distemper again occurred in one of the wards which was prevented from spreading, it is said, by Mr Ackerman, the Governor, who, at Dr Hales's direction, disinfected all the wards with the fumes of burning brimstone. Newgate was now regarded as hopeless, and when the matter came up before Parliament in 1767, an order was passed to pull the old prison down, and build a new one in its place.[1]

---

[1] The foundation stone of the new building was laid in 1770. It

Hales had supposed that an attempt to improve the sanitation of Newgate would have some consequence in the outside world. When the Duc de Noailles, the Commander of the French army at the battle of Dettingen, heard about it, he approached Dr Hales through M. Mazeas, his librarian, "of the Society of Navarre and F.R.S.", asking for an account of it that "so far as in him lay, he might promote having the same done in the French prisons and hospitals". This request, which was duly complied with, had an important sequel later.

Hales and Pringle attributed the "gaol distemper" to the direct physical consequences on the body of bad air, and not to infection with lice carrying the organisms of the disease. How convincing must have seemed the case of the lad John Dobie, who was forced to venture down the main shaft of the ventilator at Newgate! This attitude was natural at the time, as physical factors were regarded as being of paramount importance in the pathogenesis of disease, and of bacteriology and infective agents nothing was known. We now realise that no amount of ventilation, however perfect, could have abolished the gaol distemper in Newgate and the Savoy. The success of his methods cannot have been as great as he honestly supposed; but it is likely that the introduction of ventilation did actually do much to prevent the spread of the disease in hospitals and prisons, and improve the sanitation of ships and mines.

The particular method he practised was in many

---

was the new building, and not the old, which was burnt out in the Gordon riots of 1780.

cases unnecessarily cumbersome, and Sutton's simpler
device would have often served much better. But
it must be remembered that he had to deal with ships
as they were then constructed, and with prisons as
they were already built. Hospitals are now planned
with some regard to the principles of ventilation.
On land, proper construction is usually sufficient,
and on sea, the introduction of steam has simpli-
fied the whole problem. His ventilator was a step in
evolution only. In its crude form it did not survive
long, but the principle of mechanical propulsion of
air, which he advocated, still persists, and in difficult
cases, such as mines and tunnels, where ordinary
methods prove insufficient, artificial ventilation is
always practised, although by simpler and more
effective means.

CHAPTER XII

Old Age. Later Years at Teddington. The Royal Society of Arts. Applied Science. His International Reputation. A Royal Appointment.

HE was now an old man. When his ventilators were installed in Newgate, he was already seventy-five.[1] Since his wife died, he had lived alone, but in his old age his niece, Sarah Margaretta, daughter of his brother, Robert Hales, Clerk to the Privy Council, came to keep house for him at the Parsonage in Teddington. He had outlived most of his contemporaries. His brother, Sir Thomas Hales, was dead and his nephew had succeeded to the family title. His neighbour Pope was dead; Lord Egmont was dead too. He still paid frequent visits to town to attend the Georgia Board and meetings of the Royal Society, and his last entry in the register at Farringdon is dated May 20th, 1748, which shows that he was there when he was seventy-one. After that he never went again, and the parish was left to Mr Lipsett's care.

In these later years, in spite of all the other calls upon his time, the village church[2] at Teddington was

[1] At the age of eighty-one he was painted by Thomas Hudson. The portrait (Frontispiece) now hangs in the National Portrait Gallery in London. A mezzotint was engraved by McArdell. It was also engraved (line and stipple) by Hopwood (with a representation of his garden below showing some botanical experiments in progress) and published in Thornton's *Elementary Botanical Plates*.

[2] A new church has been built at Teddington, but the old church still stands very much as Hales left it.

to a large extent rebuilt (Plate XIV). The population of the parish had increased during the long period in which he had been minister, and the church was now too small to accommodate "the number of Parishioners that ought to resort thither to join in the Worship of Almighty God". Alterations were begun in 1743, when he had to remonstrate with some of them who arrived late at services, and they complained that they could not hear the bells:

Mem.—That it being found by long experience that the three Bells, which are inclosed in the Tower of this Church, can be heard at but a very little distance when the wind blows contrary, to the great inconvenience of the Parishioners, especially those who live the more distant; It was in the year 1748 agreed to inlarge three of the Tower Windows; and at the expense of private contributions of the principal inhabitants to place a lantern on the Tower, in the room of the Shingled Spire; in which to hang a loud Bell, to be heard at a much greater distance, not only for the benefit of the serious and well disposed, but also as a constant memento to the Careless, the Negligent and the Profane; who with the wicked in Job are but too apt to say, "Who is the Almighty that we should serve Him? And what profit should we have if we should pray unto him?" (Job xxi. 15). The inscription on the Bell is "Worship God. 1743." The weight of the Bell is 179 Pounds. The whole expense was £51. 07. 00.

Mem.—That this Parish Church of Teddington being too small to contain the number of Parishioners that ought to resort thither to join in the Worship of Almighty God, by consent of the Parishioners met in vestry, it was agreed to have it inlarged by building a new Ile on the North Side with the same dimensions as the South Ile. And having procured a licence from the Bishop of London for doing it dated 21st of August 1753 the said North Ile was built, the same year, with a Gallery and Pews. The whole Expense was—£382. 19. 00. Part of which Expense, was defrayed by the money which was raised by the Sale of the New Pews, at the Price of nine Shillings the Square Foot, which amounted to £130. 05. 00. There was care taken to have the Roof very strong and durable; not only by setting the Rafters near enough; but also by having laths of Heart of Oak, so thick that it was necessary to punch Holes through them for the six penny nails; And every Tile had either a Pin or a six penny nail. And the ridge Tiles were an inch thick, and two inches deeper than common Ridge Tiles, so that by reason of their weight and greater breadth, they cannot be blown off, as the Common Ridge Tiles are too apt to be.[1]

The expenses incurred in building the new aisle were only partly met by the sale of the new pews at nine shillings a square foot. As this source failed to meet the entire cost, he contributed £200 himself:

1753. Agreed and Ordered that the Rev. Mr. Cecil Wray Goodchild doe return ye thanks of this Vestry to ye Rev. Dr. Hales for his intended honourable donation of two hundred pounds towards the intended North Isle as an addition to this church.[2]

In the following year the churchyard was enlarged, and, as the heavy bell had proved too much for the wooden belfry in which it had been hung, further alterations to the church were necessary:

About the year 1734 I prevailed with Mr. Perkins then the Lord of the Manor to enlarge our church yard 15 feet on the North Side and 18 feet on the East Side in all 2190 square feet. In the year 1754 his son Mr. Tryon Perkins granted an enlargement of 65 feet on the East Side viz. 4550 Square Feet. The Sum of both the enlargements is 6740 feet. And at the

---

[1] Teddington Parish Registers.
[2] Vestry Minutes, Council Offices, Teddington.

West end of the Church Yard it was enlarged by taking 750 Square Feet out of the Road. And at the same time the Pales of the adjoining Fields being brought out into the road, 450 Square Feet of Land were thereby added to the fields.

In the year 1754 the old Timber Tower which stood on the west end of the church was pulled down; and a new Brick Tower built, on which was set the Lantern, which six years before had been erected on the Timber Tower, for the Sake of having a loud Sounding Bell.

This Lantern cost	£50.
The brick tower cost	£210. 10. 02.
Total for enlarging the church and the new tower	462. 10. 8½.
Besides £130. 0. 0 raised by sale of pews.[1]	

In the parish register is his inventory of the church plate, with the weight of each piece given with characteristic accuracy to a grain:

An account of the Communion Plate. 1742.

	pds.	oz.	pwts.	gr.
The Flagon weighs 1716	2	5	0	0
The Tankard given by Colonel Miggot 1721	3	1	17	21
The Cup 1728	1	11	12	21
The Salver 1716	1	1	1	14
Total	8	3	8	8

A curiously chased and Guilt Silver cup given by a Gentlewoman who desired to be unknown to Teddington. 1759. The weight. 30 ounces.

The visitor to the old church at Teddington will

---

[1] Teddington Parish Registers.

see a large square tombstone quaintly sandwiched
in between the churchyard wall and the side of the
tower. This is the tomb of Isabel, Dowager Countess
of Denbigh, the widow of the sixth Earl, who came to
live near Teddington in her declining years with
her sister, Lady Blandford, and is said to have cultivated a friendship with the aged Dr Hales for a
similarity of tastes and pursuits.[1] These two old
ladies were intimate with Lady Suffolk who, since
her second husband's death, had lived a retired
life at Twickenham, and both were the source of
great amusement to her nephew, Lord Buckinghamshire. While Ambassador at St Petersburg,
he often wrote about them to his aunt.[2] His wife
kept him well informed with local gossip, and
when Lady Denbigh bought a grave in Teddington
churchyard close to the tower of the church under
which Dr Stephen Hales was buried, he wrote to
Lady Suffolk:

St. Petersburg,
Nov. 18. 1763.

Lady Buckinghamshire informs me of the purchase which
Lady Denbigh, carrying her worldly views to the very last
stage of mortality, has lately made. Very different are the
objects of the two sisters; but each seems to be much directed
by sensuality: the one has fixed her attention upon a Mus-
covite (*Count Woronzow*), who is very much alive, the other
upon a departed philosopher. With regard to the first, the
extremity of christian charity may indeed suppose her
attachment to be merely to the mind of the young gentleman,
and that not the least intemperate idea is blended in their

[1] Rev. Daniel Lysons, *Environs of London*, III, 503, London,
1795.
[2] Lewis Melville, *Lady Suffolk and her Circle*, London, 1921.

sentimental connection: but far other must be the animal views of your neighbour, who with such premeditation provides that her corporeal parts may be squeezed close to the remains of Dr. Hales; for as to his soul, she is certainly much more likely to find it anywhere than in Teddington churchyard. I do not excel in fancy, yet will mention a thought that occurs to me, which you may recommend, if you approve it, to the good countess. She may purchase of the sexton of Teddington those venerable relics which she so greatly prizes, and probably at a much less expense than what she payed for the contiguous mould: these, with reverence due, must be consumed upon a funeral pile, and the hallowed ashes gathered in an urn, which should be deposited in her bed chamber, till time has made her clay a proper subject for the same operation; then let her dust be mixed with his, and incorporated with the soil of some pleasant mound at Strawberry Hill. The pious owner (*Horace Walpole*) will plant a myrtle upon the sacred spot, there long to flourish, the vegetating monument of their mutual affection....

Your most affectionate nephew,

BUCKINGHAMSHIRE.[1]

In spite of the many jokes that must have been made at her expense, Lady Denbigh persisted in her intention. "Bury me in wool", she wrote in her will in 1766, five years after Hales's death, "in a Grave in Teddington Churchyard which I have bought for that purpose and give twenty guineas to Mr. Cousens to bury me and ten pounds for him to give to the poor at Teddington".[2] At her death in the following year this wish was carried into effect. She was buried close up against the tower of Tedding-

---

[1] British Museum Add. MSS 222629, f. 96. (I have been unable to discover Lady Buckinghamshire's original letter.)
[2] The will is in Somerset House.

ton church, and on her tomb are inscribed the
following lines:

> With lively talents and an open heart
> Superior to the fallacies of Art,
> Grac'd by that innate dignity of soul
> Which neither threats nor bribes could once control,
> Second in high nobility to none,
> See Denbigh lies beneath this humble stone.
> A large benevolence each thought refined
> Like Hales, a generous friend of human kind,
> With love of philosophic learning fraught
> She wisely practised what his virtues taught.
> Then sealed his praises with her parting breath
> And graceful courts his last remains in death.[1]

At the age of seventy Dr Hales was chosen by the
President and Fellows of the Royal College of
Physicians to preach the annual Crounian Sermon in
the church of St Mary-le-Bow. He selected his
favourite subject, "The Wisdom and Goodness of
God in the formation of Man", and took as his text,
Job x, 11, 12—*Thou hast clothed me with skin and flesh,
and hast fenced me with bones and sinews. Thou hast
granted me life and favour, and hath not thy providence
preserved my spirit?*[2] Two years later he received a
visit from John Wesley. "I rode over to Teddington", wrote Wesley in his diary, "Dr. Hales sent
after dinner to desire our company and showed us
several experiments": and then this comment:

---

[1] These verses were probably written by Dr John Cousens, Hales's
successor at Teddington (1761–1791), who published a book of
poems entitled, *The Economy of Beauty* (1772).
[2] *The Wisdom and Goodness of God in the formation of Man: being
an anniversary sermon preached before the Royal College of Physicians:
according to the institution of Dr. Croun.* Published in 1751.

"How well do philosophy and religion agree in a man of sound understanding".[1]

In his old age he continued his experiments, but his mind had lost the vigour of youth, and some of the problems to which he now devoted himself seem a little trivial. When, however, scientific methods might help or protect the public, he was still ready to step in. In 1747, he investigated the preparation of "Tar Water":

> To ev'ry med'cine is assigned its part,
> Senna is purging, Saffron warms the heart;
> Blood sweetening juice to Sassafras is given,
> To Tar drink,—every virtue under Heaven.[2]

Three years before, Bishop Berkeley of Cloyne had advocated its medicinal value, and in his *Chain of Philosophical Reflections and Inquiries concerning Tar Water*, had set forth an account of the many cures he believed it to have achieved. So rapid was the growth of its popularity as a remedy, that in the same year a "Tar Water Warehouse" was established behind the Thatch'd House Tavern in St James' Street, and its value was testified to by Bishop Hildesley, Edward Young, Samuel Richardson, Laurence Sterne, and Henry Fielding. In his writings on the subject, Hales exhibited considerable caution. He separated out a number of different constituents of tar water according to their rates of solubility, and came to the conclusion that the discrepancies observed in the results of treatment depended on the haphazard way in which it was prepared. He concluded *An Account*

---

[1] Diary of John Wesley, July, 1753.
[2] *Gentleman's Magazine*, 1747, XVII, 81.

*of some Experiments and Observations on Tar Water:
Wherein is shown the Quantity of Tar that is therein,*[1]
by cautiously expressing the hope that "the Light
given by these Researches, might be of use in skilful
hands, for regulating and adapting the due Propor-
tions of the acid and oily Principles, to different Cases
and Constitutions". "This is the proper Province
of the Physicians", he said, "which I am no ways
qualified to meddle in".

His next published paper was entitled: *An Examination of the principal Purging Waters, especially
that of Jessop's Well.*[2] In 1751, new medicinal
waters had been discovered at Glastonbury, rising
from a spring near Chain Gate. A pump room was
opened in 1753, and Society, forsaking Bristol,
Bath, and other spas, flocked to Glastonbury. The
popularity of the new resort soon received a check.
Before the year was out, the *Public Advertiser* an-
nounced that the waters had been submitted to a
celebrated chemist for analysis, who was unable to
detect in them any constituent, beyond some excess
of iron, to which any therapeutic value could possibly
be attributed. A passage in Butler's *Memoirs of
Mark Hildesley* discloses the celebrated chemist's
name:

Hales analysed mineral waters; and, from the pure love of

[1] *An Account of some Experiments and Observations on Tar Water:
Wherein is shown the Quantity of Tar that is therein. Which was read
before the Royal Society. To which is added a Letter from Mr. Reid
to Dr. Hales, Concerning the Nature of Tar, and a Method of obtaining
it's Medical Virtues, free from it's hurtful oils: Whereby also the
Strength of each Dose may be the better ascertained.* First edition
published in 1747, and a second in the same year.
[2] Hales, *Phil. Trans. Roy. Soc.* 1750, XLVI, 446.

truth and humanity, detected the impositions of those, who would have recommended common water to the afflicted, as a specific for all disorders. This he particularly exemplified in the Glastonbury waters; and in those of a spring not far from Godstone, in Surrey, which were very much extolled in the newspapers of the time for their great virtues, but clearly shown by Dr. Hales to possess no other properties than those of common spring water.

His interest was now centred almost entirely on applied science, and in 1754 he played an active part in the foundation of the Royal Society of Arts. On March 2nd, a meeting was held at Rawthmell's Coffee House in Henrietta Street, Covent Garden, to discuss the formation of "a Society for the Encouragement of Arts, Manufactures, and Commerce". This was attended by Viscount Folkestone, Lord Romney, Henry Baker, F.R.S., Gustavus Brander, F.R.S. and a director of the Bank of England, James Short, an optician and astronomer, John Goodchild of Teddington, Nicholas Crisp, a watchmaker, and the Rev. Dr Stephen Hales. The meeting first considered a suggestion to offer two prizes, one for the discovery of cobalt, and the other for the successful growth of madder in the United Kingdom. They then resolved "to bestow premiums on a certain number of boys and girls under the age of sixteen, who shall produce the best piece of drawing, and show themselves most capable when properly examined, it being the opinion of all present that the Art of Drawing is absolutely necessary to many employments, trades, and manufactures". In the following month, Viscount Folkestone was elected first President, and James Theobald and Stephen Hales, Vice-Presidents. The

Society developed rapidly, and in ten years its annual income had risen to over three thousand pounds.[1]

He published further papers,[2] but in these later years it was his ventilators that engrossed him more than anything else. Without doubt he regarded them as the most important discovery that he had ever made; he had not thought of them until he was sixty-five, and now they became the child of his old age. In addition to the primary purpose for which they had been designed, he suggested that they might be applied to a number of other useful purposes, such as drying gun-powder at the powder mills, and, when experimenting with his windmill ventilators for the Admiralty on the "Sheerness" and "Prince", it occurred to him that similar ventilators might prove very useful in keeping corn, malt, and other cereals, stored in granaries, dry and free from insect pests.

I therefore wrote an account of this Design to Mons. *Du Hamel* at *Paris*, who is Inspector of all the Ports in *France*, and at the same time proposed to him to make use of the same Method to preserve great Quantities of Corn in Granaries, by the same Means.—He was so pleased with the Proposal, that he immediately fixed a Windmill, on a great Public Granary at *Paris*, which by working large Ventilators, blows Plenty of fresh Air upwards through the Corn, which so effectually preserves the Corn, that it is like to become a National Practice; of which he has sent me a

---

[1] Sir Henry Trueman Wood, *Journ. Roy. Soc. Arts*, LIX, 767.
[2] "A Proposal to check in some Degree the Progress of Fires", *Phil. Trans. Roy. Soc.* 1748, XLV, 277, and *Some Considerations on the Cause of Earthquakes*, 1750 (see also "On the Cause of Earthquakes", *Phil. Trans. Roy. Soc.* 1750, XLVI, 669). The latter paper was suggested by the earthquake which shook London in 1750. (See *The Letters of Sir Horace Walpole.*) This paper was translated into French: *Sur les Tremblements de la Terre.*

particular Account, with Drafts describing how it is done. I have written him Word, that where it can be had, a Water-Mill will do much better.[1]

More important was his suggestion that ventilators might be employed to keep mines free from asphyxiating and explosive "damps". Mr Emmerson, Rector of Middleton, near Barnard Castle in Yorkshire, put this idea into practice in one of Lord Darlington's lead mines situated in his parish:

In the Drifts, while digging to the Air-shafts, the Air is very noxious; so that a candle will burn only when held inclining sideways. But Mr. *Emmerson* having placed a small Ventilator, at the Entrance of an Adit, that was digging 50 Fathom to a new Air-shaft, where the Miners complained much of the Badness of the Air when they were got about 20 Fathoms, insomuch that they could work but few hours at a time; yet when the Air was renewed through a long Trunk, which reached from the Ventilators to the miners, they could then work all day with Pleasure. This cheap and easy Method of Relief is, therefore, not only of great Benefit to the Health and Lives of the Miners, but will also be very profitable to the Proprietors and Owners of the Mines. On communicating the Success of this Method of ventilating Drifts while digging, to Mr. *Percival* at *Bristol*, he put it in Practice in his Mines in *Cornwall*, and that with so good Effect, that it is like to become a general Practice in that County. Large ventilators are now making, by a model which I sent, to be fixed in a coal mine at *George Bowes*, Esq., Member of Parliament for the County of *Durham*.[2]

[1] Sir Stephen Theodore Janssen, Bart., *A Letter to the Lord Mayor, the Aldermen, the Recorder and the Gentlemen of the Committee appointed for the rebuilding of Newgate. With an appendix*, London, 1767. See also Hales, *Gentleman's Magazine*, 1745, XV, 354 and 360; 1746, XVI, 315, and his *Description of Ventilators*, 1743, and *Treatise on Ventilators*, 1758.

[2] Hales, *Treatise on Ventilators*, London, 1758.

One day, Mr Littlewood, a shipwright at Chatham, came to see him at Teddington. "He came purposely", he says, "to communicate to me an ingenious Contrivance of his, soon to sweeten stinking Water, by blowing a Shower of fresh Air thro' a Thin Pipe, full of small Holes, layed at the Bottom of the Water. By this means, he told me, he had sweetened the stinking Bilge Water in the Well of some Ships; and also a Butt of Stinking Water in an Hour, in the same manner as I blew Air up thro' Corn and Gunpowder". This visit led indirectly to the invention of an important technical method:

> I have lately happily, most unexpectedly, discovered an easy and effectual Method to distil great Quantities of Water with little Fuel; which I was led to by the following Incidents, *viz*. Mr. *Shipley*, Secretary of our Society, *for the Encouragement of Arts, Manufactures and Commerce*, brought me acquainted with Mr. *William Bailey*, of *Salisbury-Court*, the Author of many ingenious Contrivances; who shewed me, in a small Model of a Tin Vessel, a Method, by which he has happily increased the Force of the Engine to raise Water by Fire, *viz*. by lifting up some of the boiling Water, at every Stroke, by means of a conical Vessel with small Holes in it, full of Tow; whereby the Quantity of the ascending Stream or Wreak was considerably increased. This led me to think, that a greater Quantity of Liquor might also by this means be distilled; but on Trial I found the Increase to be but one twelfth Part, tho' considerable in the expanded Form of Steam. Hence I was led to try what would be the Effect of causing an incessant Shower of Air to ascend thro' the boiling Liquor in a Still; and this, to my Surprise, I found on Trial to be very considerable.

If a current of air was blown through boiling water, the quantity distilled was more than doubled. He

communicated this method to the Royal Society in
1756,[1] and also described it in a separate tract: *An
Account of a Useful Discovery to Distil Double the
Usual Quantity of Sea-Water, by Blowing Showers of
Air up through the Distilling Liquor.*
This invention was undoubtedly important; it is
a method now frequently practised in experimental
chemistry and extensively employed in a large number of manufacturing processes. Apart from this, the
work of these later years hardly bears comparison
with his other experiments; it was the work of an
old man, and lacked the vigour and imagination of
his early days. But his classical experiments on
animal and vegetable physiology were by this time
known throughout Europe, and his reputation as a
scientist was international. *Vegetable Statics* had
been translated into French by the naturalist, Buffon, in
1735, and *Haemastatics* by De Sauvages in 1744; both
were translated into German (1748), Dutch (1750),
and Italian (1756).[2] His book on ventilators quickly
appeared in a French edition. In 1755, Sir Hans
Sloane, the veteran physician, died. He was succeeded as President of the Royal Society by Martin
Folkes, but it was Dr Hales who was elected to take
his place as British representative, and one of the eight
Foreign Members of the Royal Academy of Sciences
in Paris.[3]

[1] Hales, *Phil. Trans. Roy. Soc.* 1756, XLIX, 312. See also *Gentleman's Magazine*, 1757, XXVII, 503.

[2] In England *Vegetable Statics* and *Haemastatics* went through
several editions under the joint title of *Statical Essays*, vols. I and II
respectively. A 4th edition of *Vegetable Statics* and a 3rd of *Haemastatics* were published in 1769.

[3] *Gentleman's Magazine*, 1753, XXIII. He was also elected a
member of the Academy of Sciences at Bologna.

The "good Doctor" was now a well known and generally respected public figure. Prince Frederick of Wales was in the habit of riding over from his residence at Kew to see the curious experiments in which he was almost constantly engaged. After the Prince's marriage, the Princess Augusta frequently accompanied him on these visits to Teddington, and she came to have a great regard for Dr Hales. When the Prince died in 1751, and his eldest son, George, now thirteen years of age, became the immediate heir to the throne, Dr Hales was appointed Clerk of the Closet to the Princess Dowager.[1] Later, there was talk of appointing either Dr Hales or Dr Johnson tutor to the young Prince of Wales. In a letter dated "Strawberry Hill, Dec. 11th, 1752", Horace Walpole wrote to Sir Horace Mann:

The preceptor is as much in suspense as the Governor. The Whigs clamour so much against Johnson, that they are regarded—at least for a time. Keene, Bishop of Chester, has been talked of. He is a man who will not prejudice his fortune by any ill placed scruples. Among other candidates, they talk of Dr. Hales, the old philosopher, a poor good primitive creature, whom I call the Santon Barsisa; do you remember the hermit in the Persian tales, who after living in the odour of sanctity for above ninety years, was tempted to be naught with the King's daughter, who had been sent to his cell for a cure? Santon Hales, but two years ago accepted the post of Clerk of the Closet to the Princess (of Wales), after literally leading the life of a studious anchorite till past seventy. If he does accept the preceptorship, I don't doubt but by the time the present clamours are appeased, the wick of his old life will be snuffed out, and they will put Johnson in his socket.[2]

[1] *Gentleman's Magazine*, 1751, XXI, 188.
[2] *Letters of Sir Horace Walpole.*

George II had quarrelled with his son, Prince Frederick, and Court society was split into two factions: those who sided with the King, and a Leicester House party. Dr Hales was in favour with the followers of the late Prince of Wales, but, after his death, the Princess was over-ruled on the question of a suitable tutor for the young Prince. Neither Hales nor Johnson was actually appointed to this post, although she succeeded in procuring the appointment of Dr Hales to be her own chaplain, and also chaplain to her son.[1] These appointments were not mere formalities. He was in constant attendance on the Princess; at Teddington he was close to her summer residence at Kew; when she left the country, he would follow her to London: "Happening Yesterday to be in Town, I find yours at my Lodging, but please to direct to me here (Teddington), till the Princess returns to reside at *Leicester-House.*" The lodging, which he kept for this purpose, was "Mrs. Batchelor's" in Duke's Court, Westminster. It was this added call upon his time, rather than any infirmity of age, that now led him to take the Rev. Cecil Wray Goodchild, son of Mr John Goodchild, the wax chandler at Teddington, as a curate to help him in his parish.

Hales visited Kew frequently to give the Princess practical advice in the management of her gardens:

The Princess will build a hot greenhouse, next spring at Kew, with a view to have exotics of the hottest climates, in which my pipes,[2] to convey incessantly pure

[1] *Gentleman's Magazine*, 1751, XXI, 428.
[2] See Hales, "Purification of Air in Greenhouses", *Gentleman's Magazine*, 1757, XXVII, 165.

warm air, will probably be very serviceable. And as there will be several partitions in the greenhouse, I have proposed to have the glass of one of the rooms covered with shutters in winter to keep the cold out, which will make a perpetual spring and summer, with an incessant succession of pure warm air. What a scene is here opened for improvements in greenhouse vegetation![1]

In addition, he did all he could to provide indoor amusements for the Princess, her ladies, and her children. When John Ellis,[2] to whom the above letter was addressed, sent a collection of different kinds of sea weeds to the Palace, Hales wrote:

Duke's Court.
Feb. 3. 1752.

Sir,
    I thank you for sending me the beautiful Sea-moss Landscapes, which I conveyed to the Princess in your name, for which she was very thankful and much pleased, as were the Prince of Wales, Prince Edward, and the Princesses. She desires the favour of you to procure her some varieties of Sea Mosses. I believe Harwich will be one good place, if you know any one there. The Princess will pay any expense it may occasion. I will write to Mr. Pullein at Dublin, to desire

---

[1] This building was the large hot-house, 110 feet long, which, according to the privately printed *Records of the Royal Botanic Gardens, Kew,* by the late John Smith, A.L.S., "was erected (in 1761) by Sir William Chambers, the Royal Architect, being at that time the largest hot-house in the country, and in after years known as the 'Great Stove'". It stood not far from the Temple of the Sun, but was pulled down in 1861. The old *Wistaria Sinensis,* now coiled on a circular frame, was once trained upon its brickwork.

[2] John Ellis (1710–1766), probably brother of Henry Ellis, Governor of Georgia, was a marine biologist who published a book on the natural history of corals, dedicated to the Princess, in which he established their animal nature. He also described a new genus of plants which he named Halesia in honour of Dr Stephen Hales (*Phil. Trans. Roy. Soc.* abridged edition, 1760, p. 508).

him to send me some, and to my nephews in Kent, to desire
them to get some on the Dover, Whitstable and Hearne shore.
I conclude, if I direct them to wash the mosses in fresh water,
and lay them thin to dry, it will suffice to preserve them well.
I shall write also to Dr. Whytt at Edinburgh, to get me some
moss. Thus you see a king's or princess's word runneth very
swift, as Solomon observes. The inclosed is for Mr. Pullein,
which I have sent open for you to add anything, or to inclose
a letter. Please also to direct it.

I am, etc.,

STEPHEN HALES.[1]

When Ellis, as requested, despatched a further con-
signment of sea weeds, Hales replied:

I carried the collection of Red Sea-mosses, which you
sent me, to the excellent Princess, for which she was thankful
and well pleased. And this day I showed her the method of
spreading them, which she soon practised herself, and liked
very much; my nephew, Sir T. Hales, having got me a few
mosses from Dover. But pray let me know how you glue
them on with gum arabic. I guess you wet the paper with it,
after the mosses are laid in their places dry. As the Princess
designs to put several ladies on this agreeable amusement, it
will be well to furnish her with plenty of these mosses. I have
desired Dr. Salter of Yarmouth to direct a parcel of them to you.[1]

A fortnight later he wrote: "I found the Sea-moss
picture, with the *Fucus*, at Kew, which happened very
well. I gave it to the Princess, and showed her the
manner, which you taught me, to expand the
Fucuses, which she was pleased with. This may
probably put her upon making some pictures".[1]

One day at Leicester House, for the children
perhaps, he constructed an ingenious machine to

[1] Sir James Edward Smith, *A Selection of the Correspondence
of Linnaeus and other Naturalists*, vol. II, London, 1821.

expedite the preparation of "syllabub". The King's chaplain gives some account of it:

The only articles, of that sort, that I know of, are: That Dr. Hales hath actually published; what has been some time talked of; a tube of tin, with a box of the same, at the lower end of it (like a box for a Great Seal) that is full of very small holes. This engine, with the help of a pair of bellows, blows up cream into syllabub, with great expedition. This complex machine has already procured the Dr. the blessing of the housekeeper of this palace, and of all such as she is, in the present generation (who know the time and labour required to whip this sort of geer): and will cause his memory to be had in remembrance, by all housekeepers, in the generations that are yet for to come.[1]

Through the influence of the Princess he might have gained preferment in the Church, for he was nominated a Canon of Windsor by the King. This appointment, however, he felt bound to refuse:

Declining to accept it, he immediately waited upon his Royal Patroness, and prevailed on her to waive the honour so kindly intended for him; preferring his retirement at Teddington to any other situation, as being more favourable for his philosophical pursuits. His circumstances, he said, were such as entirely satisfied his desires, and an ampler income would be only a greater incumbrance.[2]

Such conduct, the refusal of an appointment in the Church so much coveted by most divines, must have called forth much criticism and comment. Collinson, his contemporary, could not understand it:

[1] The Rev. Edmund Pyle, Chaplain to King George II, in a letter to his friend the Rev. Samuel Kerrich, November 1st, 1758. Albert Hartshorne, *Memoirs of a Royal Chaplain*, London, 1905.

[2] Rev. Weeden Butler, *Memoirs of Mark Hildesley, D.D., Bishop of Sodor and Man*, London, 1799.

That a man so devoted to philosophical studies and employments, and so conscientious in the discharge of his duty, should not desire any preferment which would reduce him to the dilemma either of neglecting his duty, or foregoing his amusement, is not strange; but that he should refuse an honourable and profitable appointment, for which no duty was to be done that would interrupt his habits of life, can scarcely be imputed to his temperance and humility without impeaching his benevolence; for if he had no wish of anything more for himself, a liberal mind would surely have been highly gratified by the distribution of so considerable a sum as a Canonry of *Windsor* would have put in his power, in the reward of industry, the alleviation of distress, and the support of helpless indigence.[1]

So, apart from his royal chaplaincy, the only other ecclesiastical appointment he ever held was that of Proctor for the clergy of the diocese of Winchester.[2] He remained Clerk of the Closet and Chaplain to the Princess, however, until his death, when he was succeeded by the Rev. Edward Young. In accepting the post, Young paid the following tribute to his predecessor:

I have taken some hours to consider of the very kind offer your Grace is so good to make me. I am old, and, I bless God, far from want; but as the honour is great and the duty small, and especially as your Grace seems desirous I should accept it, I do accept it with great gratitude for your remembrance of one who might easily and naturally be forgotten. The honour indeed is great, and in my sight greater still, as I succeed to so great and good a man. Would to God I could tread in all his other steps as well as this.

[1] Peter Collinson, *Gentleman's Magazine*, 1764, XXXIV, 273; *Annual Register*, 1764, vol. VII, Characters, 42.
[2] *Dictionary of National Biography*.

Mark Hildesley, Bishop of Sodor and Man, had for twenty years, as Vicar of Hitchin, been a friend and neighbour of Edward Young. Hales also was a friend of Hildesley, a friendship which dated from their early years, for Hildesley's father owed his presentation to the living of Murston, Kent, to Thomas Hales of Bekesbourne. It was therefore natural that Samuel Richardson, writing to the Bishop on September 24th, 1761, should comment on Hales's death, and Young's appointment to succeed him:

> I have the great pleasure of congratulating you on Dr. Young's promotion, as he is the immediate successor and heir of one of the best divines, and soundest Christians, and usefulest genius that ever graced a court, or a nation—Dr. Stephen Hales. This, I know, is a circumstance that your Lordship will hear with pleasure.[1]

To this the Bishop replied:

> Your paragraph relating to Dr. Young, did, as you rightly judged, give much pleasure; not so much as altogether on his account, as of the family he is likely to prove a blessing to, by supplying the great loss her Royal Highness and her offspring have suffered in the death of her late pious and worthy curator, in her domestic spiritual concerns. I wrote to good Dr. Hales, the 15th of October last, and, notwithstanding the usually uncertain passage of letters to and from hence, through the various hands they are committed to, by sea and land, I received an answer from him of two folio pages, close wrote, dated the 25th of the same month; at the conclusion of which, he says, "This is a long letter for one in his 84th year." As my father had the honour of dispensing the first rudiments of his education, the doctor thought proper to transfer some part of that regard he had for his tutor to the less worthy son.[1]

[1] J. Paul de Castro, *Edinburgh Review*, 1920, ccxxxi, 78.

Of the sincerity of his religion, and of the purity and rigid discipline of his life, there can be no question. To these his contemporaries testified. "He was remarkable for social virtue and sweetness of temper; his life was not only blameless, but exemplary to a high degree". Nothing, it is said, lessened "his natural and unwearied disposition for doing good and relieving distress". Nevertheless, he was not in advance of his generation in his sense of social justice. He had done much to mitigate the horrors of the slave trade, but he justified it as being in keeping with the teaching of Christianity. He had prevented the spread of disease and reduced the mortality in gaols, but he left the death sentence for theft, imprisonment for debt, and public executions, pass uncriticised. He was satisfied with the laws of the country, and only once, in connection with the gin trade, did he make any attempt to alter them. On the other hand, he had devoted more than half of his life to the discovery of methods that would promote the welfare of mankind, irrespective of class, race, or creed:

He began his enquiries into Natural knowledge very early in life, and continued them uniformly as his darling amusement, being engaged in experiments till within a few weeks of his death. His industry had likewise this farther excellence, that it was always pointed at the general good of his fellow creatures, agreeable to the unlimited benevolence of his heart; and being animated with the success of some of his more useful discoveries, his knowledge appeared to everybody near him to feed his mind with a nourishment which gave him, in decline of life, and even in its last stages, that vigour and serenity of understanding, and clearness of ideas, which so few possess, even in the flower of manhood; and which he used often to say, he valued as the most perfect of all human pleasures.[1]

"As I perceive you loved the good old man", wrote Gilbert White to a friend, "I do not know how I can amuse you better, than by sending you the following anecdotes respecting him, some of which may not have fallen within your observation. His attention to the insides of ladies' tea-kettles, to observe how far they were encrusted with stone that from thence he might judge of the salubrity of the water in their wells:—his advising water to be showered down suspicious wells from the nozzle of a garden watering-pot in order to discharge damps before men ventured to descend;—his directing air-holes to be left in the out-walls of ground rooms, to prevent the rotting of floors and joists;—his earnest dissuasive to young people, not to drink their tea scalding hot;—his advice to watermen at a ferry, how they might best preserve and keep sound the bottoms or floors of their boats;—his teaching the housewife to place an inverted tea-cup at the bottom of her pies and tarts to prevent the syrop from boiling over, and to preserve the juice;—are a few, among many, of those benevolent and useful pursuits on which his mind was constantly bent. Though a man of a Baronet's family, and of one of the best houses in Kent, yet was his humility so prevalent, that he did not disdain the lowest offices, provided they tended to the good of his fellow creatures. The last act of benevolence in which I saw him employed was at

[1] Rev. Weeden Butler, *Gentleman's Magazine*, 1799, LXIX, 9.

his rectory of Farringdon, the next parish to this, where I found him in the street with his paint-pot before him, and much busied in painting white with his own hands the tops of the foot-path posts, that his neighbours might not be injured by running against them in the dark ".[1]

[1] J. E. Harting, *Gilbert White's Natural History of Selborne*, 2nd ed. with letters not included in any previous edition of the work, London, 1876.

CHAPTER XIII

The Seven Years' War. The Last Experiment. Death and Burial.

THE peace of his declining years was marred by war. The opening phases of the seven years' struggle with France were disastrous on both sides of the Atlantic:

In America things went even worse than in Germany. The inactivity of the English generals was contrasted with the genius and activity of Montcalm. Already masters of Ohio by the defeat of Braddock, the French drove the English garrisons from the forts which commanded Lake Ontario and Lake Champlain, and their empire stretched without a break over the vast territory from Louisiana to the St. Lawrence. A despondency without parallel in our history took possession of our coolest statesmen, and even the impassive Chesterfield cried in despair, "We are no longer a nation".[1]

In prisons and hospitals the deaths from sickness far exceeded the numbers killed in battle. Foreseeing this evil day, and knowing the inevitable consequences of war, Hales had already corresponded with the French, Du Hamel, the Duc de Noailles, and M. Mazeas, on prison and hospital sanitation. With some hope of success he now laboured unceasingly throughout these depressing years to get Louis XV to order the installation of ventilators into the prisons where British soldiers were confined. In these endeavours he was at last successful. His ventilators were installed in some at least of the French prisons with, it is said, considerable reduction in the

[1] J. R. Green, *A Short History of the English People*, London, 1903.

death-rate among the British prisoners. On this occasion he was heard to say that he hoped no one would inform against him for corresponding with the enemy!

Pendant une des guerres contre la France, Hales, après des longues sollicitations, obtint, dit-on, de Louis XV, l'ordre de faire pratiquer des ventilateurs dans les dépôts où l'on retenait les prisonniers anglais. Des rapports, qu'il disait, en riant, à cette occasion, qu'il espérait que personne ne se porterait son accusateur comme correspondant avec l'ennemi.[1]

In 1756, the year in which the war began, he performed his last experiment:

June 7, the Wind S.W. cloudy, the Thermometer at 58 Degrees, 13 live Gudgeons were put into two Gallons of fresh Pond-water in a Pail A; and a like Number into Pail B, at 10 Minutes before 7 in the Morning. At 50 Minutes past 7, two in B began to be sick; at 8, half of them came up for Air, and showed Uneasiness; at 15 Minutes past 8 two are dead; at 30 Minutes past 8, eight more turned Belly upwards; at 8 Minutes past 9, five are dead in B, and five more sick; at 30 Minutes past 9, seven are dead, and four sick, two well; and 30 Minutes past 10, eight are dead; at 11 two only alive, and also well, though they showed some Uneasiness by their raising their Mouth to the Surface, which they continued to do till nine, when they were taken out of the Water. The water in Pail A was ventilated from 10 Minutes before 7, to 6 in the Evening, by blowing every quarter of an Hour Showers of fresh Air up thro' it, with 25 Strokes of the Bellows; by which means the Fish continued all well, laying quiet at the Bottom: at six we ceased to ventilate; for an Hour and a half after which, there were no Signs of Sickness; after two Hours two of them showed Signs of Uneasiness; and at nine most of the Fishes turned Belly upwards, and lay at the Bottom dead or dying. By comparing this Event

[1] Michaud, *Biographie Universelle.*

with that at eight in the Morning, we see that there is more Air in this Ventilated water than in the Pond-water, as is probable by the Gudgeons living longer in it, without Ventilation, than in the Pond-water.

Tho' from these Experiments it is manifest, that Fish die for want of constant Supplies of fresh Air in the Water, yet when taken out of the Water very lively, they soon die, notwithstanding the Surfaces of their Gills are then exposed to the immediate Contact of the Air; which shows that either the Air does not enter from the Gills to the Blood, from the open Air, as it does from the Water; or that the Circulation of the Blood is stopped by exchanging their proper Element, Water, for Air; as the Circulation of the Blood of Land Animals is soon stopped by immersing from Air into Water. Hence we see the Benefit of frequently replenishing the Water with fresh Air, which we find is necessary not only to preserve the Life of Land Animals, but also of Fish; as also the Use of their Gills, to spread in thin Sheets fresh Supplies of Water, that they may the better come at the Air in the Water; for which Purpose both Sides of their Gills are furrowed with many fine Furrows, not only thereby to enlarge their Surfaces, but also more minutely to divide the Water, whereby to come at the Air in it.[1]

So at the age of seventy-nine he returned from applied science to physiology again, and after forty years completed his long series of experiments on respiration. "We have good reason", he writes, "to be diligent in making farther and farther researches; for tho' we can never hope to come to the bottom and first principles of things, yet in so inexhaustible a subject, where every smallest part of this wonderful fabrick is wrought in the most curious and beautiful

[1] Hales, *An Account of a Useful Discovery to Distill double the usual Quantity of Sea-Water, etc.* 2nd ed. with Appendix, London, 1756.

manner, we need not doubt of having our inquiries rewarded with some further pleasing discovery; but if this should not be the reward of our diligence, we are however sure of entertaining our minds after the most agreeable manner, by seeing in everything, with surprising delight, such plain signatures of the wonderful hand of the divine Architect, as must necessarily dispose and carry our thoughts to an act of adoration, the best and noblest employment and entertainment of the mind".[1]

He had advanced biological science by his work on the circulation of the blood, the flow of sap, the chemistry of respiration, and the growth of bone. He had played an active part in procuring the Gin Act of 1736, and had been largely responsible for the ultimate success of the colony of Georgia. By his work on ventilation he had established one of the first principles of preventive medicine. He had ministered faithfully to the parish of Teddington for over fifty years, and in the last scene of his active life we see him triumphant, reducing the mortality among British soldiers in French prisons! He had served science and humanity, his King and his Country:

> Poets heap Virtues, Painters Gems at will,
> And shew their zeal, and hide their want of skill.
> 'Tis well—but, artists! who can paint or write,
> To draw the Naked is your true delight.
> That Robe of Quality so struts and swells,
> None see what Parts of Nature it conceals:
> Th'exactest traits of Body or of Mind,
> We owe to models of an humble kind.

[1] Hales, *Vegetable Statics*, 4th ed. p. 319.

> If Queensbury to strip there's no compelling,
> 'Tis from a Handmaid we must take a Helen.
> From Peer or Bishop 'tis no easy thing
> To draw the Man who loves his God, or King:
> Alas! I copy (or my draught would fail)
> From honest Mah'met,[1] or plain Parson Hale.[2]

At the age of eighty he settled down to his fireside and his books. Georgia was a flourishing colony, and the Trustees had surrendered their powers to the Crown. The Royal Society of Arts had been founded. The windmill was working over Newgate, and his ventilators had been installed in the Savoy; his invention had been adopted in a score of public institutions in his own country, and also in hospitals in France. Teddington church had been enlarged, and when, in 1760, Mr Richard Lipsett died, Hales appointed Gilbert White, the naturalist, to be curate-in-charge at Farringdon. There was only one task to which he had set his hand that still remained unfinished. In 1747, the Gin Act had been repealed. In 1751, largely due to his own labours and those of Fielding and Hogarth, a third Act had been passed, but its provisions were far from being strict enough to satisfy him. On Sept. 17th, 1757, he wrote to the Rev. William Henry:

It behoves all who have the real Interest of Mankind at Heart to persevere in their Endeavours to rouse them to a just Abhorrence of spirituous Liquors, the most Destructive *Hydra*; and if many more could prevail on themselves

---

[1] "Mah'met, servant to the late King (*George II*)—said to be the son of a Turkish Baffa, whom he took at the siege of Buda, and constantly kept about his person" (Wharton).

[2] Pope, *Moral Essays*, Epistle II, "To a Lady". J. Wharton, *The Works of Alexander Pope*, vol. III, 223, London, 1797.

Plate XIV. Teddington parish church in the XVIIIth century

(From a print in Teddington church)

to be as much in earnest as you are, then much might be done. Tho' I thank God, I have been blessed with Success in promoting several Things which will be of lasting Benefit to Mankind, yet nothing I have done, has given me near the Satisfaction, that the public Testimony, which I have for 26 Years past borne against these infernal Spirits ten different Times, has given me: And as I intend soon to begin to print my second Volume on Ventilators, I have in the strongest Terms expostulated on the Subject; Hoping, that as Ventilators are coming into more and more general Use, so my Book on the Subject will probably be proportionately dispersed about the World, In which I have given my last dying Testimony against them, I being this Day, I bless God, *eighty-years* old.[1]

In the following year his last book was published:

A TREATISE ON VENTILATORS. Wherein An Account is given of the Happy Effects of the several Trials that have been made of them, in different Ways and for different Purposes: Which has occasioned their being received with general Approbation and Applause, on account of their Utility for the great Benefit of Mankind. As also of what farther Hints and Improvements in several other useful Ways, have occurred since the Publication of the former *Treatise.*

He at once sent a copy to Mark Hildesley in the Isle of Man, and, in reply to the Bishop's acknowledgment, wrote to him again on May 16th, 1758:

My good Lord,

I am much obliged to you for your kind letter of April 11th, and for the favourable reception of my book: in

[1] Rev. William Henry, *A New-Years-Gift to Dram-Drinkers,* London, 1762.

which I hope there are many things of so great benefit to mankind, as will hereafter have a considerable influence on the affairs of the world, for the better; especially in relation to those mighty destroyers, *drams*; and that, not only of the lives, but also of the morals, of mankind. With a view to which, I have sent sixteen copies of this book, with its first part, to several nations of Europe; especially the more Northern as far as Petersburg; and am just going to reprint the first part, so much abbreviated, as to bind up well with the second part in one six-shilling book; principally with a view to send two or three hundred of them, at the first opportunities, to all our colonies in America, from the Southern to the most Northern....As to your observation, "that I have lived to eighty without drams", it puts me in mind of an observation of the late bishop Berkeley; viz., "That there was in every district a tough old dramist, who was the *devil's decoy* to draw others in". Upon the whole, the open public testimony that I have, for near thirty years past, borne against *Drams*, in eleven different books, or newspapers, has been matter of greater satisfaction to me, than if I were assured that the means which I have proposed, to avoid noxious *Air*, should occasion the prolonging the health and lives of an hundred millions of persons....

> I am, my Lord, with the greatest esteem,
>
> your Lordship's obliged humble servant,
>
> STEPHEN HALES.[1]

In a letter dated November 21st, 1759, to Ellis, the marine biologist, he tells how he had sent a thousand copies of his book "to all our colonies in America, purposely to rouse the nations, not to poison themselves with strong drams, but

---

[1] Rev. Weeden Butler, *Memoirs of Mark Hildesley, D.D., Bishop of Sodor and Man*, London, 1799. The original letter is to be found among the MSS at the British Museum.

to make them weak, to the standard of Nature's cordial wine". "And I have sent", he said, "a parcel of these books to Governor Ellis, to whom pay my best respects. I fear the climate will not agree with him".

On December 23rd he wrote to his old friend, William Stukeley:

Dear Sir,

I write this at the desire of George Bedle of this parish, and a freeman of the City of London on the behalf of his son Thomas, eight years old; whom he is desirous to get into Christ's Hospital by your assistance.

Mrs. Adamson tells me that you are so good as to endeavour the continuance of the allowance of £20 from the Hospitals to the distressed Mrs. St. Armand, who has met with cruel usage for many years from the family she married into.

Thank God, Ventilators are coming into esteem, for the salutary effects of them in our Fleets, where, by their means, whole squadrons enjoy perfect good health. While I am writing of this it occurs to me it would be of great benefit to the youth of Christ's Hospital to have Air Trunks pass through the ceiling of the Rooms, where the children are long. The Trunks would convey off the foul Air that arises from them, and that without the inconvenience of any cold Air descending through them. They are now much used in many places, as over the House of Commons, the Court of King's Bench, Garrick's Play House and in many Hospitals and Gaols, and in all the Gaols for the French Prisoners, who find great benefit by them, as the Commissioners of the sick and wounded do assure me. It is of great consequence towards Youths being bred up hale and hardy, to breathe fresh Air. We see how hale the children of cottagers look, who usually set with the door of the house open.

The expence of these Trunks is very little. As Mr. Yeoman who lives in little Peter Street Westminster has put up most of those above mentioned, it may be well to have his Advice where and how to fix them, but he will not charge to be employed in putting them up.

I am, Sir,

Your obliged Humble Servant,

STEPHEN HALES.[1]

In 1758, his niece Sarah Margaretta, who had been keeping house for him, became engaged to the Rev. William Johnson, Rector of the parishes of Nettlestead and Teston in Kent; according to the register he had been a frequent visitor at Teddington for some years. Hales married them himself in the church at Teddington.[2] A few months later, he wrote out with his own hand his last will and testament:

IN THE NAME OF GOD AMEN, I Stephen Hales of the Parish of Teddington Middlesex, an unworthy member of Jesus Christ, in the Church of England, being through the abundant Mercy of God in Health of Body, and enjoying that measure of Understanding and Memory, with which it has pleased God to bless me, do hereby constitute and appoint this my last Will and Testament, and desire it may be received as such, thereby revoking and annulling all former wills by me made, First I humbly commend my soul to God my Maker, whensoever it shall please him to call for it, beseeching his most gracious acceptance of it through the all sufficient merits and mediation of my compassionate Redeemer, who I trust will not reject me when I come to him for mercy, humbly beseeching God to prepare me for the time of my dissolution, and then to take me to himself, into that eternal rest and peace and felicity which he has prepared for all that love and fear his holy name. As for my Body, I desire it may be decently interred, without pomp or state,

[1] Bodleian Library, Oxford.
[2] *Gentleman's Magazine*, 1758, XXVIII, 196.

or giving gold rings, and without a leaden coffin, at the Discretion of my Executor and Executrix hereafter named, under the new Tower of Teddington Church, in comfortable Hopes of a happy Resurrection at the last Day from the Dishonours of the Grave into Glory. As for my worldly Goods, with which it has pleased God to bless me, and make me his Steward of, I dispose of them in the following manner, first desiring all my Debts may be paid, viz. As to my copyhold dwelling House at Teddington, with the out houses, yard, and garden, adjoining, I do hereby devise, will and bequeathe the same to my dear niece, Sarah Margaretta, the wife of the Rev. Mr. William Johnson, Minister of Teston near Maidstone in Kent, and her Heirs for ever. All my bound Books at Teddington, which my Executor hereafter named, shall think proper to be sent to Georgia, I give and bequeathe for a public parochial Library to such Town or Parish in Georgia in America, the Governor shall think fit to appoint. The carriage of them thither to be at the expense of my Executor and Executrix hereafter named. I give ten pounds to be expended by my successor at Farringdon in Hampshire in horn Books, Primers, Psalters, and New Testaments, for the use of the poor children of that Parish. Item I give and bequeathe, to the incorporated society for propagating the Gospel in foreign Parts, the sum of one hundred Pounds to be by them layed out, as occasion shall offer, in purchasing Books on the pastoral duty, to be from Time to Time given to the several successions of Ministers and Missionaries in our plantation in America. Item I give to Elizabeth Hooper a work woman, the Daughter of the late widow Susannah Hooper, who was my servant, the sum of forty Pounds. Item I give to Mary Hole a work woman, who lives in the Great Armoury near Deans Yard Westminster, the Sum of twenty Pounds. Item I give to Mary the Widow of John Jones late a Hosier at High Wickham, she now living next to the Parish Head in Swallow Street Piccadilly, the sum of one hundred Pounds, and in case of her death I give the said sum of one hundred Pounds to her only child and daughter Catherine

Jones. Item to each of my two servants, who shall be such at the Time of my death, I give the Sum of fifteen Pounds. All the rest and residue of my Money, Goods, or Chattels, I give and bequeathe to my said dear niece Sarah Margaretta, the Wife of the said William Johnson hereby constituting her and her husband, executor and executrix of this my last Will and Testament. In witness whereof I have hereunto set my Hand and Seal this thirtieth day of October, in the year of our lord One Thousand Seven Hundred and fifty nine, Stephen Hales.

Signed, sealed, published and delivered, by the said Testator for and as his last will and Testament, the day of the date hereof, in the Presence of us who have hereunto subscribed our names as Witnesses, in the said Testator's Presence, and at his Desire.

John Gunner
Richard Fry
John Fielder.[1]

In April, 1760, his curate, Goodchild, for some reason went away. This, as several entries in the parish register show, brought his niece, Sarah Margaretta, with her husband, the Rev. William Johnson,[2] back to live with him in the Parsonage at Teddington. It was in this house that their child, his great-niece, was born and died:

July 14. 1760. Anne Johnson was buried, aged 6 weeks.

Hales lived just long enough to see the young George III ascend the throne of England. He died before the Peace of Paris, but in his last years he witnessed the restoration of his country's prestige under

---

[1] The original will is in Somerset House, London.

[2] Johnson apparently remained at Teddington until Hales's successor, Dr John Cousens, came in May, 1761. Johnson himself died in the autumn of the same year. His widow subsequently married a clergyman called Negus.

the administrative genius of the elder Pitt. The year 1759 was one of British triumphs the world over: September brought the news of Minden, and a victory off Lagos; November, the tidings of the capture of Quebec, and the French defeat at Quiberon. The British triumphs meant much, but to him they were not everything. Humanity still suffered, and so he laboured on, confident in the knowledge that he had done "many things to promote the welfare of mankind", certain that he could do but little more. Less than three weeks before his death, in a letter written to Dr Swithin Adee of Oxford, he spoke of publishing a new edition of his book on ventilators, mentioned some experiments he had recently made on the different degrees of saltness of sea water brought to him from different latitudes, and of a quaint idea, which he had recently communicated in a paper to the Royal Society, on the benefit to be derived from wetting the body with salt water. "If the trial were made", he said, "in twenty tents to wet the soldiers' bodies with salt water in very cold weather, it would probably give some light unto the matter";—and then a little wearily—"but I know, by very much experience, that the *vis inertiae*, that strong power of indolence in mankind, is too great, to attempt useful discoveries by proper trials; and without them useful discoveries cannot be made".[1]

[1] "Experience, however, from extreme trial, has fortunately come in aid, upon this very interesting subject; and has fully confirmed, by mere accident and sharp necessity, the truth of our good doctor's hypothesis. Amidst the peculiar difficulties and distress, which Captain William Bligh and his eighteen officers and men suffered, in April, May and June, 1789, during their escape from his mutinous crew of the *Bounty*, in a small open boat, the wringing of their

His last entry in the parish register at Teddington, now in a feeble hand, is dated November 4th, 1760. On the 25th he wrote to the Rev. Dr Bradley at the Observatory in Greenwich Park:

> I thank God, Ventilators in Ships, and Air Trunks in Gaols and Hospitals etc., prove Salutary beyond my most sanguine expectations: And tho' these things are of greater Benefit to Navigation than the much desired Discovery of the Longitude, yet I desire no other Reward, than that greatest of all Rewards, which I enjoy, viz: the pleasure of having done something for the benefit of Mankind.[1]

A letter, written only a few days before his death to the Rev. William Henry, shows that his mental vigour was still unchanged, and his boundless faith unshaken:

> I am sorry that there is a Drawback, and Bounty to encourage the Exportation of these worse than infernal Spirits, in order to poison other Nations as dear to God as ourselves. Could we export these mighty Destroyers to the Inhabitants of the Moon, or of Saturn's Satellites, I

clothes through the sea water, after being drenched with continual rains, and then putting them on wet, was found not only a great refreshment, but the best preservative also against the mortal effect of cold and rheumatism. This is strikingly evinced in captain Bligh's most pathetic narrative, which he thus concludes: 'With respect to the preservation of our health, during a course of sixteen days of heavy and almost continual rain, I would recommend to everyone, in a similar situation, the method we practised; which is, to dip their clothes in the salt-water, and wring them out, as often as they become filled with rain. It was the only resource we had, and I believe was of the greatest service to us; for it felt more like a change of dry clothes than could well be imagined. We had occasion to do this so often, that at length all our clothes were wrung to pieces; for, except the few days we passed on the coast of Holland, we were continually wet, either with rain or sea'". Rev. Weeden Butler, *Memoirs of Mark Hildesley, D.D., Bishop of Sodor and Man*, London, 1799.

[1] Bodleian Library, Oxford, MS Bradley, 45.

should be zealously and utterly against it, as being an effectual Means to debase and destroy God's Creatures there. Were there a Confederacy to consult about establishing the Kingdom of *Satan*, and destroying all the wise and gracious Designs of Christianity; could they, or even the infernal *Divan*, devise a more effectual or expeditious Way to do it, than by holding forth within the Reach of all those intoxicating Spirits, which so greatly debase human Nature, and absolutely drive out all Sense of Religion?[1]

"With a vigour and alacrity which toil could not damp, nor age diminish, he delighted to promote the honour of his God, by advancing the best welfare of mankind. In this employment, blessed with serenity of temper, he calmly waited for death, as an acquaintance long familiarised to his mind".[2]

Hales died at Teddington on January 4th, 1761, after a short illness, at the age of eighty-four.

* * * * *

On a winter's day his body was carried from the house where he had lived so long, and laid to rest under the tower of Teddington church as he had directed in his will. His nephew by marriage conducted the service, and his "dear niece", Sarah Margaretta, was the chief mourner at the grave. On the stones of the floor of the church at Teddington they had this inscription carved:

Here is interred the body of Stephen Hales D.D., Clerk of the Closet to the Princess of Wales, who was Minister of this

---

[1] Rev. William Henry, *A New-Years-Gift to Dram-Drinkers*, London, 1762.
[2] Rev. Weeden Butler, *Memoirs of Mark Hildesley, D.D., Bishop of Sodor and Man*, London, 1799.

Parish 51 years. He died the 4th of January 1761 in the 84th year of his age.[1]

A monument,[2] erected to his memory by the Princess Augusta, stands in Westminster Abbey, but his body lies buried, according to his own wish, under the tower that he built for the church which he had loved so well.

* * * * *

After nearly two hundred years, let us adapt John Wesley's words: how well did science and religion agree in this man of sound understanding.

THE END

---

[1] This inscription, now almost obliterated, was copied on to a brass plate on the side wall of the tower by certain botanists of the Royal Society in 1911.

[2] It was executed by Wilton, and stands next to Handel's monument. Below is the following inscription:

Stephano Hales, S.T.P. Augusta, Georgii Tertii regis optimi mater, P. Quae, viventem, ut sibi in sacris ministraret elegit, mortuum, Prid. Non. Jan. MDCCLXI, octogesimum quartum agentem annum, hoc marmore ornavit.

INDEX

INDEX

Ackworth, Sir Jacob, 159
Act, the Gin, of 1736, 119, 122
Adee, Dr Swithin, letter from Hales to, 243
Admiralty, experiments on Hales's ventilator, 166, 167
Agriculture, Hales's interest in, 55
Air, absorbed by animals, 103; absorbed by plants, 96; fixed by plants, 99; free and fixed, 98
Animal physiology, 22–42, 87, 90–107
Animal respiration, 101
Animals, air absorbed by, 103; cruelty to, 55, 56, 57
Apparatus, rebreathing, 106, 107
Aristotle, 94
Arran, Earl of, Chancellor of Oxford University, recommends Hales for the degree of Doctor of Divinity, 117
Arterial resistance, 33
Arteries, pressure in the, 24
Artery, pressure in pulmonary, 37
Arts, Royal Society of, 217
Astronomy, lectures on, by Roger Cotes, 19
Atheism and the Church, 77

Bacon, Francis, 58, 116
Bacon, Nicholas, 10
Beck, Thomas, 8, 9
Bekesbourne branch of family of Hales, 1, 2
Bene't College, description of, in 1696, 6; Dr John Spencer, Master of, 4; Dr Thomas Greene, Master of, 4, 20; Dr William Stanley, Master of, 4, 7; Master and Fellows in 1702, 8, 9, 10; some former Fellows of, 5; Stephen Hales: admitted a Fellow of, 11, admitted a Pensioner of (1696), 4, elected a Fellow of, 8, resigns his Fellowship of, 52
Bentley, Richard, Master of Trinity College, 12, 13, 77; "Boyle's Lectures," 78

Bequests by Stephen Hales, 241, 242
Berkeley, Bishop, 80; advocates tar water, 215
"B.L. of Twickenham," *An Accurate Description of Newgate*, 195, 197, 198
Bleeding vine, the, 71
Blood, circulation of the, 23; in the lungs, velocity of, 39
Blood pressure, 24 *sqq.*
Bond, Dr, Regius Professor of Physic (1857–82), 5 n. 4
Bones, growth of, 87
Borelli, 23; his theory, 86
Boyle, Hon. Robert, 77, 90
"Boyle's Lectures," 7, 78
Bradley, Rev. Dr, letter from Hales to, 244
Bray's Legacy, Dr, 131, 140; Hales trustee of, 118, 140
Bridgeman, Sir Francis, 44
Bridgeman, Sir John, presents living of Teddington to Hales, 43
Bridgeman, Sir Orlando, 43, 44
Briggs, William, *Ophthalmographia*, 5
Buckinghamshire, Lord, letter to Lady Suffolk, 212
Bugden, Hales ordained Deacon at, 11
Bull, Michael, 10, 11
Butler, Rev. Weeden, on character of Hales, 88, 89, 230, 245

Cage, William, offers living of Farringdon to Hales, 52
Calculations on the output of the heart, 30
Calculus, work on the, 112
Cambridge, education at, in 1704, 7
Canon of Windsor, Hales nominated, but declines, 226, 227
Capillarity, 70, 74; experiments on, 66
Capillary blood pressure, 40
Carbon dioxide, 106

Fawcett, Thomas (Stukeley's tutor),
 10, 17, 19
Fellowship of Bene't College,
 Hales resigns his, 52
Flow of sap, 63; cause of the, 70;
 reversibility of the, 69
Frederica, settlement at, 173,
 180
Fulham, Hales ordained Priest at,
 12
Function of leaves, 100

Galileo, 90
Gaol distemper, 190, 206
Garden, Dr, account of slave trade,
 161
George II, *Haemastatics* dedicated
 to, 116
Georgia, colony of, 235; attacks
 against Trustees of, 185; Board
 of Trustees, 135; Captain Henry
 Ellis appointed Governor of,
 188; claimed by Spain, 180, 181;
 condition of people in, 176;
 debate in the Commons on, 184;
 differences of the Trustees, 142
 sqq.; discontent in, 177, 178;
 emigrants sail for, 136; Established Church in, 140; financial
 difficulties, 179; foundation of
 (1732), 132, 133; Hales a Trustee
 of, 118; Indians from, 170;
 John Wesley before Trustees of,
 175, 176; objects of the Trustees,
 138 *sqq.*; progress of, 170 *sqq.*;
 slave law of, repealed, 187; slaves
 prohibited in, 172; the Wesleys
 go to, 173; Trustees' anniversary
 meeting, 137; Trustees of, surrender their Charter to the
 Crown, 188; Walpole's attitude
 towards, 180 *sqq.*; work of the
 Common Council, 139
Gin, introduction of, 119
Gin Act of 1736, 119, 122, 235
Gin drinking, Hales writes against,
 120
Gin Riots, the, 123
Glastonbury, medicinal waters at,
 216
Goodchild, Rev. Cecil Wray, curate
 at Teddington, 223

Greene, Dr Thomas, Master of
 Bene't College, 4
Grew, Nehemiah, 59, 63, 94, 95
Growth, of bones, 87; of plants, 85

"Haemastatical Papers" read to
 the Royal Society, 115
Haemastatics, dedicated to George
 II, 116; published, 116; trans-
 lated, 221; written, 113
Hales and Mayow, experiments
 by, 104 *sqq.*
Hales, Anne, 114
Hales, Catherine, 114
Hales, Sir Christopher, Attorney-
 General (1529), Vice-Chancel-
 lor and Master of the Rolls, 1
Hales, Sir Edward, Lieutenant
 of the Tower, a Lord of the
 Admiralty and a Privy Coun-
 cillor, 2 n.
Hales, Edward, of Tenterden, 1
Hales, Elizabeth, 114
Hales, family of, 1–3; Bekes-
 bourne branch of, 1, 2; Wood-
 church branch of, 1, 2
Hales, Sir John, Baron of the
 Exchequer (1522–39), 1
Hales, John, of Tenterden, 1
Hales, Mary, Stephen Hales's
 sister, 114; his wife, 88
Hales, Sir Nicholas, 1
Hales, Sir Robert, of Bekesbourne,
 guardian of Stephen Hales, 3
Hales, Sir Robert de, Prior of the
 Hospital of St John of Jerusalem
 and Admiral of the Fleet, 1
Hales, Robert, 114, 208
Hales, Sarah Margaretta, 208, 245;
 marries Rev. William Johnson,
 240
Hales, Stephen, 2; addresses him-
 self to Parliament, 120, 121;
 admitted a Fellow of Bene't
 College, 11; admitted a Pen-
 sioner of Bene't College, 4;
 anecdotes of, 230, 231; appointed
 Chaplain to the Princess of
 Wales, 223; appointed Clerk of
 the Closet to the Princess of
 Wales, 223; appointed "Perpetual Curate" of Teddington,

Parish Register, Farringdon, 54; Teddington, 46, 47, extracts from, 209 *sqq.*, quaint entries in, 47

Parliament, *see* Commons, House of

Pasteur, 84

Penance, public, at Teddington, 49; at Farringdon, 54

Percival, Viscount, 118; *see also* Egmont, Lord

Perfusion experiment, a, 34

Peripheral circulation, 32

"Perspiration rate," 61

Pews, sale of, at Teddington church, 46

Philosophical Experiments published by Hales, 146

Phlogiston theory, the, 92

Physiological Essays, by Robert Whytt, 42

Physiology, comparative, 31; of animals, 22–42, 87; of plants, 59–75, 85–87, 94–101

Pictures, sea-weed, 224, 225

Pitcairn, David, Physician to St Bartholomew's Hospital, 5 n. 4

Plants, air absorbed by, 96; air fixed by, 99; growth of, 85; "imbibing force" of, 67; nutrition of, 94; physiology of, 59–75, 85–87, 94–101

Poor relief at Teddington, 51

Pope, Alexander, 55; tribute to Stephen Hales, 235

Porlock, Somerset, Hales Rector of, 52

Preservation of meat, 148

Pressure, capillary blood, 40; in pulmonary artery, 37; of the sap, 67; root, 71, 72

Priestley, Joseph, 95

Primate, the, visited by Indians, 171

Pringle, Sir John, 195, 203, 205

Prisons, ventilation of, 189 *sqq.*

Pulmonary artery, pressure in, 37

Pulmonary circulation, 36

Ranby, Mr, Surgeon to the Royal Household, 112, 113

Ray, John, 59, 60

Rebreathing, apparatus, 106, 107; experiment, 102

Religion and science, 76 *sqq.*

Respiration, and combustion, 90 *sqq.*; chemistry of, 91; of animals, 101; of fish, 233, 234

Respirator, Hales suggests, 107

Richardson, Samuel, comments on Hales's death, 228

Riots, the Gin, 123

Root pressure, 71, 72, 74; experiments on, 73

Royal Academy of Sciences in Paris, Hales foreign member of, 221

Royal Family patronise Hales, 222

Royal Navy, ventilation of ships of, Chap. ix, 169

Royal Society, papers communicated to, 60, 73, 109, 115; award Copley Medal to Hales (1739), 130; "Haemastatical Papers" read to the, 115; Hales elected Fellow of, 58; Hales elected member of Council of, 110; letter from Hales to President of, 115

Royal Society of Arts, 217

Sachs, Julius von, 74

St Paul's Cathedral, Hales married in, 88

Sap, flow of, 63; cause of the flow of, 70; pressure of the, 67, 68, 71, 72; reversibility of the flow of, 69

Savoy Prison, Hales visits, 190, 191

Science and religion, 76 *sqq.*

Sciences, Royal Academy of, in Paris, Hales foreign member of, 221

Scott, Clement, Fellow of Bene't College, turns papist, 5, 6

Scott, John, 10

Sea-gauge, a, 148 *sqq.*

Sea-weed pictures, 224, 225

Sermons at Teddington, 45

Seven Years' War, the, 232, 233

Sheldrake, Richard, 8

Ships, dry rot in, 165; life on, 145 *sqq.*; ventilation of, 151

"Simpling" expeditions, 18

Slave law of Georgia repealed, 187

For EU product safety concerns, contact us at Calle de José Abascal, 56–1°, 28003 Madrid, Spain or eugpsr@cambridge.org.

www.ingramcontent.com/pod-product-compliance
Ingram Content Group UK Ltd.
Pitfield, Milton Keynes, MK11 3LW, UK
UKHW010347140625
459647UK00010B/893